To Matt Spence
For your continued support
and contributions to ProGrid

INTANGIBLES

Exploring the Full Depth of Issues

C.W. (CLEM) BOWMAN

National Library of Canada Cataloguing in Publication

Bowman, C.W.
Intangibles: Exploring the Full Depth of Issues

ISBN 0-9739339-0-9

Typeset in Sabon and Frutiger
Printed and bound in Canada

GRAFIKS
PUBLISHING

Published by:
Grafiks Marketing & Communications
Publishing Division
Sarnia, Ontario, Canada N7T 8B9

To Marjorie, Ann and John,
for help with the ABCs,
and of course the Ds,
for the name, and for
the independent axes.

Preface

Alex Lowy
Co-author, *"The Power of the 2 x 2 Matrix"*

Economists like to speak of incentives and contingencies; attach enough of the right sort of consequence to a market or work situation, and in most cases you will control the outcome. Operations research and human resource specialists apply this principle to managing performance when they advise businesses to quantify and track the important aspects of production, cautioning that we "manage what we measure." Accountants are wont to apply standard and accepted measurement practices to conduct assessments of value and changes in value. The parts of a business that cannot be described in standard ways are regarded as off balance sheet, and generally given less weight.

Reassuring as these discipline-based approaches may be on the surface, they too often miss the target entirely. The problem with applying such "folk wisdom" is that in complex situations involving people, politics and markets, the most important factors influencing outcomes and behavior are often beyond easy apprehension and description. This creates a rather significant dilemma, what might be called the "measurement paradox." Should you ignore or disqualify "fuzzy" but important data and measure what can be measured directly with precision and reliability, or should you base decisions and findings on terribly flawed, approximate or subjective observations?

As with many dilemmas of this kind where one is seemingly faced with two incomplete and often unsavory options (think of poor Abraham's choice – to sacrifice his son Isaac or to disobey God), the answer lies in somehow transcending given limitations and constraints to find a more suitable alternative at a higher logical level. Systems thinkers sometimes describe this as *both-and* rather than *either-or* thinking wherein elements of paradoxically opposed factors find a way to co-exist, and in so doing enrich rather than detract from understanding.

As scientists and serious researchers we want to apply the best tools of our trade in a rigorous and conscientious manner, but what do you do when the method misses the objective – when what you're measuring isn't what really matters the most. Kurt Lewin, author in 1951 of Field Theory in Social Science, and the original management consultant, made the sobering observation that the "the map is not the territory." Translated: Your tools may indeed be sharp, but are they the right tools to reflect what is really going on?

Go back in time a mere few thousand years and science and philosophy were one. In a fashion, Clem Bowman takes us again in this book to where the two disciplines usefully intersect, and offers methods that cut the Gordian Knot. With Gregory Bateson, he enjoins us to ponder questions of category rather than content, asking not only about how much of x is present, but how much more or less of it would constitute a difference that matters. To answer this, we need to address issues of meaningfulness and relationship that come before and create the context for measurement. In the words of one of my early mentors, Mathew B. Miles, author of *Qualitative Data, an Attractive Nuisance*, Clem Bowman is a "soft-nosed positivist," with one foot planted in the scientific methods and traditions of his training and the other equally firmly rooted in the murkier philosophical questions of meaning.

The outcome of his work as attested to in the case studies described in this book is a courageous and practical contribution to decision-making. If you buy certain premises… that often the most important factors in tough evaluations are ignored or misrepresented because they are hard to measure, that in most, possibly all instances of complex decision-making there are two over-riding criteria that define the issue, and that by modeling these you increase clarity and quality of choice, then Clem and his colleagues at ProGrid are on to something powerful and much needed in a world of increasing complexity.

As one who regularly works in the margins, helping business leaders to make sense of important but often faint and vague market signals, I wholeheartedly accept these premises, and appreciate the contributions of ProGrid thinking to making those essential yet elusive intangibles a little more visible and measurable.

Foreword

Dr. R.B. (Robert) Church
Chair Emeritus, Alberta Science and Research Authority

The evolution of the interface between basic science discoveries and their application in engineering and biosciences to provide innovative products, processes and/or services has changed dramatically in the last few years. With the advances in information management and computing science, it is now possible to provide unique visual presentations of data in formats never before possible.

The peer review system is like democracy in that it has its faults but remains the best alternative for allocating scarce resources to researchers or projects in the basic sciences. It is based on the proven concept that excellent researchers, with outstanding track records, will be the most productive in a discipline. Granting agencies such as the Medical Research Council and the Natural Science and Engineering Research Council were spun out of the National Research Council in Canada to address the question of "how to fund basic and applied science" for the benefit of the public sector and for the development of new products and processes.

In the same time frame as new developments in information management and computing power were taking place, huge multidisciplinary science projects, from space exploration to innovative industrial processes, were being tackled globally.

Clem Bowman is a pioneer in the management of huge complex science-engineering challenges. Projects had to take new frontiers in cutting edge science through to new processes, products and services. In doing so, a "new concept of peer review" evolved which addressed the allocation of resources to the entire innovation continuum.

In the 1970s Clem, as the first Chairman of the Alberta Oil Sands Technology and Research Authority (AOSTRA), developed a strategy for a billion dollar project to develop the "tar sands" (now known as oil sands) in Northern Alberta. The challenge was to define the diverse factors and problems from the discovery of knowledge to process and product development in a remote area.

AOSTRA Research Chairs were selected by peer review to deal with such diverse basic science projects as "tailings sand biota" to anti corrosion materials.

The results are bison grazing on land created from reclaimed tailings to new anti corrosion coatings and processes, which are an essential part of the "trillion dollar" oil sands operation in Alberta today.

In the 1980s, as President of the Alberta Research Council, Clem once again faced the question of how an organization charged with technology development and innovation assesses the allocation of resources to challenging proposals. The links between the discovery of new knowledge and the development of new processes and products, the drivers of economic success, were being refined.

In the 1990s, in collaboration with other experienced science and technology managers such as Ron McCullough, formerly with Spar Aerospace, Clem applied the power of data analysis with a unique language ladder, which he called ProGrid. This created a whole new type of peer review, which addressed the full spectrum of the innovation continuum.

In the last ten years, science and innovation strategies have been developed by the Alberta Science and Research Authority in a number of areas. All had in common the philosophy that excellent researchers working in an environment that promotes development of products, processes and services for the public good would yield economic success in a knowledge economy.

The problem was "how does one evaluate and rank the many challenging proposals in areas as diverse as medical discovery, agribusiness, high tech, to energy resources?"

We were fortunate in being able to work with Clem's team on an evolving ProGrid system. The case studies presented in this book reflect the impact that ProGrid has had not only in creating and developing innovative technologies but also in providing a medium for multidisciplinary communication between individuals across the knowledge spectrum.

In a rapidly developing world in which basic knowledge discoveries, global communication and product innovation are key to economic and social success, it is only fitting to also have rapidly evolving tools, such as ProGrid, for evaluating each stage of the innovation process.

Acknowledgements

We live mainly in a one-dimensional world, one that has us rising in the morning and following a fairly straight line until we close down shop at night. But add a second dimension and life becomes richer, albeit more complex, especially if we start thinking about tomorrow or issues that may conflict with the desires of today. In one of my semi-retirements, this one in the early 1990s, I began doing just that, pondering the enormous importance of intangibles, and the significance of two overarching dimensions. Various associates of mine joined in these musings, the ultimate result of which was the ProGrid® methodology described here.

A relatively small group of colleagues formed the nucleus of this effort. These original "ProGridders" include, more or less in the order they joined the challenge, J.R. (Ron) McCullough, G.B. (Gerald) Dyer, Gregor Robinson, Bruce Fountain, Alan Winter, Lise McCourt, F.A. (Fred) Christie, J.W. (John) Kramers, Bill MacMillan, Chris Jones and Keith Jones, the last two unrelated and known inside as the "Jones Boys." To each I owe enormous thanks for their contributions in charting a smoother course over rough terrain.

And there were others. Gerry Heffernan, and Jeff Parr of the Clairvest Group provided wise business advice over many years until we were ready to 'fly on our own.' Rob McLean teamed up with Ron McCullough to extend an on-line version of ProGrid into post-Enron applications. Dale Homeniuk helped John Kramers in the transition from our initial spreadsheets to user-friendly software, which includes highly valuable suggestions from many ProGrid users. Jim Hutch, with his huge smile, provided help and encouragement as ProGrid evolved. Fraser Barnes has seen the opportunity for ProGrid to provide a compelling value proposition to address the challenges organizations are experiencing with their evaluation processes, in a variety of markets.

Thanks also to the many individuals in both the public and private sector who went against conventional thinking to try ProGrid and become its champions. A partial list would include Jac van Beek, Garry Sears, Bob

Hipkin, Grant Allan, Peter McGeer, Ian Rowe, Peter Day, Glen Smeltzer, Paul Johnson, Steve Moran, Karen Ford, Keith L. Jones, Bob Church, Ian Strang, Duke DuPlessis, Carmen Charette, Matt Spence, Jacques Magnan, Linda Humphreys, Richard Thornley, Mark Taylor, Tina Blake, Steven Kenny, Brad Johns, Larson Brodner, Abbas Taeb, Karen Beliveau, Ralph Christian, Freda Molenkamp, Joan Unger, Ron Dyck, Ray Bassett, Scott Wright, Jim Baker, Malcolm Drury, Ross Bricker, Len Bolger, Eddy Isaacs, Surindar Singh, Steve Vossos, Neil Taylor, Nadine Cyr, Ted Heidrick, and Darren Hutton, again more or less in the order they joined the cause. Many became chapter contributors or participants in the case studies that are presented.

C.W. (Clem) Bowman

Contents

ProGrid® Methodology and Trademarks are protected Intellectual Property, but as with many business support tools in the marketplace, there are ample opportunities to share experiences and learnings. We encourage readers to contact and work with us in meeting the challenges described in this book.

Profits from the sale of this book will be used to augment the C.W. Bowman Chemical Engineering Scholarship Fund at the University of Alberta.

Notes from the Author

In the words of one of the Reviewers, "this is a short book, with 7 chapters that cover the "What" and the "So What?" of ProGrid's approach to evaluating what cannot be measured. It is also a long book, with 19 chapters dedicated to case studies – actual and potential uses of the ProGrid® methodology."

Chapter 1 provides the entire structure needed to apply ProGrid Methodology.

Chapters 2 to 6 describe five challenges that face modern competitive economies: the pressure to accelerate innovation, the drive to commercialize new technologies, the search for good governance, more effective government procurement, and the need to define and track societal goals. Select the topics of interest to you; they all build on a common evaluation structure.

Chapter 7 documents what has been learned to date and presents some huge challenges for future ProGrid enthusiasts.

Then, if you want to learn the details from the practitioners on the ground, move on to the Case Studies in Part Two.

Chapters 8 through 10 pertain to the front end of the innovation chain, research infrastructure and early stage research proposals.

Chapter 11 is an effort to apply what has been learned in evaluating research proposals to a different arena, government procurement, which has suffered from lack of a credible due process.

Chapters 12 through 20 extend further down the innovation chain, getting into the first stages of commercial assessment, with the introduction of the "people side" in Chapter 19.

Chapters 21 to 25 drill deeper into the innovation chain, moving from making decisions on proposals to evaluating and tracking the performance of organizations toward short and long-term goals.

Chapter 26 is an overview of the software side of ProGrid. This has evolved to keep pace with growing expectations of ProGrid users for real-time user-friendly graphical interpretive charts and reports.

PART ONE

What Intangibles Are All About

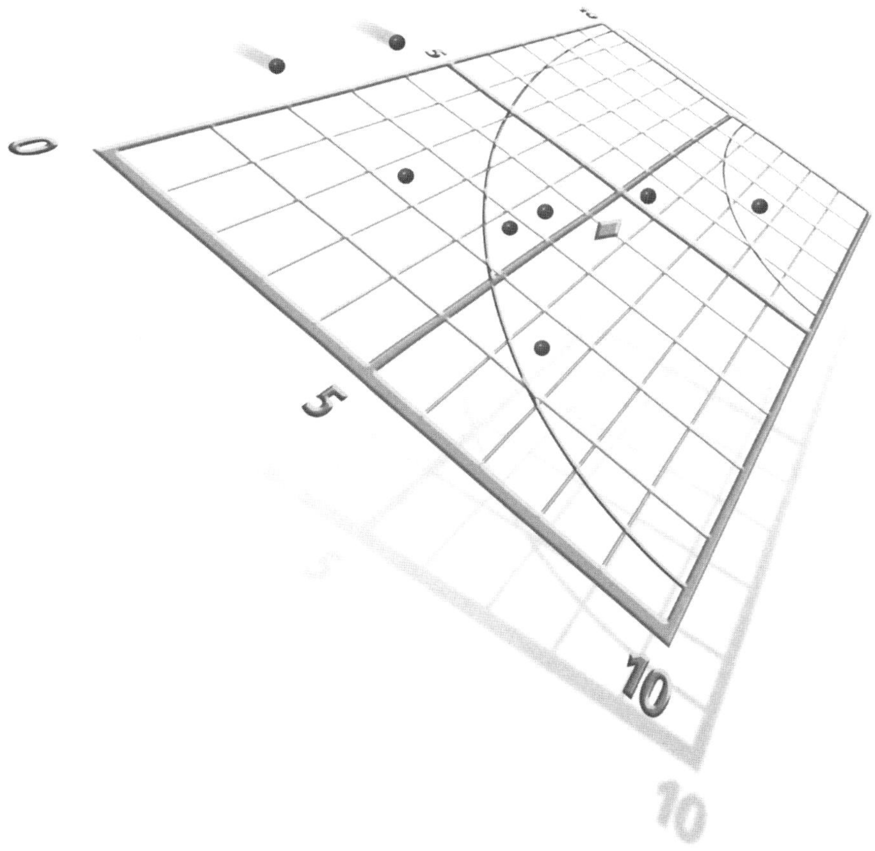

1 Intangibles: Important and Immeasurable

Ask your colleagues what's important to them and out will come pictures of their family, if these are not already sitting on their desk. If they talk about their house, it won't be about the bricks and mortar – it more likely will be the view of the river, the valley or the mountain that they see from their window. Meeting one's future spouse may have a greater effect on one's life that any other single event. What could be more intangible than the events leading up to this chance encounter?

Bottom line: we cannot measure the things that are really important. But their value is real, a point Canadian author Margaret Atwood made when she stated in an interview: "Art is the highest form of entrepreneurship – the artist creates value out of nothing." A prime example is Michelangelo's David, a priceless statue carved out of a stone that would otherwise be of negligible value.

A characteristic of intangibles is that the value lies to a large extent in the eye of the observer. While the painting "Voice of Fire" was worth millions of dollars in the eyes of those selecting art for the National Gallery of Canada, others felt that given a case of spray paint, they could readily create a replica of the three coloured bands.

Time also comes into play when comparing tangibles and intangibles. Tangible assets normally depreciate over time; intangibles often realize their value only over time. Watch how the value of famous paintings increases dramatically from one auction to the next.

The human body could be considered as the most powerful intangible of all. Over 90% of the human body is a combination of oxygen, carbon and hydrogen, the balance looking like the periodic table. Although the composition does not vary much among people, the final product certainly does—just look at Michael Moore and Pamela Anderson. The "Artist" in these cases demonstrates a keen sense of humour!

Evaluating what you cannot measure – we do it all the time! This book describes a disciplined methodology, with a clear and justifiable paper trail.

In the Eyes of the Accountant

Accountants have taken the phrase "what cannot be measured cannot be controlled" to the point where they've ruled the world of commerce for most of recent history. Indeed, tangible assets were assumed to represent the majority of the wealth of companies. With assets suited to accurate assessment, we see the phrase "bean counting" coming into vogue (albeit in a somewhat derogatory fashion). The accountants' view of the world has been the cornerstone of national and international commerce. The metrics developed for GAAP (Generally Accepted Accounting Principles) provide an essential universal framework for transactions among commercial enterprises.

But tangible assets form only one part of the wealth of a company or a nation. The book value of a company frequently has poorly represented its strength, either by overlooking future potential or exaggerating the long-term value of manufacturing processes and products. An entire industry has been set up to document the difference between a company's book value and its market value. Through the concept of Intellectual Capital, the components of which are shown in Table 1.1, we see assets which cannot be quantitatively measured, but would be costly to develop or replace if lost. In short, they are intangible.

TABLE 1.1
Components of Intellectual Capital

<table>
<tr><th colspan="4">Intellectual Capital</th></tr>
<tr><th colspan="3">Structural Capital</th><td rowspan="3">Human Capital (knowledge, skills, capabilities, motivation of people)</td></tr>
<tr><th colspan="2">Intellectual Assets</th><td rowspan="2">Systems, Processes, Relationships (with customers, suppliers etc.)</td></tr>
<tr><td>Intellectual Property (patents, trademarks)</td><td>Codified Knowledge (documents, drawings, software)</td></tr>
</table>

Of the FORTUNE 500 companies first listed (in 1954), two-thirds were off the list 40 years later.[i] Would we have been able to predict their demise with better knowledge of the strength of their intellectual capital?

The Market Understands Intangibles

The value of companies lies between two bookends, Book Value and Market Value. Book value represents the depreciated value of all the tangible assets accumulated over a period of time—the bricks and mortar, production equipment, and inventory. These are the factors that accountants can identify and measure and are the basis for valuing assets. But market value typically lies well above this figure, representing the promise that comes from intangible assets—the people, processes, brand names, and intellectual property.

FIGURE 1.1
Hidden Values

An iceberg (Figure 1.1) is a good representation of intangible assets, with 90% of its mass hidden below the water surface. Nevertheless, we know it's there. And we ignore it with "Titanic" consequences.

TABLE 1.2
Market to Book Value Ratios (typical 2005 values)

Company	Ratio Market/ Book Value
General Motors	3.2
Microsoft	4.6
IBM	6.0
Genentech	7.9
Pfizer	12.3
GlaxoSmithKline	13.3

Examples of the difference between the market and book values of companies are shown in Table 1.2. As the "promise" grows, the ratio of market to book value increases, in some cases exceeding the 9 to 1 ratio for hidden to visible ice.

Over the past decade, companies in areas such as software and information technologies have produced market to book value ratios far in excess of those shown in Table 1.2, all based on promises that attracted enormous investments, only to see the real value of some of those promises eroding to essentially zero.

Evaluating the Promise

Know any venture capitalists? Ask them how they value start-up companies and they'll likely say they "have their ways" of predicting future success. But if you probe, they may admit their real test is to meet the CEO or the entrepreneur behind the business, with a warm feeling in the gut becoming the ultimate basis of an investment decision. While most venture capital companies can point to many successes, there are just a few home runs. Indeed, "success" is usually measured by having one big success in 10, with another two or three surviving. The balance, a venture capitalist will acknowledge, are ultimate failures. The reality is that continuing a high success rate is a more difficult challenge – many venture capital companies simply approach sector averages over time. Evaluating intangibles is usually claimed to be an art, one that involves the weighing of subjective factors in some indefinable way deep inside the human brain.

But what if we could add science to the process? Could we place a value on intangibles? Ten years of research and practical applications have led to a powerful five-step methodology for doing just that – evaluating what cannot be measured:

1. Identifying the Overarching Objectives
2. Defining an Evaluation Matrix™ of Criteria
3. Establishing metrics through Language Ladders
4. Evaluating the Intangible
5. Plotting the results on an Evaluation Grid

Overarching Objectives

Many decisions in life involve two overarching factors, or objectives, each of which may be conflicting and in apparent opposition. Lowy and Hood[ii] note the "tension" that is involved in complex situations, one that is generated from "two conflicting needs." With more than 50 examples of this tension documented, they show that through resolution, a new and higher level of success can be achieved.

This two-dimensional aspect of decision-making was noted in a previous publication related to intangible assets[iii]. Examples of these conflicting objectives are many; the short term versus the long term, the important versus the urgent, quality versus price, growth versus profitability, the vision versus the execution, personal life versus business pressures. Once the second dimension is recognized and understood, the pathway to understanding and using intangible assets becomes much clearer.

There are many examples of companies failing due to a one-dimensional strategy. A single product strategy, for example, eventually fails as the product reaches maturity. Focusing on the quarterly bottom line and neglecting long-term survival is another example of one-dimensional thinking. Unfortunately the tendency for individuals and organizations is to operate in that one-dimensional mode. Why? It's an easy pathway that avoids the huge challenge (and choice) of incorporating a second dimension. Those who can think naturally in two dimensions have a tough time if they work in a strongly one-dimensional organization. In short, they don't fit very well. Indeed, ambitious people do not stay in these organizations. Although the strong ones may stay, fighting for and making a difference, others stay and become moulded into rigid one-dimensional thinkers.

These competing forces frequently have a time dimension, such as short and long-term goals. Often they will have a mandated dimension, such as an emphasis on research and teaching in universities. The tension between funding basic and applied research is another example.

John Polanyi, a Nobel prize winner in chemistry, has eloquently and effectively demonstrated the positive impact of curiosity-oriented basic research[iv]. But the other dimension is equally important. Man has reached the moon and the Alberta Oil Sands are now contributing half of Canada's hydrocarbon demand, two major mission-oriented research endeavours that required extensive basic and applied research working hand in hand.

Peter Hackett has drawn the analogy to DNA[v], with "two complementary strands of DNA, a culture of creativity in individuals and a culture of innovation in societies. The one patterns the other."

When two competing objectives are orthogonal to one another, their net effect can be assessed using geometry. In their resolution, a vector is generated which provides the "energy and aim" necessary for success, as noted by Lowy and Hood. If the objectives are opposing (180 degrees apart in direction), a resolution is not possible.

The case studies in this book illustrate effective methods for selecting and validating the two overarching objectives that need to be determined as the first step in making decisions and evaluating performance.

Evaluation Matrix

The Evaluation Matrix is the backbone for evaluating intangible assets and contains criteria central to the evaluation. A convenient example is an action that most take at least once and sometimes several times in a lifetime—buying a house. The process is normally a consultative one, involving family members reaching consensus on priorities, values and expectations. The entire process is illustrated in Figure 1.2.

Through discussion, the following overarching objectives are established:

- Quality of the building
- Attractiveness of the environment

An Evaluation Matrix contains the criteria desired for both the building and the neighbourhood environment, with the overarching objectives shown as the headings for the first column and the third column respectively. Criteria are tabulated in the appropriate

FIGURE 1.2
Buying a House

Selecting the Overarching Objectives

1. Quality of the building
2. Attractiveness of the environment

Establishing the Evaluation Matrix

Building	Connectors	Environment
1 Features	**4** Price	**7** Location
2 Quality	**5** Resale	**8** Lot
3 Upgradability	**6** Maintenance	**9** Neighbourhood

Building the Language Ladder

e.g. Features (four bedrooms, three bathrooms, large family room, full finished basement, two-car garage)

A. Missing more than two requirements
B. Missing one or two requirements
C. Meets requirements
D. Exceeds requirements

Evaluating the Choices

	House					
Criteria	**1**	**2**	**3**	**4**	**5**	**6**
1	A	C	D	C	B	C
2	B	C	C	B	B	B
3	A	C	C	D	B	A
4	A	C	C	B	B	C
5	C	C	C	B	B	B
6	B	C	C	A	B	A
7	A	C	C	A	B	C
8	C	C	B	C	B	C
9	B	C	C	D	B	D

Plotting the Results

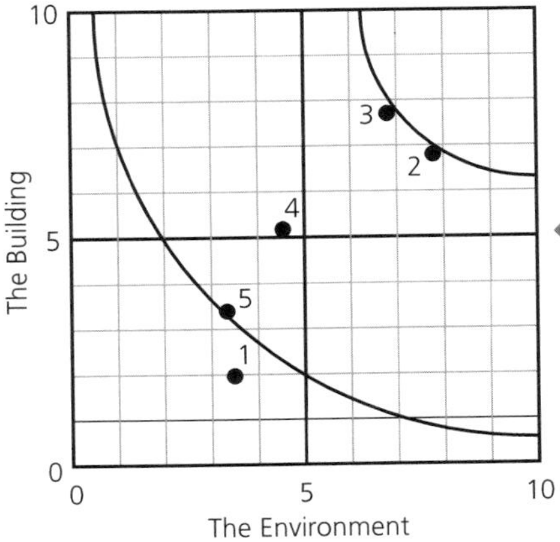

columns, with those influencing both overarching objectives in the middle column—Connectors (sometimes called Enablers).

Language Ladder™

Statements, which serve as measurements for the evaluation, can be prepared, for simplicity expressed in Figure 1.2 as one statement with four levels of expectation. Four-level Language Ladder statements are used in most of the examples in this book.

Language Ladders are not a new concept and have long been used for illustrating intangibles. A fresh wind blows in your face, a pleasant experience. The wind speed can be measured and a tangible number associated with it. But the wind itself and the emotions that it raises? Those are surely intangible.

Consider the Beaufort Scale (Table 1.3), developed in 1806 as a result of frustration with the way people described weather. Captain Francis Beaufort of the British Admiralty found imprecise expressions such as "moderate winds" or "a big storm" lacking certainty and accuracy of definition in the minds of non-observers.

Beaufort sought to match information about the wind's speed to numbers that could be universally recognized and accepted by simple observation. Thus in a calm (Beaufort Scale 0), smoke rises vertically. At Beaufort Scale 1(light air), the direction of the wind direction is shown by smoke but not wind vanes. These are simple observations to which a number can be applied for each new progressive level and which can be clearly understood by users – in this case, often uneducated mariners.

This 13-step Beaufort Scale from 0 (calm) to 12 (hurricane) is an early example of a Language Ladder that seeks agreement on words to describe an intangible event and then gives it numerical equivalent.

By 1838, the now Admiral Beaufort, as Hydrographer to the British Admiralty, witnessed his scale accepted as the standard for the measurement of wind (there were no accurate wind instruments at the time) by the British Navy. Eventually it was adopted by many sea-going nations worldwide.

TABLE 1.3

The Beaufort Scale - 1838

Beaufort Number	Name	Wind speed (mph)	Description
0	Calm	<1	calm; smoke rises vertically
1	Light air	1-3	direction of wind shown by smoke but not by wind vanes
2	Light breeze	4-7	wind felt on face; leaves rustle; ordinary vane moved by wind
3	Gentle breeze	8-12	leaves and small twigs in constant motion; wind extends light flag
4	Moderate breeze	13-18	raises dust and loose paper; small branches are moved
5	Fresh breeze	19-24	small trees in leaf begin to sway; crested wavelets form on inland waters
6	Strong breeze	25-31	large branches in motion; telegraph wires whistle; umbrellas used with difficulty
7	Near gale	32-38	whole trees in motion; inconvenience in walking against wind
8	Gale	39-46	breaks twigs off trees; generally impedes progress
9	Strong gale	47-54	slight structural damage occurs; chimney pots and slates removed
10	Storm	55-63	trees uprooted; considerable structural damage occurs
11	Violent storm	64-72	very rarely experienced; accompanied by wide-spread damage
12	Hurricane	73-136	devastation occurs

Author Scott Huler[vi] cited the 110 words of the Beaufort Scale as "the best, clearest, and most vigorous piece of descriptive writing I have ever seen" or, as he described it, "science put in poetry."

Beaufort embraced the quotation from "A Manual of Scientific Enquiry, Third Edition, 1859 that "Nature, rightly questioned never lies."

Others who followed saw the logic and wisdom of taking observations and assigning them a numerical equivalent, especially in converting intangible observations to data, thus improving the quality of information in a variety of activities.

The Modified Mercalli Earthquake Intensity Scale provides descriptions of 12 stages of increasing intensity of earthquakes. For example, at Scale I an earthquake is not felt and marginal; at Scale VI dishes are broken and many are frightened, running outdoors; at Scale XII damage is nearly total[vii]. Other examples of similar applications include the five levels of the Fujita Tornado Damage Scale[viii] and five levels of the Saffier-Simpson Hurricane Scale[ix] with the too familiar Categories One to Five describing expected wind damage and the impact of surging water levels, a horrifying experience as testified by those that survived the 2005 hurricane Katrina in the Southern United States.

Why not just numbers without the description? An early version of ProGrid used a 10-point scale to measure the degree of adherence or progress. Users, however, pointed out that a rating of "7" may be very different from person to person. Even so, a 10-step language scale was found to be impractical. Some evaluation methodologies employ a two-point binary scale, an example of which is used for compliance in fields such as the safety of production environments. If two fire extinguishers are required per production area, you either meet the requirement or you don't. While users of the ProGrid methodology have tested various scales, most now use a four-step ladder, thus avoiding a middle "safe" region.

The term "ladder" is useful in that it provides a good physical representation of the problem, as shown in Figure 1.3. The four-step ladder starts with A and progresses upward to D. Short sentences with key words are used to express the intent of each step in this ladder and sentences are constructed to fit the evaluation task at hand.

FIGURE 1.3
Generic Language Ladder

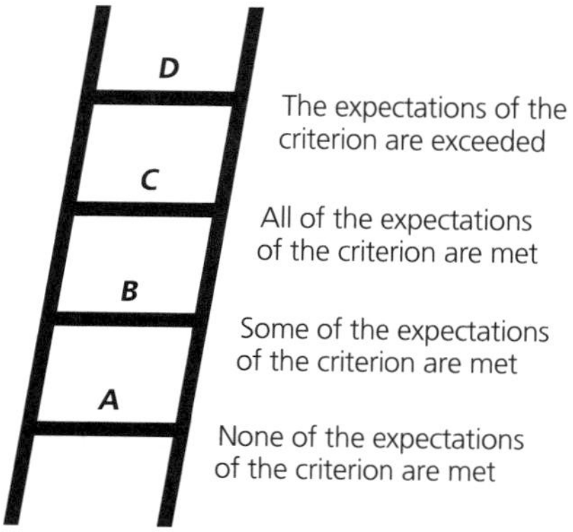
D
The expectations of the criterion are exceeded
C
All of the expectations of the criterion are met
B
Some of the expectations of the criterion are met
A
None of the expectations of the criterion are met

Why does the ladder start at A and end at D, which is the reverse of the terminology used in academia for grading purposes? Starting a journey at "A" is a logical starting point, permitting the journey to be extended beyond "D". Extending the reach of the ladder is a useful concept in personnel evaluations involving staff promotions. Plus, the case studies described in later chapters in this book are hardly "academic exams." Rather, they illustrate trajectories for increasing the value of assets and improving performance over time, in theory and in practice without limits.

The quality of the process depends initially on the correct structure for the Evaluation Matrix and then ultimately on the quality of the Language Ladder's design. The words used to describe the steps in the Ladder should represent meaningful separations and be understandable by evaluators. In effect, the Language Ladder provides the "dictionary" definition for the A, B, C, D's.

Establishing the Grid

The results of an evaluation can be shown in the form of an Evaluation Grid (as shown previously in Figure 1.2), using the overarching objectives as its axes.

Literature is replete with examples of four-box grids, representing a range of evaluation tasks. The Lowy and Hood[ii] array of more than 50 matrices is a comprehensive compilation of examples of tasks to which this methodology could be applied. Lowy and Hood summarized the issue that all four-box users have faced, in their instruction "place yourself in one of the boxes." Easier said than done but it's a challenge that has been addressed and solved by the ProGrid methodology. The case studies presented show how to measure where you are in a four-box grid, with clear and convincing documentation.

R-Values – The Ranking Scale

Deciding whether to measure progress in the grid from the origin (0,0) or from 10,10 is critical. Measuring progress from 0,0 provides credit for any movement in the grid, regardless of direction, which is appropriate, for example, in deciding on staff promotions where an employee's strength may lie primarily in one dimension,

FIGURE 1.4
Comparison of R-value Scales

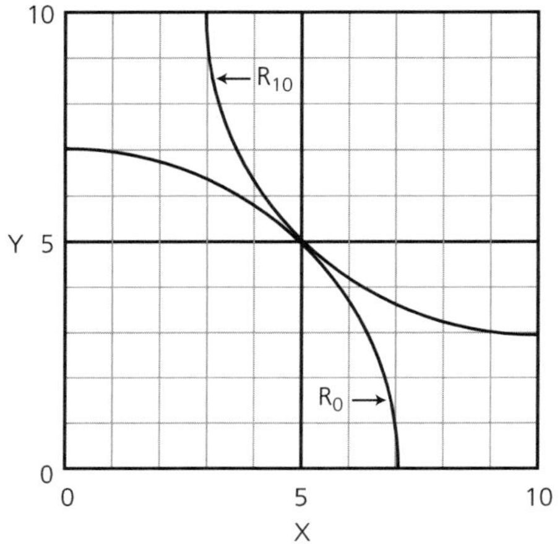

and progress in that dimension should be rewarded. By contrast, a commercial technology-intensive venture may require progress in both axes; measuring the distance from the ultimate 10,10 goal would be a more appropriate metric. The difference between these approaches is illustrated in Figures 1.4.

Grid travel can be expressed as an R-value, which can be calculated in two ways:

- R_0 – a measure of the distance travelled from the point 0,0
- R_{10} – a measure of the distance to travel to the point 10,10

The R-values can be defined mathematically such that a grid position of 0,0 is equal to 0% and a grid position of 10,10 is equal to 100%, for both R_0 and R_{10}. The two curves in Figure 1.4 both have R-values of 50%, and meet at 5,5. As the curves diverge from the diagonal, the difference between R_0 and R_{10} increases.

Regardless of which R-value definition is used, all points along an R-value arc can be considered to be "equal" with respect to the two competing overarching objectives, but with a different weighting of values.

Exclusion Zones

It is essential that the grid axes be relatively independent. This means that the overarching objectives that are plotted on these axes can be achieved independently. The degree of "independency" dictates how much of the grid is accessible for plotting purposes. If all criteria in the Evaluation Matrix are apportioned fully to one or the other axis, the full grid is accessible. If one or more criteria are apportioned to both

FIGURE 1.5
Exclusion Zones

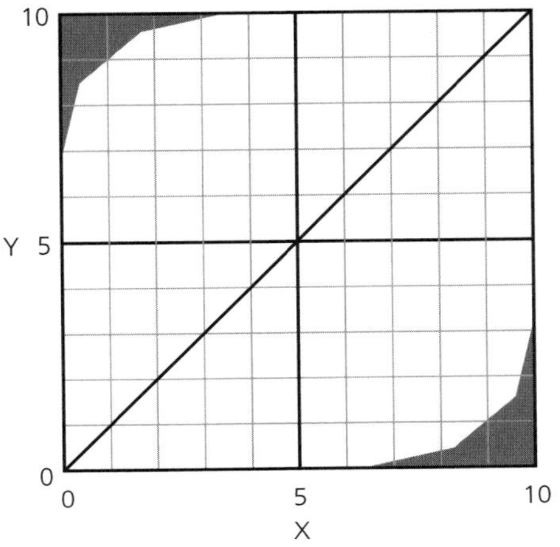

axes, then some parts of the grid around the points 10,0 and 0,10 are not accessible (as seen in Figure 1.5). It is important that these zones are not excessively large. If they are, it means that there are too many criteria that influence both axes. If carried to the limit, only the diagonal is accessible and in this case, the axes are no longer independent. The example shown represents a realistic case in which the two exclusion zones in the upper left corner and the lower right corner are reasonably small.

FIGURE 1.6
Evaluating in a Three Dimensional World

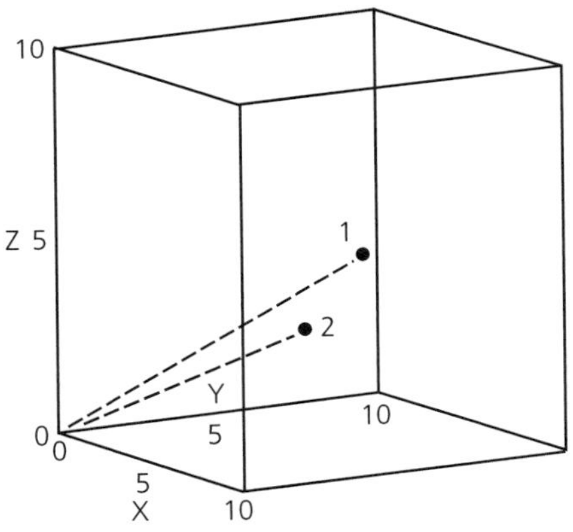

But why only two dimensions?

We live in a world of three dimensions; four if we include time. While ProGrid methodology will work with three dimensions, the results being displayed as a cube (Figure 1.6), no significant advantages have been evident to date using a three dimensional approach. At the same time, there is nothing implicit in ProGrid methodology that prevents an evaluation in n-dimensional space. While a graphical display of the results would not be possible, a quantitative comparison of the intangible asset under consideration could be made, the R-value representing the distance from a defined point in n-dimensional space.

The Decision Process

Organizations using the ProGrid methodology have their own decision processes to meet their specific goals and requirements. In most cases there is an individual, or group, that prepares an application for funding or a proponent who presents a proposed course of action. Reviewers or evaluators typically assess the merits of the application/proposal. And decision-makers seek the advice of those who initially screen the applications/proposals.

A Comparison with Peer Review

Organizations providing funds for scientific projects in a formal competition typically use a Peer Review process to select winning projects. This time-honoured process has served the scientific community well in the past and will continue to be a mainstay of project selection. Applications, which normally consist of rigorously detailed descriptions of the planned research, also include papers describing previous related research and the curriculum vitae of principal investigators, documentation equivalent to a complete business plan for a commercial venture. The review process involves other researchers with experience in the area involved, part of the normally accepted work load that could consume several days to complete.

Yet peer review has its limitations. For example, when the volume of applications is large (several hundred or more), or there is a near-term business implication requiring a wider spectrum of experience of the reviewers, or there is a need for a high level of transparency in the review process and the need for a more consistent basis of providing feedback to applicants (both successful and unsuccessful), the need for modification of the standard peer review process is clear.

The major complaint against standard peer review is summed up by the phrase "fatigue" – by both applicants and reviewers alike.

Organizations that have used the methodology described in this book have reported the following advantages.

- Comprehensive – ensures that all key aspects have been addressed (open architecture)
- Achieves consensus – provides input from all stakeholders
- Rapid – busy experts are willing to participate in the review process
- Disciplined and reproducible
- Graphical and easily understood
- Ranks a large number of opportunities in a portfolio
- Provides a corporate database and memory
- A self-learning methodology, constantly improving
- Focuses on issues key to making difficult decisions

Importance of Self-Assessment

Most of the active users of the methodology include self-assessment as a fundamental part of the process. As the purpose of benchmarking is to improve the performance of an organization, it is critical that the organization be actively involved in the process since it will have the prime responsibility for acting on the results.

Self-assessment is also frequently employed when ProGrid is used as a decision-assist, particularly in enabling reviewers to rapidly validate an assessment. The clarity in which the applicant/proponent is able to make a case for action is an important input in the process.

Nevertheless, self-assessment is not a prerequisite for using the ProGrid methodology. Indeed, in certain situations it may prove to be appropriate to leave out self-assessment, or at least not to disclose its existence to reviewers. In such cases, sufficient information needs to be included for reviewers to make an independent judgment. Don't fall back on the traditional approach – providing masses of information from which reviewers have to extract key information on which to base their opinions.

Other Approaches

If intangibles are so important, why are rigorous methods not in use for their evaluation? In fact, many approaches have been developed, such as those described below:

The Risk Management Matrix of the Boston Consulting Group

This was a technique that used four-quadrant grids for displaying performance using Relative Market Share and Growth as its two axes. As noted in the review by Millet and Honton[x], these terms represent cash generation and cash use respectively and are thus not strictly independent. Millet and Honton note that portfolio analyses methods, of which the Boston Consulting Group Risk Management Matrix is an example, are "not only highly judgmental, but also highly arbitrary (even biased)." Such methods are qualitative and the axes are unscaled. The position of a technology in these matrices is not subject to quantitative examination by other evaluators.

The Kepner-Tregoe Decision Process

This technique, which lays out key criteria for a selection process and uses a numerical scale to rank alternative choices[xi], is particularly useful in problem solving as it identifies the likely cause of an undesirable event by listing and weighting potential causes. This approach illustrates the importance of having clearly-defined criteria and separating them into "musts" and "wants."

The Blake Managerial Grid

The Blake grid is used to optimize the balance between people-focused and production-focused human resource practices.[xii] Using a grid that displays and compares different personnel behaviour practices, the technique shows how subjective factors can be organized into meaningful patterns.

The Myers-Briggs Personality Test

This evaluation test reveals the personality traits of individuals by using carefully-defined statements and randomized selections of preferred statements.[xiii] Useful in improving group dynamics by valuing different approaches to solving problems, Myers-Briggs uses a scale of statements to establish comparative performance levels.

Although useful for specific tasks, these approaches do not provide a process for assessing the value of intangible assets and integrating them into an effective management system. A 10-year search for such a system led to the approach described in this book, which is now known as ProGrid.

The ProGrid methodology can be used by:

- Governments to provide fair and objective procurement practices.
- Granting agencies to provide an effective national innovation capacity.
- Investors to identify and track winning technologies.
- Shareholders and regulatory authorities to assess the effectiveness of governance practices
- By a nation to establish and monitor long-range societal goals

These are huge claims for a process that is still relatively immature. However, with the history of Enron and other examples of unacceptable performance, the existing evaluation approaches have failed to achieve a desired level of performance. In the next five chapters, we will describe how the methodology has been used to address major challenges in which intangible factors are the drivers.

[i] *Forty Years of the 500,* Carol J. Loomis, Kathleen C. Smyth, Suzanne Barlyn, Volume 131, No. 9, 40th Anniversary Issue, page 182

[ii] *The Power of the 2 x 2 Matrix,* Alex Lowy, Phil Hood, 2004, Jossey-Bass (Wiley)

[iii] *Evaluating Intellectual Capital – Part I,* C. W. Bowman, *Canadian Chemical News,* January 2001

[iv] John Polanyi, *Assessing the Role of Basic Research in Science Policy.* Science Forum, 9, June, 1969

[v] Peter Hackett, Innowest 2004, Presentation Nov 17, 2004, Calgary, Alberta, Canada

[vi] Huler, Scott, *Defining the Wind,* Crown Publishers, New York, 2004, ISBN 1-4000-4884-2

[vii] http://hvo.wr.usgs.gov/earhquakes/felt/mercalli.html)

[viii] http://www.tornadoproject.com/fscale/fscale.htm

[ix] http://www.charlottecountyfl.com/Emergency/hurricane/

[x] *A Manager's Guide To Technology Forecasting And Strategic Analysis Methods,* Stephen M. Millet and Edward J. Honton, Battelle Press. 1991

[xi] http://www.kepner-tregoe/index.html

[xii] *The Managerial Grid,* Robert R. Blake and Jane Mouton, Gulf Publishing Company, Library of Congress Number 64-14724, 1964

[xiii] http://www.oise.on.ca/~cengel/coop.mbcareer.htm

2 Innovation – The Competitive Advantage

Innovation is the hallmark of nations in today's fiercely competitive global environment. But as pointed out by Peter Hackett[i], there are two critical inputs required to become a highly innovative country: people with the skills and imagination to extend the boundaries of what is possible, and a supportive and response society that can capture economic and social value from the resulting advances in science and technology. Canada as an example has made some bold moves to increase its innovative capacity, and this has led to major increases in leading edge infrastructure, world-class research programs and incentive programs that recognize entrepreneurial achievements.

Still, it is not yet possible to measure quantitatively a country's or a company's innovative capacity. There is no entry for innovation on a balance sheet, other than a token footnote about the importance of a company's people. Innovation excellence is based on many intangible factors and its crucial value is more easily recognized by its absence. Let's look at how ProGrid® methodology has been used to capture the two interlocking strands of the innovative process, addressing first the need for major new research infrastructure, then a major expansion in R&D effort, including the need for enhanced training and incentive programs.

Refurbishing Infrastructure

A prevalent and long-lasting problem in research organizations, both public and private, has been maintaining physical infrastructure. Organizations and countries must maintain their infrastructure at the leading edge of efficiency and effectiveness if they are to be globally competitive. Further, they must invest in infrastructure matched to new opportunities at the very forefront of research.

Universities and hospitals in Canada raised the country's poor record of ongoing infrastructure investment as a major concern in the early 1990s. In response, in 1997 the federal Canadian government created an independent non-profit organization, the Canada Foundation for Innovation (CFI), providing funding support for infrastructure in universities and hospitals. An enormous success, the CFI's budget of $3.65 billion funds up to 40 percent of a project's infrastructure costs, in partnership with eligible institutions and their funding partners from the public, private, and voluntary sectors. Total capital investment by all involved will exceed $10 billion by 2010.

The original legislation under which the CFI was established set out seven key objectives.

1. Provide infrastructure to support research in Canadian universities and hospitals.
2. Support economic growth and job creation
3. Enhance capacity for innovation
4. Strengthen training and research careers
5. Attract and retain research workers
6. Promote networks and collaborations

When the CFI was launched, executive and senior management ultimately selected ProGrid as the best fit for its broad mandate and anticipated high volume of applications. As the first step, the Quality of Proposals and the Benefits to Canada were selected as the overarching objectives, which became the headings in the first and third columns in the Evaluation Matrix™ shown in Table 2.1.

TABLE 2.1
The CFI Evaluation Matrix

Quality of the Proposal	Capacity for innovation	Benefits to Canada
The Research	Need for the Infrastructure	Potential Benefits to Canada
The Researchers	Training Highly Qualified Personnel (HQP)	
	Research Collaboration and Partnerships	

The CFI originally had nine cells in their matrix but found that they could discriminate proposals using six. How do we know if we have the right number? Experience has shown that if there are less than six, some of the criteria may have too broad a span and be difficult to measure. If there are more than 12, there are two possibilities; criteria are included that are not crucial to the evaluation, or there are a number of interlocking decisions that cannot be addressed at the same time or on the same scale. The latter can be handled by a process involving cascading matrices, where there is a set of interconnected matrices at successively lower levels (ie: greater levels of detail), each having six to 12 criteria. Lowy and Hood[ii] suggest that seven is the maximum number of themes that can practically represent the issues involved in a decision process.

FIGURE 2.1
CFI's First Major Competition

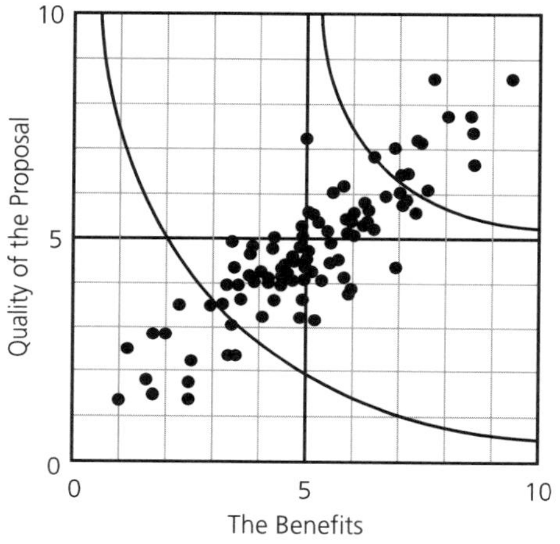

CFI receives many hundreds of proposals a year and it is essential that their peer review process be heavily automated and respectful of reviewer time. The results from the initial competition are shown in Figure 2.1

Alberta was one of many provinces in Canada that established its own infrastructure program, recognizing early that having a separate application process would create additional applicant and reviewer fatigue, a major complaint of the research community. Alberta adopted the basic structure of the CFI Evaluation matrix, adding two cells to cover specific Alberta requirements as shown in Table 2.2.

TABLE 2.2
The Alberta Infrastructure Matrix

Quality and Innovation	Process	Strategic Benefits
The Research	Need for the Infrastructure	Potential Benefits of the Research to Canada
The Researchers	Training of Highly Qualified Personnel (HQP)	
	Research Collaboration and Partnerships	
Strategic Alberta Fit		Capacity for Research Excellence

Establishing World Class Research Programs

Canada has been criticized for decades for its low investment in R&D, for long periods barely above one per cent of GNP. More recently, progress has been made, in part due to the establishment of new Provincial and National Centres of Excellence.

One of those, Materials Manufacturing Ontario (MMO), has used ProGrid methodology to select research proposals which meet two overarching objectives, the potential Advance in Science and Engineering and the Economic Impact on Ontario, as shown in Table 2.3.

TABLE 2.3
MMO's "Enabling Projects" Evaluation Matrix

Advance in Science and Engineering	Enablers	Economic Impact on Ontario
Engineering and/or Science Advance	Enlarging the HQP Pool	Industrial Receptor Capacity
Capability to Execute	Pervasiveness	Market Impact
	Industry Involvement	

Since adopting ProGrid in 1997, MMO has refined its Language Ladder™, resulting in well-defined and separated steps, as illustrated in Table 2.4 for Industrial Receptor Capacity.

TABLE 2.4
MMO's Industrial Receptor Capacity

Industrial Receptor Capacity:	
A	It is anticipated that there will be receptor companies in Ontario for the technology but these have not been contacted.
B	Receptor company(ies) with the capacity to exploit the technology in Ontario have been contacted and have expressed in writing (letter attached) commercial interest.
C	Receptor company(ies) with the capacity and market access to exploit the technology in Ontario have expressed in writing (letter attached) a commitment to track the progress of the technology and their intent to identify specific opportunities for commercial use in their Ontario operations.
D	Receptor company(ies) with operations in Ontario who have demonstrated capacity, skills, and market access to aggressively develop and market the technology have expressed in writing (letter attached), their expectation that they will exploit/use the technology in their Ontario operations.

Training and Incentives

The bedrock of innovation is the people whose ideas and skills drive the process. The graduate training programs of academic institutions (leading to a Masters or a Ph.D. degree) is integral to the research enterprise. They serve as the principal source of future researchers, and also as a source of person power for research during their formal graduate training. As graduate programs are resource intensive in terms of student time, faculty supervisor time, and university infrastructure, the number of available positions is limited as compared to the undergraduate university population. The Alberta Heritage Foundation for Medical Research (AHFMR) selects students to work on

FIGURE 2.2
Database of AHFMR's Applications

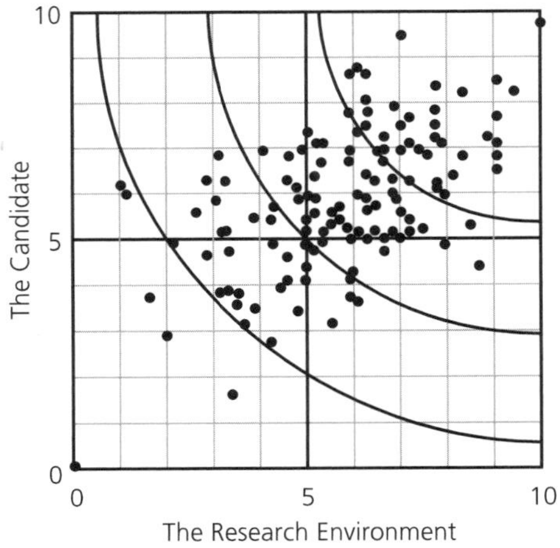

TABLE 2.5
AHFMR's Evaluation Matrix for Student Selection

The Candidate	Linking Factors	The Research Environment
Academic Record	Role of Trainee and Linkage to Supervisor's Research	Supervisor's Research Record
Research Experience	Overall Impression of Project	Training Environment
Letters of Reference		

research projects under the guidance of established researchers, using a committee-based peer review assisted by ProGrid software.

The overarching objectives for the competition are the qualifications of the candidate student and the research environment provided by the supervisor, which are highly independent factors, as shown in Table 2.5.

The results from the first five years using this approach are shown in Figure 2.2. The spread in the data in this grid reflect the high level of independence of the axes. In the bar chart (Figure 2.3), the results from a specific Proposal are shown compared to the database average, which helps focus on strengths and weaknesses of that application.

FIGURE 2.3
Profile of Strengths and Weaknesses

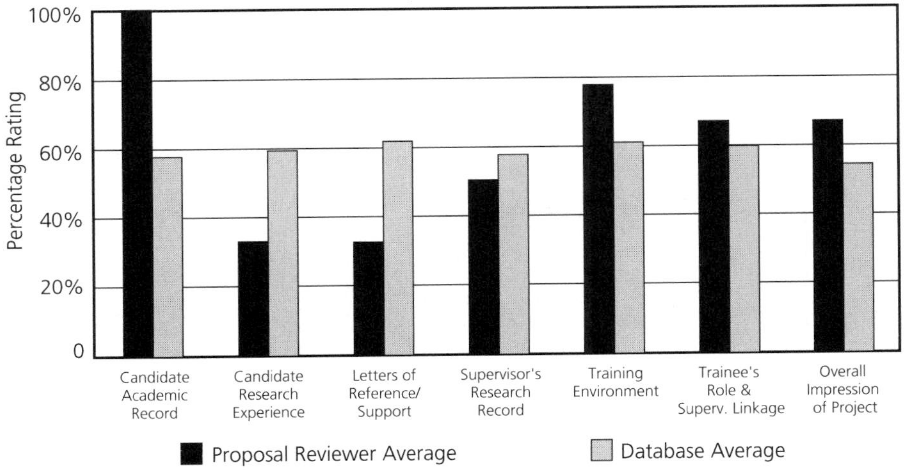

The power of this approach is demonstrated by a much broader distribution in the ratings of applications compared to the earlier more traditional evaluation approach (Figure 2.4).

FIGURE 2.4
Distribution of Applicant Ratings

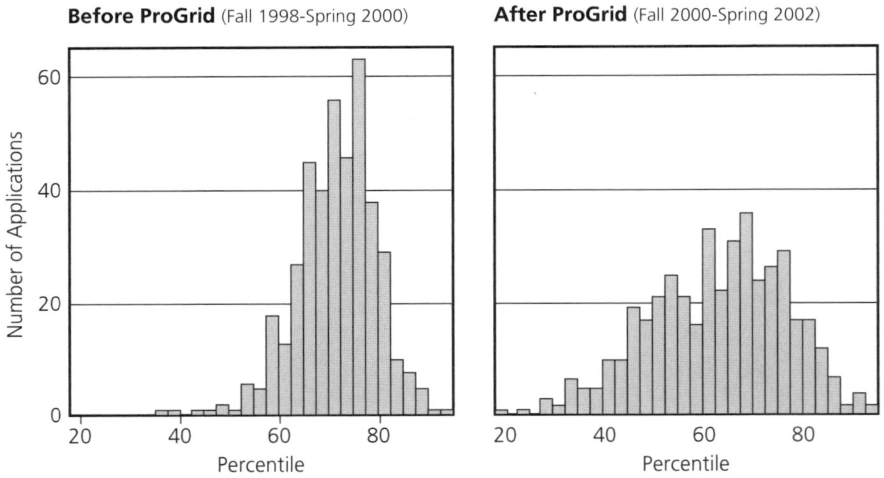

The Ontario Ministry of Natural Resources (OMNR) has also used ProGrid in evaluating research staff with respect to the quality of their research and their ability to transfer the results to the Ministry and industry. Three levels of staff were evaluated as shown in Figure 2.5. The triangles represent staff in the lower RS3 category, the circles represent staff in the middle RS4 category and the diamonds represent staff in the top RS5 category. As individual staff members improve in their research and technology transfer accomplishments, merit

FIGURE 2.5
Performance Appraisal

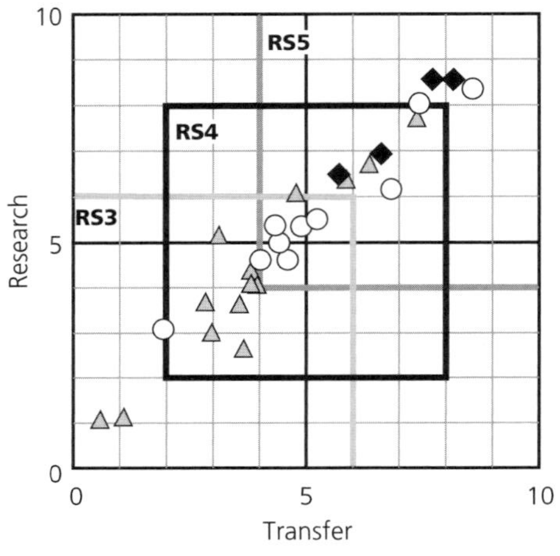

FIGURE 2.6
Contributions of Staff

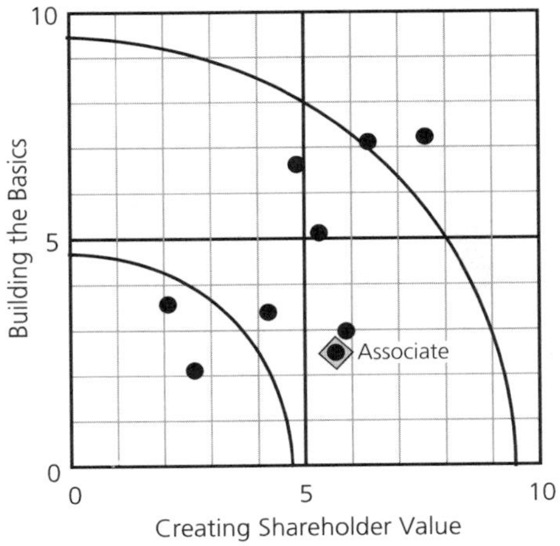

and promotion decisions become evident and justifiable.

Rewards and incentives are an important driver in the innovative process. Professionals in most disciplines are hired to, and are committed to, increase shareholder value in their organizations. They do this in part by undertaking a multitude of day-to-day activities focused on building their own capabilities and the overall strength of the organization, essentially "building the basics."

Creating Shareholder Value and Building the Basics thus form the two overarching objectives of a performance evaluation process. An example for a team of professionals is shown in Figure 2.6. The rating for a specific associate is compared with colleagues, and used as the basis for promotions and for bonus pool distribution. The ratings were provided by colleagues in a 360-degree process (i.e. by those above, below and in lateral organizational positions).

In this example, the curves are drawn concentric with the point 0,0, using R_0 as a measure of chart progress (as defined in Chapter 1). This approach does not penalize a staff member who makes a contribution on one axis only.

In a complex organization, individual staff would not be expected to make major contributions in all of the defined criteria. Excellent performance in one or two criteria, often referred to as "spikes," could easily be recognized and rewarded, as illustrated in Figure 2.7.

FIGURE 2.7
Example of Performance Profile

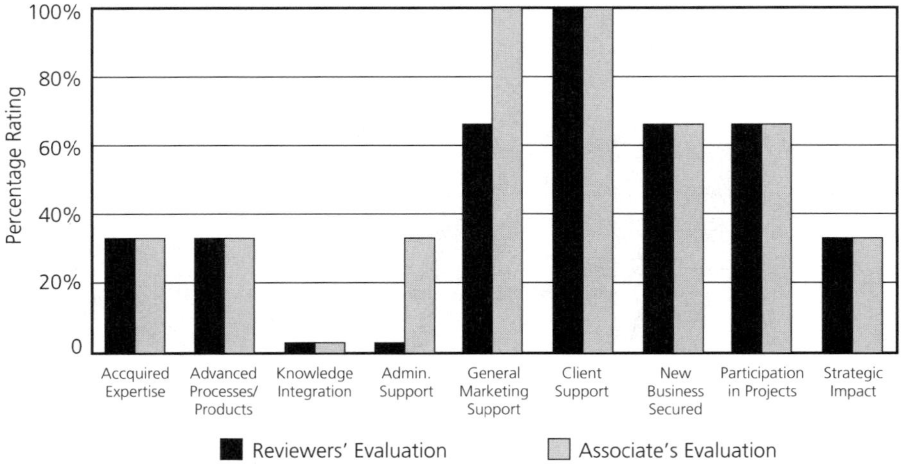

The full texts of the case studies related to innovation are provided in:

Chapters 8, 9 – Infrastructure

Chapter 10 – Research Programs

Chapters 14, 19 – Training and Incentives

[i] Peter Hackett, Innowest 2004, Presentation Nov. 17, 2004, Calgary, Alberta, Canada

[ii] *The Power of the 2 x 2 Matrix*, Alex Lowy, Phil Hood, 2004, Jossey-Bass (Wiley)

3 New Technologies – The Economic Engine

The development and commercialization of new technologies is the trademark of globally-competitive nations. Supporting fundamental research is but one part of the process; the establishment of a strong receptor capacity is equally important, again evidence of the twin strands of innovation. There is a chain of receptors in the commercialization process, starting with early stage funders such as Angel Investors and Venture Capitalists.

Identifying new ideas that have the potential for transforming the marketplace is the goal of all early stage investors. Two overarching objectives that are useful for this purpose are the quality of the venture and the potential market impact, as shown in Table 3.1.

TABLE 3.1
Evaluation Matrix for Early Stage Ventures

The Venture	The Connectors	The Impact
Advance Over Current Commercial Practice	Customer Validation and Acceptance	Market Size and Growth
Competitive Advantage	Business Plan	Market Share
Current Development Status	Business Team Experience and Capacity	Competition
Capability to Complete Technical Development	Investor Support	Financial Returns to the Venture Capital Investor

Governments are prepared to wait for new ideas to develop over time; private investors on the other hand expect to see evidence of early commercialization, such as positive responses from the market, as illustrated in the Language Ladder™ for Customer Validation and Acceptance (Table 3.2).

TABLE 3.2
Language Ladder™ for Customer Validation and Acceptance

	The products/processes/services provided by the concept:
A	have not yet been evaluated by potential customers. Preliminary market studies may indicate that a potential market exists.
B	have had limited evaluation by potential customers but they have confirmed the concept has potential value to them.
C	have been fully tested by potential customers who have confirmed their commercial interest and are prepared to place firm orders for the purchase of development quantities.
D	have been accepted for commercial use by two key customers (as identified in their business plans) and these customers are placing repeat orders.

The profile chart of strengths and weaknesses is an important indication of future potential, with the example in Figure 3.1 indicating a modest advance (left two bars), but with encouraging market prospects (right three bars). In this example, the ratings provided by the Proponent as part of a self-assessment are reasonably consistent with the average ratings of a group of assessors. This provides encouragement that the Proponent has a realistic understanding of the venture and its market potential.

FIGURE 3.1
Profile Chart

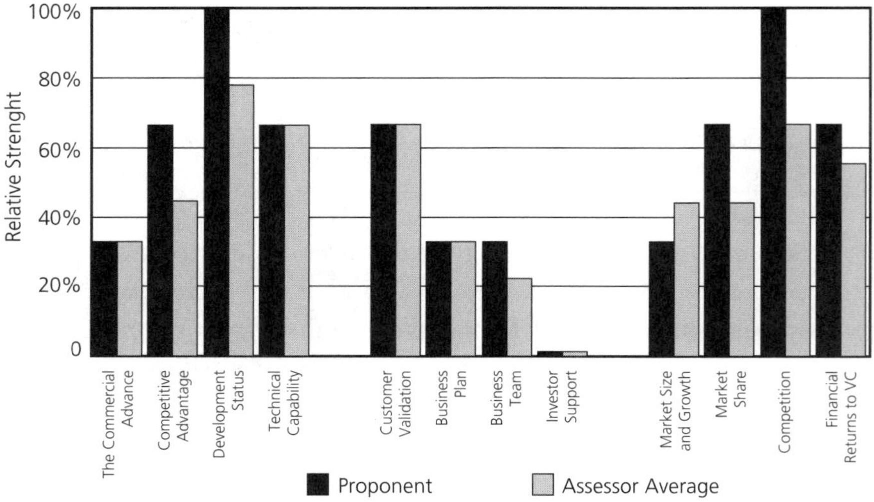

FIGURE 3.2
AHFMR Technology Commercialization Database

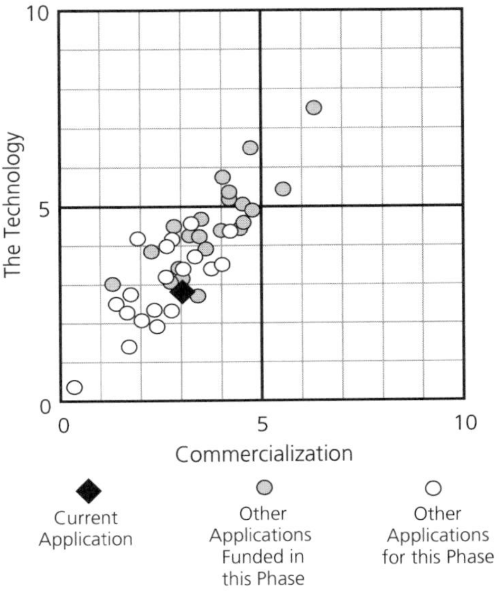

The Alberta Heritage Foundation for Medical Research (AHFMR) has adapted this approach for its Technology Commercialization Program, designed to assist innovators with the transfer of new health-related ideas and scientific findings into successful commercial products and services. The database of applications is shown in Figure 3.2. The overarching objectives were defined as the strength of the Technology, and the progress towards Commercialization, reflecting the name of the program. Since the applications tend to be early stage ventures, with many evolving out of university research programs, most of the projects fell in the lower left hand quadrant.

The space between the steps in the Language Ladder statements is territory for making improvements. AHFMR uses a feature of ProGrid® methodology called Sensitivity Analysis that predicts possible upsides and downsides based on the current position of the project. An example is shown in Figure 3.3. This provides zones of upsides and downsides, each based on changes that are controllable by the project team (Proj.) and those that may result from changes in the external environment (Ext.). Periodic reassessment of the venture will provide a trajectory, which will indicate the extent to which the upsides and downsides are realized.

FIGURE 3.3
Sensitivity Analysis

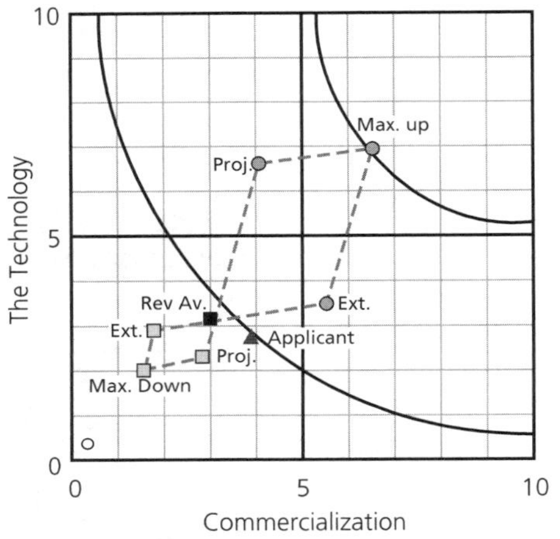

FIGURE 3.4
AVAC Ltd. Database

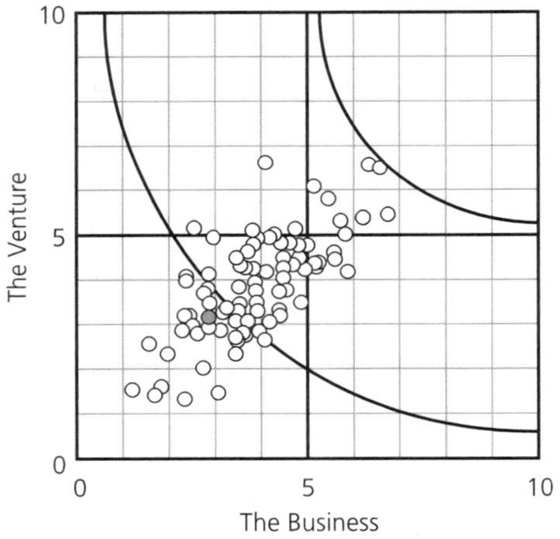

This approach can be applied to any technology support program, regardless of field. Figure 3.4 shows the database for proposals submitted to AVAC Ltd., a program for supporting value-added initiatives in the agri-food area.

One of the advantages is the ability to share applications among funding bodies and to facilitate the transfer of technology. One such grouping is the Agriculture Funding Consortium comprising:

- Alberta Agricultural Research Institute (AARI)
- Alberta Crop Industry Development Fund Ltd. (ACIDF)
- Alberta Diversified Livestock Industry Development Fund (ADLIDF)
- Alberta Livestock Industry Development Fund Ltd. (ALIDF)
- AVAC Ltd.
- Agriculture and Food Council (AGFC)

Entrepreneurship education has now become a popular course in many universities. ProGrid methodology provides a solid framework to help students understand the issues involved in preparing and evaluating business plans. A methodology similar to that shown in Table 3.1 has been used as a teaching and evaluation tool in senior undergraduate engineering and MBA level classes at the University of Alberta. Many of the business plans developed by students have been successful in business plan competitions. The feedback that each student group receives has been an important benefit.

As development proceeds, higher level of investments and more detailed due diligence are needed. In the example shown in Table 3.3, each cell in the Evaluation Matrix is expanded, resulting in 37 criteria in total. Technologies at various stages of maturity are shown in Figure 3.5. A technology may follow a specific trajectory in this grid, with spurts of advance in technical strength and commercial strength.

TABLE 3.3
Thirty-Seven Criteria for Technical and Market Readiness

Technical Strength	Enabling Strengths	Commercial Strength
Technical Framework • scientific basis • advance on prior art • uniqueness • pervasiveness	Commercial Readiness • current stage of development • level of development required • complexity of scale-up	Market Characteristics • market acceptance • competitor's strength • regulatory compliance • regulatory leadership • market impact • geographic reach
Level of Verification • proof of concept • system integration • external validation	Proprietary Strength • patent/copyright position • competitive IP • trademark strengths • know-how requirement • scope for improvement	Margin and Profit Potential • cost reduction opportunities • competitor's price sensitivity • speed of commercialization • price-margins
Project Team • technical credentials • technical networks • understanding market needs	Technological Durability • avoidance • dependence on other products • duplication • robustness • obsolescence	Commercialization Channels • investment availability • market trials • partners • marketing networks

FIGURE 3.5
Searching for the Winners

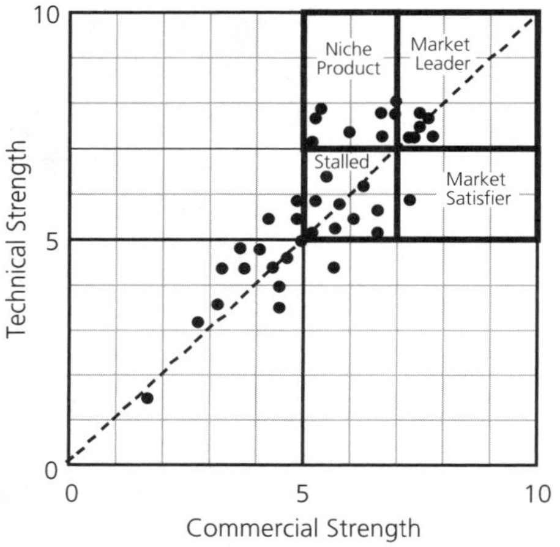

Ventures in the "stalled" zone may represent the case of a relatively mature technology that has a flat profile with the serious weaknesses improved but with no outstanding strengths to take it to a higher grid position – not something venture capitalists like to see.

The full texts of case studies addressing technology commercialization are given in Chapters 12, 13, 15, 16, 17 and 20.

4 Good Governance – Post Enron Best Practices

Audit Best Practices

In the late 1990s, some aspects of corporate management were like driving on the "autobahn" – few posted limits and thus few enforceable consequences. As the complexities of corporate structures and activities grew, the old, well-established "rules" (based largely on GAAP – Generally Accepted Accounting Principles) became less able to deal with the ability of persons or groups within corporations to bend them to what they thought might be best. In some cases, this bending of the rules was well intentioned – in some cases not. Some had the intent of protecting or enhancing shareholder value in the corporation – some were focused solely on the individual. Some resulted from incompetence, some from failure of process, and some from criminal intent.

The results are well publicized – Enron, WorldCom, Adelphia, Hollinger, Nortel, etc. These and others resulted in a global focus on "Failures in Governance," particularly in the light that these failures have cost investors many billions of dollars. Over and above the monetary losses is a loss of investor confidence.

As a consequence, governments and regulators introduced both legislation and regulations to define a new set of "speed limits" and penalties for rule breakers. Many of these are designed to protect against the negative experiences of the past but not for the improvement of standards of governance in whole; rather they limited instances of bad governance. Significant debate goes on about whether or not some of the new regulations to limit "bad practices" will lead to "best practices." Need proof? One initiative is to ensure that all members of a board of directors are independent, thus preventing the possibility of insider dealings. But this could mean a board has no members who really know the business, a factor seen in the past to be an essential element of a corporation able to generate healthy returns for shareholders.

The new "speed limits," which focus on governance processes and financial reporting, are codified in the U.S. Sarbanes-Oxley Act. In Canada, Canadian Securities Administrators adopted Multilateral Instrument 52-110 and stock exchanges such as the TSX, NYSE and NASDAQ have revised their rules and manuals. The limits defined new regulations and obligations for companies, the individuals within them and the professional organizations supporting them. While penalties were potentially severe and implementation was to be almost immediate, the new environment was so demanding and complex that in the area of audit and reporting it was generally acknowledged that there were not nearly enough audit professionals in all of North America to do the work required to be compliant. In fact, significant numbers of corporations were given permission to delay their initial filings for just this reason.

The Canadian Institute of Chartered Accountants (CICA) is the organization that provides accreditation for public accounting professionals across Canada. It determines and publishes practice standards and manuals. It is a world leader in creating new tools and "best practice" guides to continually advance the standards of practice for not only its members but also for the clients they serve.

One such publication is *"Integrity in the Spotlight, Opportunities for Audit Committees"* which provides best practices for Audit Committees well in advance of the new regulations. Reviewed in light of the practices that led to prominent audit and governance failures and the new regulations, it was obvious that Integrity would help Audit Committees meet the new requirements. But the framework would also help with continuous improvement in the efficiency and effectiveness of practices of both Committees and their members. A number of organizations had begun to apply *Integrity* in part or in whole based on the efforts of individuals who had read and espoused its principles.

Based on the best practices in this publication, CICA launched the *Audit Committee Performance Support System (ACPSS),* based in part on ProGrid® methodology. One example of a Language Ladder™ is shown in Table 4.1.

TABLE 4.1
Language Ladder for Review of Accounting Policies

	Accounting Policies
A	The Audit Committee does not review and discuss the company's accounting policies and their relationship to GAAP as part of its review of the annual financial statements.
B	The Audit Committee reviews the accounting policy note to ensure completeness and acceptability with GAAP as part of the approval of the financial statements.
C	The Audit Committee discusses with management and the external auditor the acceptability, degree of aggressiveness/conservatism and quality of underlying accounting policies.
D	The Audit Committee carries out discussions with management and the external auditor to ensure that the underlying accounting policies, disclosures, and key estimates and judgements are considered to be the most appropriate in the circumstances (within the range of acceptable options and alternatives).

Audit Committees are able to carry out a self-assessment of their practices against 114 best practices, grouped into 29 matrix cells, to produce a profile chart such as shown in Figure 4.1. The grey areas identify where improvements are needed to achieve expected performance.

FIGURE 4.1
Audit Committee Performance

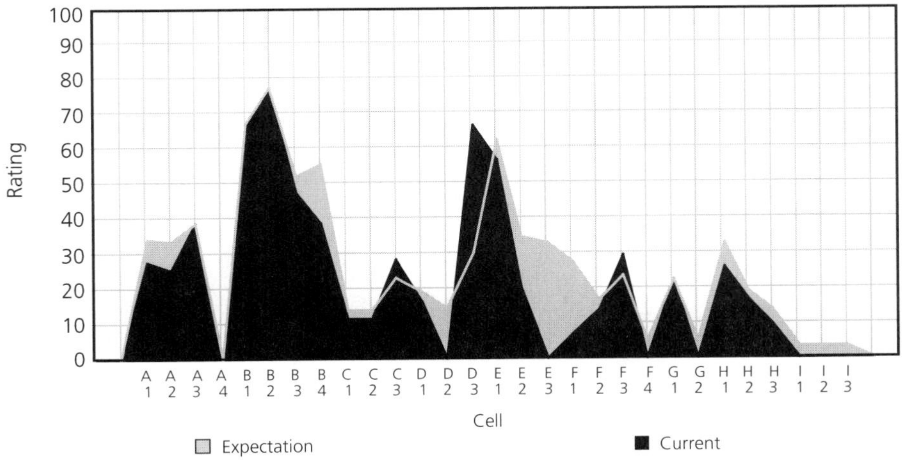

Shareholder Value

The challenge for companies is not just to have an effective audit function but to ensure that good governance is pervasive throughout their organization. Focusing only on audit and accounting functions does not ensure that an organization is doing its best to produce shareholder value. Thus, two key overarching objectives for a company are to achieve organizational excellence and high business performance, reflected in the Evaluation Matrix that includes the elements identified in Table 4.2. The term Level Zero indicates that the evaluation is at the level of the Board of Directors and senior management.

TABLE 4.2
Level Zero Company Evaluation Matrix

Organizational Excellence	Enablers	Business Performance
Vision/Mission	Human Resources	The Products
Governance	The Business Plan	The Markets
Intellectual Capital	Production Practices	The Competition

To ensure a company is well aligned at all levels in the organization, we can drill down into each cell of this matrix to produce underlying matrices (Level One), as shown in Table 4.3. Each of the criteria from the Level Zero Evaluation Matrix has an underlying Evaluation Matrix. (This illustrates a specific ProGrid tool for this purpose with a total of 60 Level One cells).

As an example, the underlying matrix for the Governance cell is shown in Table 4.4. The influence of good governance is seen at various levels in the organization, with important external impacts.

The process of drilling down can be extended to Level Two, with the Evaluation Matrix for the Board of Directors cell shown in Table 4.5.

The results of a Board of Directors evaluation is shown in Figure 4.2, with the heavy solid lines showing current performance and the two shaded circles representing the expected performance if the C and D levels in the associated Language Ladders are achieved.

TABLE 4.3
Level One Divisional/Operational Level Evaluation Matrices

Vision/Mission		
A1	B1	C1
A2		C2

Human Resources		
A1	B1	C1
A2	B2	C2
	B3	

The Products		
A1	B1	C1
A2	B2	C2
A3		

Governance		
A1	B1	C1
A2	B2	C2
A3	B3	C3

The Business Plan		
A1	B1	C1
A2	B2	C2
A3		

The Markets		
A1	B1	C1
A2	B2	C2

Intellectual Capital		
A1	B1	C1
A2	B2	C2
A3		C3

Production Practices		
A1	B1	C1
A2	B2	C2

The Competition		
A1	B1	C1
A2		C2

TABLE 4.4
Level One Governance Evaluation Matrix

Commitment to Governance	The Connectors	The External Impact
Board of Directors	Organizational Structure	Industry Relations
Shareholders	Audit and Evaluations	Public Relations
Senior Management	Succession	The Environment

TABLE 4.5
Level Two Board of Directors Evaluation Matrix

Attributes	Roles/Processes	Impact
Experience	Strategy and Policy	Internal Impact
Knowledge	Planning	External Impact
Independence	Performance	Strategic Impact
Commitment	Staff Relations	Leadership

FIGURE 4.2
Current Evaluation of a Board of Directors

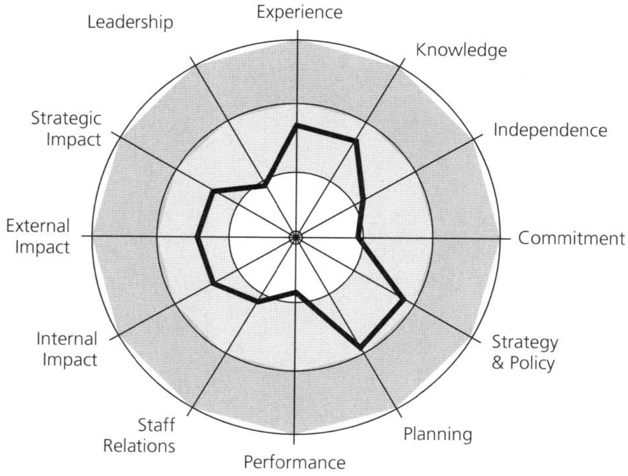

We began this chapter with a discussion of how a recent emphasis on governance has led to an array of regulatory requirements, the reaction of governments to blatant acts of malfeasance and fraud. We then introduced a methodology by which corporations can attain high levels of performance that meet the fiduciary requirements expected by regulatory authorities and, at the same time, meet the expectations of shareholders.

While the methodology may be more complex than the decision-making tools outlined elsewhere in this book, the information needed is no different than what is required for the effective management of any organization. Once the overarching objectives are established by the Executive and approved by the Shareholders all parts of the organization must be in alignment, with performance measured and reported in a full and comprehensive manner. The actions required to move from the current to desired future states should be known and understood by all stakeholders.

Good governance in public bodies is also getting increased attention. Philanthropic organizations, for example, have responsibilities for effective stewardship of their grants. Public sector research organizations have mandates that include contributions to the "public good".

An international benchmarking study was undertaken to compare the practices of both public and private sector research organizations. With two overarching objectives (Generation of Intellectual Capital and Deployment of Intellectual Capital) the study compared current and desired future states. Surprisingly, none of the organizations, public or private, were satisfied with their current positions as shown in Figure 4.3.

The pubic sector bodies wish to put more emphasis on technology deployment and less on the generation of new intellectual capital, which raises the question of whether public sector laboratories can put in place the necessary tight linkages among a broad range of clients. It also raises the issue of whether they would so weaken their ability to generate new technology that they fail to perform their original mission. Industrial R&D bodies recognize that they need to put more emphasis on longer-term technology and see the possibility of doing this through industry consortia.

The full texts of the case studies on Governance are provided in Chapters 21, 24 and 25.

FIGURE 4.3
How R&D Organizations See Their Future

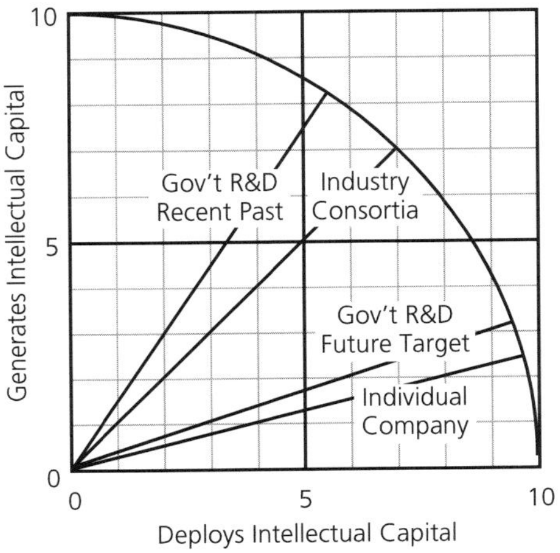

5 Government Procurement – A Troubled History

From the time that kings and their agents (and later elected governments and bureaucracies) began to collect taxes for war or public works, persons on both sides of the transactions have taken advantage of procurement situations and extracted hidden coinage or other advantages. Ancient and contemporary history is bursting with references to abuses of the public procurement system.

Examples abound with major abuses and scandals in building, supplying and maintaining the Royal Navy and Napoleon's army. All jurisdictions have examples of failed bridges and dams as a result of cheating on public contracts. Historians exploring this topic would find many cases in the building of railways and canals.

There has been a plethora of recent examples of headlines such as:

Bureaucrats mismanaged $3-billion

- audit reveals mess in grant-giving process:
  - without submission of an application form
  - approved without any internal or external consultation
  - no evidence of financial monitoring

$150-million federal deal broke rules

- audit finds:
  - contract process was not carried out fairly
  - process lacked transparency
  - incomplete or missing files

Public procurement is a big market. Purchasing by governments and other public bodies in Canada in 2000 at all levels (national, state/provincial, region/county, and local) including education and health care and other public funded bodies tops $100 billion annually or some $3,000 for each Canadian citizen.

Over recent years, a marked shift in the mix of public procurement requirements from "hard" goods to "softer" services has gone even further by the practice of outsourcing – hiring private and non-profit organizations to undertake work otherwise done by government staff. To some extent, this reflects the growth of the services sector in national economies and the requirement of public bodies to purchase these services. But it also reflects a fundamental change in political direction. Today, outsourcing is not just the preserve of right-of-centre governments, but also all governments that see the inherent efficiency advantages of a *competitive* outsourcing approach.

Whenever the decision factors move beyond the historic "lowest price wins" format, the complexity of the buy is much increased. This is because qualitative and intangible issues tend to take the ascendancy over the quantitative – indeed, the *only* quantitative criterion in services procurement is often the cost.

When Canada's Auditor General, Sheila Fraser, raised concerns over the federal government's sponsorship and advertising activities, a Commission of Inquiry was formed, prompted by cited failures of internal control systems, a lack of appropriate documentation justifying material expenditures of public money, the payment of large sums of money to private parties with no apparent value being received in return, a systematic disregard of the applicable rules including those contained in the government's own *Financial Administration Act,* a lack of competition in the selection of advertising agencies, and a general bypassing of Parliamentary procedures.[i]

With this background, we engaged in more than 40 "conversations" with people regarding the problems with public procurement as it is presently practiced in Canada. These included persons on both the policy and practice side of government procurement. It included four levels of government as well as procurement representatives from government agencies. We also spoke with the supply side – senior managers of vendor organizations whose practices include a high per cent of public sector involvement.

There is frustration on all sides. And while there is clear recognition of the problem, there is a general reluctance to seek alternative solutions. Many vendors, for example, are unwilling to tackle the existing institutional approaches themselves, and the highly-fragmented vendor industry has not shown the leadership or persistence required to attack the systemic problems head on.

We found the professional associations to be balkanized between the private and public sectors and to represent fewer and fewer of the people whose jobs are in procurement. There appears to be little academic research in the area and limited knowledge transfer.

Examples of problems involved in standard government RFPs (Request for Proposals) were cited as:

- Poorly drafted selection criteria
- Poor linkages between the organization's objectives and the services to be procured
- So-called "requirements" which do not appear in the evaluation criteria
- Unnecessary restrictions on the proposed vendor solutions
- Vendor misunderstandings, leading to wasted vendor effort
- Provision by the vendors of unnecessary and irrelevant information
- Inconsistency in the application of the selection criteria
- Opaque processing of the results
- A poor audit trail
- A challengeable decision.

To overcome as many of the deficiencies as possible, a ProGrid® process has been developed and tested for government procurement. The steps described in Chapter 1 were adopted for an RFP for selecting a Consultant to carry out a specified task. The overarching objectives were defined as the qualifications of the Consultant and the expected impact of the Results, as shown in the Evaluation Matrix™ in Table 5.1.

TABLE 5.1
Procurement Evaluation Matrix

The Consultant	Enablers	The Results
Credentials	Project Understanding	Delivery
Performance	Work Plan	Quality
Organizational Capacity	Access and Responsiveness	

The Language Ladder™ for the Work Plan cell in the Evaluation Matrix is shown in Table 5.2. The D level Language Ladder builds on the C level through an additive phrase, an approach that helps quickly differentiate the C and D levels.

TABLE 5.2
Language Ladder for Work Plan

The Work Plan covers the Approach, Organization and Management of the Project:	
A	The Work Plan has significant weaknesses.
B	The Work Plan should result in a satisfactory completion of the Project
C	The Work Plan presents a comprehensive management approach to successfully complete the Project ...
D	... AND includes some innovative ideas which provide additional value without additional risk.

The results of the evaluation of 13 proposals are shown in Figure 5.1. Each Proposal has its individual report identifying strengths and weaknesses. In this example, the decision team would assess the four proposals above the upper curve, and examine factors such as reviewer variation or any specific concerns raised by individual reviewers.

The reports document and demonstrate *in a consistent and graphical form* the ability of any competing proposal to meet the values, priorities and expectations of the procuring agency. The reports provide both an excellent *medium of accountability* and a *permanent audit trail* for future reference with respect to the following:

- Ranking of each proposal against all the other proposals
- Profile showing how each proposal rates against each set of performance criteria

- Comparison of the suppliers' self-rankings with those of the reviewers
- Comparison of criteria rankings of current applications with those of previous applications
- Degree of consensus among the reviewers

This methodology provides a decision environment that is open, fair, transparent and accountable. It gets the best out of both potential vendors and reviewers while concentrating on the issues important to the competition. It is a win/win situation for both sides, offering efficiencies and benefits to the private and public sector while taking advantage of automated reporting systems that advance the practice of public procurement.

The full text of the case study on government procurement is provided in Chapter 11.

FIGURE 5.1
Comparative Ranking of RFP Proposals

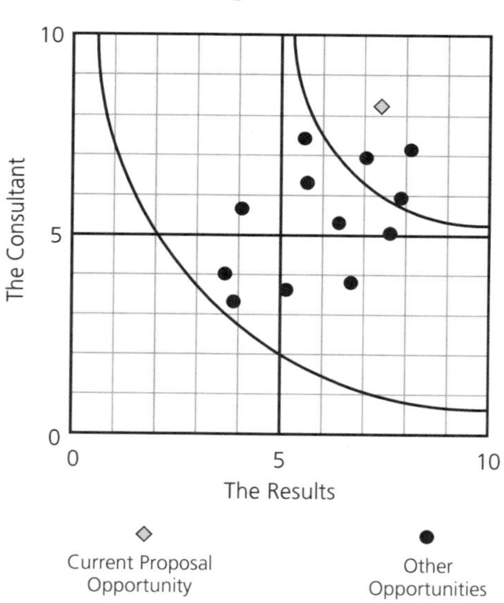

[i] http://www.gomery.ca/en/index.asp

6 Societal Goals – Setting Targets, Measuring Progress

Defining the Goals

In previous chapters, we have progressed from making personal decisions such as buying a house to evaluating the way corporations measure their progress toward long-term goals. But nations and societies have their own aspirations that can be expressed in language and the progress, or lack of it, measured over time. We have worked in one jurisdiction sufficiently to be able to demonstrate both the concepts and the impact of using the ProGrid® methodology for this purpose.

While the Province of Alberta has enormous riches in both agriculture and energy resources and has a dynamic high technology infrastructure spawned from the needs of the resource industries, it is now a thriving economic power in its own right. With its entrepreneurial culture, it is hardly surprising that Alberta has been receptive to the evaluation concepts described in this book.

Alberta has expressed its long-range goals in the Evaluation Matrix™ shown in Table 6.1. The two overarching objectives are to establish the Innovation Capacity to achieve specified Economic and Social Values, the second and third columns in this matrix. This would be implemented through a set of Strategies pertinent to sectors of the economy (the first column). Recognizing the long-term impact of its strategies, Alberta has committed to a set of Outcomes shown in the fourth column. While difficult to measure in the time-span of individual programs, these describe future aspirations. Using this matrix as the master plan, ProGrid methodology is being used to evaluate progress toward the desired future state.

TABLE 6.1
The Alberta Evaluation Matrix

<table>
<tr><th>INPUTS
Strategies</th><th>ENABLERS
Increased Innovation Capacity</th><th>OUTPUTS
Economic and Social Value</th><th>OUTCOMES
People Prosperity Preservation</th></tr>
<tr><td>Energy Research Strategy</td><td>People</td><td>Energy Processes, Products and Services</td><td rowspan="5">• Effective environmental stewardship
• Value added economic activity
• Prosperous rural communities
• Alberta made strategy for reduction of greenhouse gases
• Skilled labour force (attract, educate and retain)
• Economic prosperity
• World class infrastructure
• Attract, establish and retrain businesses
• Healthy population
• Unleashing innovation
• Industrial sustainability
• Knowledge-based economy</td></tr>
<tr><td>Life Sciences Research Strategy</td><td>Infrastructure</td><td>Agri - Processes, Products and Services</td></tr>
<tr><td>ICT Research Strategy</td><td>Strategic Projects</td><td>Forestry Processes, Products and Services</td></tr>
<tr><td>Tech. Comm. Strategy</td><td>Technology Adoption and Commercialization</td><td>Health Processes, Products and Services</td></tr>
<tr><td></td><td>Innovation Facilitating Mechanisms</td><td>ICT Processes, Products and Services</td></tr>
</table>

The organizations shown in Table 6.2 were included in the first phase of the project. The concept of cascading matrices was used to evaluate the degree of alignment of these organizations with the strategies and goals of the Department of Innovation and Science.

TABLE 6.2
The Alberta Evaluation Matrix

<table>
<tr><th colspan="3">Department of Innovation and Science (INNSCI)</th></tr>
<tr><td>Alberta Energy Research Institute (AERI)</td><td colspan="2">Life Sciences</td></tr>
<tr><td></td><td>Alberta Agriculture Research Institute (AARI)</td><td>Alberta Forestry Research Institute (AFRI)</td></tr>
<tr><td colspan="3">Alberta Science and Research Investment Program (ASRIP)</td></tr>
<tr><td colspan="3">Technology Commercialization Program (Tech Comm)</td></tr>
</table>

Each of these units developed its own set of Evaluation Matrices and Language Ladders. Their assessments of their current and future positions were prepared and then aggregated in Figure 6.1 (open points) to compare with those of the Department of Innovation and Science (solid points). Both the Department and the units reporting to the Department identified the major advances that were needed to achieve the Future 1 goals (in about five years) and the longer-term Future 2 goals (in 15 years). The units positioned themselves at a lower starting position; the specific differences behind these evaluations were identified for discussion and resolution.

FIGURE 6.1
Degree of Alignment Toward the Future Goals

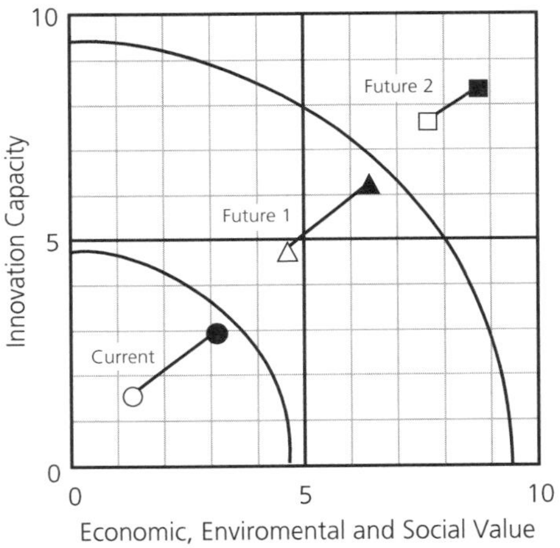

Once the long-term goals were established, the Alberta Government launched various initiatives to support the goals. The Alberta Innovation Program was an example and included two streams; Service Excellence to improve the delivery of government services and Unleashing Innovation to enhance the application of new knowledge. This competitive program, available to government departments and agencies, has helped ensure the various arms of government keep their focus on issues central to the government's strategic plan. ProGrid methodology made it feasible to assess the wide diversity of complex applications involving both tangible and intangible factors.

The Alberta Innovation Program provided the breadth to cover the spectrum of initiatives that were key to the province's strategic plan. Some sectors of the economy are so key to future prosperity that it was imperative to "drill down" into those sectors to get the specificity required to make transformative changes. An example is provided in the following section.

Technology Oil

When oil was first produced in commercial quantities in the United States and Canada[i], you only had to scratch the surface of the ground for oil to flow. A century and a half later, oil is still being discovered and produced but much of it is requires advanced technologies to recover in an economically and environmentally sound manner. This is now referred to as "technology oil." Alberta has established a comprehensive Energy Evaluation Matrix shown in Table 6.3.

TABLE 6.3
The Energy Evaluation Matrix

<table>
<tr><th>Innovation Strategy</th><th>Enablers (Innovation Capacity)</th><th>Economic, Environmental and Social Goals related to:</th></tr>
<tr><td rowspan="6">Link public and private sector partners from across Canada to work together on research to further oil sands technology, develop cleaner coal technology, reduce greenhouse gas emissions, manage water resources, improve conventional oil and gas recovery and explore alternative energy sources.</td><td rowspan="2">Energy Innovation Network</td><td>Bitumen Upgrading
• Energy Efficiency
• Diversified Products
• Environment</td></tr>
<tr><td>Clean Carbon/Coal
• Coal
• Biomass</td></tr>
<tr><td rowspan="2">Policy and Business Drivers
• R&D Incentives
• R&D Investments
• Capital Investment
• Regulatory Protocols
• Climate Change and Water Management
• Industrial Infrastructure</td><td>Carbon Dioxide Management
• CO_2 Environment
• CO_2 Use and Disposal</td></tr>
<tr><td>Hydrocarbon Recovery
• Conventional Oil
• Natural Gas
• Heavy Oil & Bitumen
• Environment</td></tr>
<tr><td rowspan="2">Innovation Framework
• People
• Infrastructure
• Global Intelligence
• Communications
• Technology Management</td><td>Alternative and Renewable Energy
• Hydrogen/Fuel Cells
• Bio-energy
• Other</td></tr>
<tr><td>Water Management
• Cross-cutting Initiatives
• Upgrading
• Recovery</td></tr>
</table>

Quantitative 2020 goals have been established for each cell in this matrix. The specific economic, environmental and social goals for the third column in this matrix are shown in Figure 6.2. This does not look like a jurisdiction that desires to be a "hewer of wood and a drawer of water."

The progress made since this project was started in shown in Figure 6.3 The two shaded outer circles represent the 2012 and 2020 targets respectively.

FIGURE 6.2
Alberta's Long Range Energy Goals

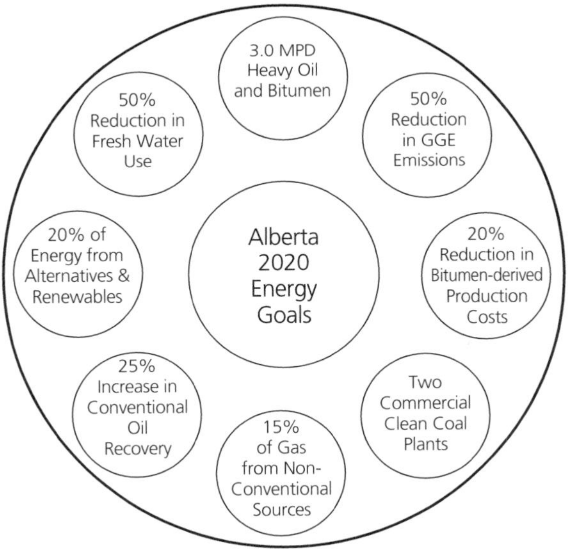

The participants in this endeavour have established major goals for the year 2020, which will transform the Canadian energy system, realizing major economic, environmental and social benefits if achieved. The value to Canada if these goals are met is expected to be huge.

The full texts of the case studies on Societal Goals are provided in Chapters 18, 22 and 23.

FIGURE 6.3
Progress Since 2003

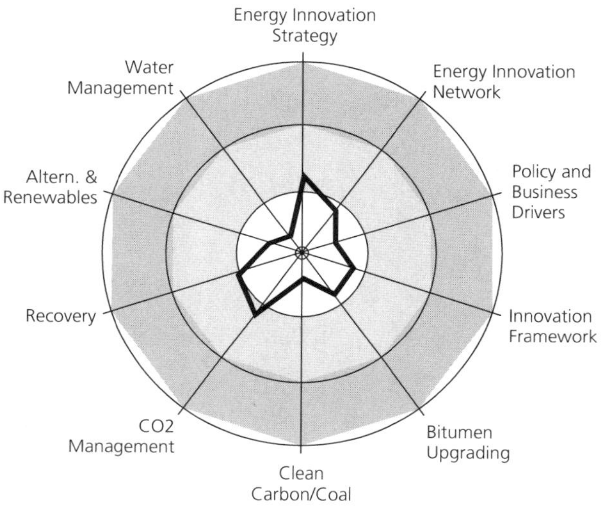

[i] Oil was first produced in commercial quantities in 1858 by James Miller Williams in Lambton County, Ontario and in 1859 by Edwin L. Drake in Titusville, Pennsylvania. *Petroleum – Prehistoric to Petrochemicals*, G.A. Purdy, The Copp Clark Publishing Company, 1957

7 What We Are Learning

More than 10 years have passed since ProGrid® methodology was first used to help in understanding and evaluating intangibles. The participants in the case studies presented in this book have developed different approaches in using ProGrid and have learned much in this process. One is tempted to refer to this as a "paradigm shift", but this over-used expression is not appropriate in that it gives the impression that the traditional evaluation approaches have been replaced by a new system.

In fact, ProGrid is still based on peer review. The expertise and opinion of reviewers remain the currency of the process. The foundations of ProGrid are the criteria, values and expectations of the sponsoring organizations. ProGrid strives to put objectivity into what is a subjective process, and seeks an actionable and supportable consensus.

The following sections present some of the key underpinnings of ProGrid.

Getting back to the Objectives

We have put considerable emphasis on the issue of two dimensions when making decisions and evaluating performance. Starting with the belief that we spend most of our time working in a one-dimensional mode, there is a need to search for the second dimension required to reach higher-level goals.

In fact, two dimensions are likely to be implicit in the mandate of an organization. The legislation establishing the Canada Foundation for Innovation (CFI) specified economic growth, job creation and the training and retention of research workers as the purposes of the program, reflected in the second of the CFI's two overarching objectives, namely the benefits of the program. The Quality of the Program was the first dimension, based on scientific excellence.

The Ontario Centres of Excellence also recognized this duality. Materials and Manufacturing Ontario was mandated to ensure that projects they supported, while meeting international standards of scientific excellence, had the potential to have a positive economic impact on Ontario.

The Alberta Heritage Foundation for Medical Research (AHFMR) provides a further example of the two dimensions. The Act establishing AHFMR states: *The Objectives of the Foundation are to establish and support a balanced long-term program of medical research based in Alberta directed to the discovery of new knowledge and the application of that knowledge to improve health and the quality of health services in Alberta.* Discovery of new knowledge is obviously a key first step; the application of that knowledge is an expected medium to long-term outcome.

The question can be asked whether the concept of two-dimensions extends across the innovation continuum. We explore this in Figure 7.1 by showing the transition from the Discovery of Knowledge to the Commercialization of Technology. The upper grid represents the "pure science" end of the spectrum. The researcher is the basic building block. Funding support is justified by the quality of the concept and a demonstrated track record. As the idea evolves into a well-defined proposal, the researcher is expected to provide information on the methodology to be employed, as represented in the next lower grid. Once a specific advance becomes apparent, the proposal must demonstrate the potential for a significant benefit as illustrated in the next lower grid. To secure investor support, the advance must eventually result in a definable product, process or service (represented by the term "product" in the next lower grid), with clear evidence of an economic or social impact. At the final stage of commercialization, the product must present a promise of significant investor value before a new business can be launched, as shown in the bottom grid. At each stage there are always two key dimensions, representing the values, priorities and expectations of the sponsors.

FIGURE 7.1
The Innovation Continuum - From Ideas to Investor Values

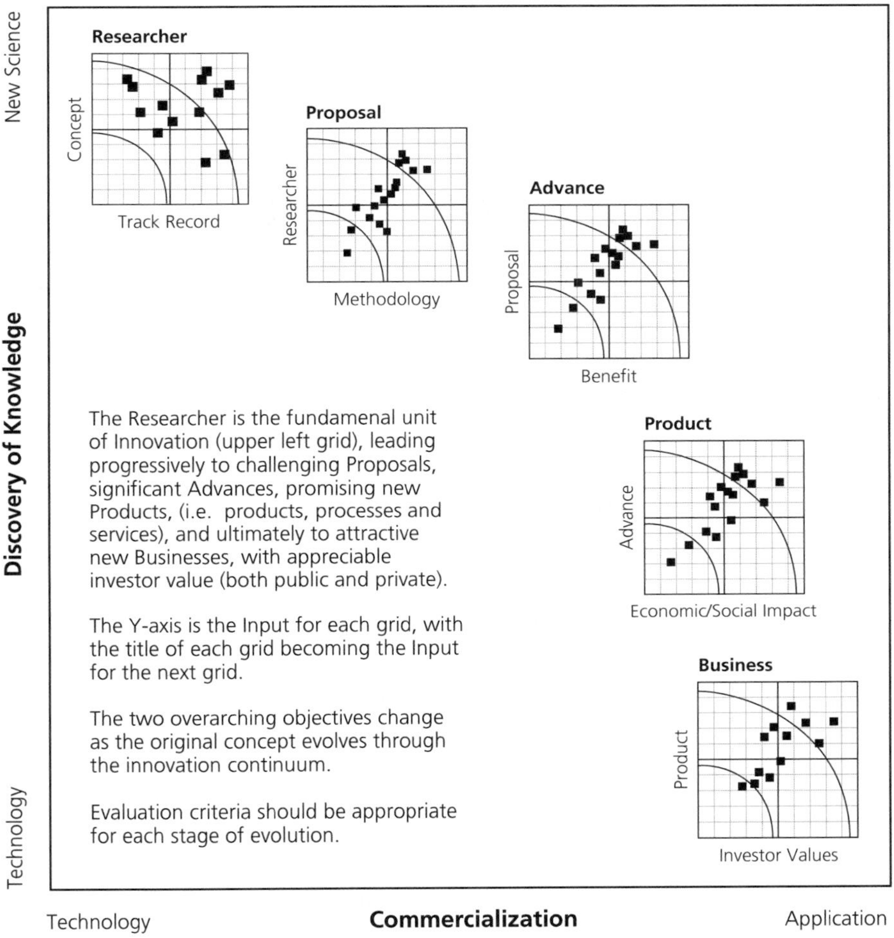

We noted in Chapter 1 that many renowned scientists are strong supporters of fundamental, curiosity-oriented basic research and are uneasy with the expectations of society that criteria other than scientific excellence be included in the decisions on research grants. For example, Lou Siminovitch, an internationally respected geneticist, has expressed concern that "governments have always placed priority on short-term strategic national objectives[i]." He notes that this devalues the importance of scientific excellence. Such concerns would dissipate if the appropriate criteria for funding were applied across the innovation continuum, as illustrated in Figure 7.1.

Each of the grids in Figure 7.1 can be considered as equally important in the innovation continuum. The grid positions have the same R-values, and are all essential parts of the process from pure science to commercialization.

The Role of the Supporting Criteria

Every qualitative and semi-quantitative process for evaluating intangible factors makes use of a checklist of supporting criteria, frequently based on an evaluator's own values and not necessarily reflecting the purposes of the program. Scoring 1 to 10 and summing the results gives the illusion of precision. ProGrid does more than provide the list of criteria; it organizes the criteria into groups that reveal the real potential of the proposal or award being considered. Some criteria clearly represent inputs, such as the assets and resources that will be used; others represent outputs, the results that are expected. Other criteria tend to be mainly supportive, such as tools and processes that will help convert inputs into outputs. Assigning the criteria into the columns of an input/enabler/output Evaluation Matrix helps to identify the significance of each criterion and provides a framework for assessing whether weak criteria can be corrected or if they are likely to be fatal flaws.

With this structure, it is feasible to design evaluation approaches to track performance over time as a guide to future funding.

Establishing Effective Metrics

"Ten out of ten" makes for a dramatic and highly visible scoring board, but unless there is substance to the numbers, the results will be questioned. The importance of language behind the numbers has been clearly demonstrated by the effectiveness of the 13-step Beaufort wind scale. The Beaufort scale provides a clear calibration for independent observers to provide the same rating based on similar observations. This is quite independent of their personal experience where at least some observers may never have experienced anything as severe as storm force winds. ProGrid methodology provides analogous calibration.

Panels and committees charged with reviewing proposals should agree in advance on criteria and their meaning. Over time, they develop effective approaches to achieving consensus on their recommendations. But if the members change frequently, reaching consensus becomes more difficult. ProGrid helps ensure that all reviewers mean the same thing when they give a numerical rating through the specification of short descriptive statements. Experience has shown it is not easy to develop meaningful and effective Language Ladders for this purpose; it is a major and sometimes tedious design task. Searching for phrases that will have the same meaning to proponents, reviewers and decision makers takes considerable time and testing, but is worth the effort.

Most ProGrid users periodically review and update their Language Ladders based on experience and evolution of the program or organizational objectives. As these objectives change, the criteria and Language Ladders need to evolve at the same time.

The Road to the Decision

It has been said that the purpose of a legal system is not to provide justice but to provide decisions. This, of course, is an overstatement, but it does illustrate that decisions must be made in the search for justice.

In the same manner, investors have to make decisions, using incomplete and imperfect information. ProGrid provides a process to organize the information that exists in a manner that ensures that the wisdom of all stakeholders is used as fully as possible.

Many evaluation methodologies in the literature, such as those using opinion surveys, collect extensive information that is progressively subdivided into finer and finer detail. As the information base grows, in desperation a long list of recommendations is prepared in an attempt to capture the essence of the evaluation task. While this information gathering process in itself is not wrong, essential information can get lost. The ProGrid process, and the software which has been developed in collaboration with ProGrid users, dramatically facilitates the condensation of large amounts of information into intuitive charts that highlight the issues to be faced in making each decision.

ProGrid users rapidly develop techniques for interpreting their specific grid and profile charts. The following are examples of patterns that help in this task.

In some applications, it would be expected that points will lie throughout the grid, without a heavy concentration along the diagonal. An example was shown in Figure 2.2, matching the qualifications of students to the research environment offered by supervisory professors. These data permit the identification of poor fit, and possibility lead to attempts at better matchmaking.

In some cases there will be a tendency to fall in one quadrant of the grid, as was shown in Figure 3.2. This represents an early stage commercialization program and would set the stage for tracking the performance of the more promising applications as they evolve in both technical and market attributes.

Portfolio managers would also look for exceptional strength in one axis, with the expectation that they might be able to add value to the venture in the weaker axis. Examples could be found in Figure 3.4.

The profile charts add important additional information. If the bars are flat and in the middle range of the ratings, this can be a signal for concern. No outstanding strengths have been identified, and most of the serious weaknesses have been partially overcome. An example of this type of "stalled" project is shown in one of the case studies in Figure 20.5. Examples of projects with more "energy" in the bars are shown in Figures 12.1 and 12.2.

Consistency among Competitions

Granting organizations that have regular competitions are faced with the need to have a cadre of reviewers available for each competition. Reviewer fatigue, a well-discussed phenomenon in the science and technology grants community, limits the number of times a particular reviewer can be called upon. How will a granting organization ensure that there is consistency from competition to competition? Having a time-tested set of language statements that all reviewers use in their assessments helps to prevent unintended shifts in values and priorities. The database that ProGrid software provides enables the funding organization to chart the pattern of ratings and to take advantage of what they have learned.

The longer-range impact of decisions will likely become apparent over time. What are the best predictors of success? What has the organization learned through its accumulated experience? If every competition is a new day, with new reviewers and no corporate memory, the learnings will be lost.

The Limitations of ProGrid

ProGrid does not make decisions. Rather, the methodology organizes information to help make sound decisions, helping applicants make their best case, reviewers to utilize their own expertise, and decision makers to make effective decisions with a clear paper trail. It represents a significant change from the conventional peer review process involving extensive meetings among reviewers exchanging opinions and ideas on long, detailed application forms and supporting documents. AHFMR has found that although the ProGrid process has led to fewer and shorter committee meetings, much of the review is done independently by reviewers with less face to face discussion of each application. To adjust to this change, AHFMR reports "there is a learning curve for the applicants, supervisors, and committee members."

Those that use ProGrid have found it to be a dynamic process that requires review and updating based on the experiences. It is not a passive process but requires the active participation of all stakeholders.

The Reaction of ProGrid Users

ProGrid methodology has significantly improved the processes used to make decisions involving intangibles as evidenced by the opinions of long time users. The views of some of these users are summarized below:

- The ProGrid analysis assists us in providing professional, objective feedback and mentoring to our clients.
- In both cases we noted substantial reductions in the time the review committee took to reach consensus.
- An altogether useful tool for a challenging job.
- It has proved to be invaluable in allowing us to fairly compare projects in very different fields of science/engineering.
- Not having to read through pages of sometimes irrelevant vendor material is a bonus for any procurement or contract manager.
- The easy-to-use ProGrid software is a cornerstone of our performance management system for science activities.

The first reaction to ProGrid is not always so positive. The initial reaction of the scientific community was suspicion, and many scientists remain skeptical. With new organizations, or those seeking to transform themselves, the response is often: "Tell us more!" This invariably leads to the exhilarating experience of linking up with a team of Innovators and Early Adopters, in the terms of Geoffrey Moore in "*Crossing the Chasm*[ii]."

We are often asked to describe the novel features of a ProGrid system. It is easy to respond that it is an effective and disciplined system for managing intangibles, but that does not really provide any understanding of what ProGrid really entails. It is the totality of the process itself, starting with the values/priorities/expectations of the user, that transforms these into a matrix of factors spanning from inputs/resources to outputs/impacts, identifying the two key overarching criteria, defining the language for the evaluation, and finally the process of getting all stakeholders working from the same page. We have been able to wrap all of these features into a compact user-friendly software package that takes most of the pain out of "the old way" of doing things. But to really appreciate the "Power of ProGrid," it is necessary to see it in action.

The Future

ProGrid methodology is effective in a wide variety of decision/performance tasks, ranging from the effective management of the careers of individuals, to the management of the assets of organizations, and ultimately to the way that organizations are structured and operated to meet the needs of stakeholders.

Applications of ProGrid methodology depend on:

- A dominant presence of intangible factors
- The need to balance two orthogonal objectives, which while not in direct conflict, must be balanced to achieve an optimal "solution"

Are there higher-level challenges that ProGrid methodology could address? The next level up the "food chain" would be understanding and managing broad social issues, which frequently get mired in public controversy without effective resolution.

The health care debate in North America is an example. The U.S. healthcare system involves a high level of private sector funding and delivery that has left 40 million people without adequate service. The Canadian system, on the other hand, provides universal coverage but can no longer keep up with evolving medical technologies and the needs of an aging population. In short, the one-dimensional solutions offered by both jurisdictions are flawed.

The environment is clearly another two-dimensional issue. Companies who understand the synergy between environmental imperatives and shareholder value will not only survive but will become market leaders. Environmentalists who view it as one-dimensional will be "pushing on a rope."

Jeffrey Simpson, a leading Canadian political columnist, has identified the balancing of rights and responsibilities as a critical two-dimensional issue in which the Canadian Charter of Rights and Freedoms protects one dimension, but says little about the issue of responsibilities[iii].

In their book on National Projects[iv], John Godfrey and Rob McLean identified a number of social and public issues that have dual dimensions, such as individual versus public initiative, equity versus efficiency, independence versus support, punishment versus prevention, and cooperation versus competition.

Rabbi Myer Schecter has referred to the conflict between a patient's religious reasons for choosing a medical course of action versus the doctor's recommendations based on modern medical science and technology. The Rabbi notes that "although each side believes there is no choice but to trump the opponent... détente is possible."[v]

How far can this concept of orthogonality be pushed? Effective conflict resolution by its nature requires more than just averaging positions. There are many regions in the world where land and security are in opposition; a satisfactory resolution will not occur until both dimensions get equal attention.

Addressing higher-level societal issues such as these would represent a great challenge for the next generation of ProGrid enthusiasts.

[i] Lou Siminovitch, *Globe and Mail,* May 24, 2005
[ii] Geoffrey A. Moore, *Crossing the Chasm, Harper Business* 1999
[iii] Jeffrey Simpson, *Globe and Mail,* June 16, 2005
[iv] *The Canada We Want,* John Godfrey, Rob McLean, Stoddart Publishing Co. Limited, 1999.
[v] *Faith in God, faith in medicine,* Rabbi Myer Schecter, *Globe and Mail,* 10 October, 2005

PART TWO

Case Studies

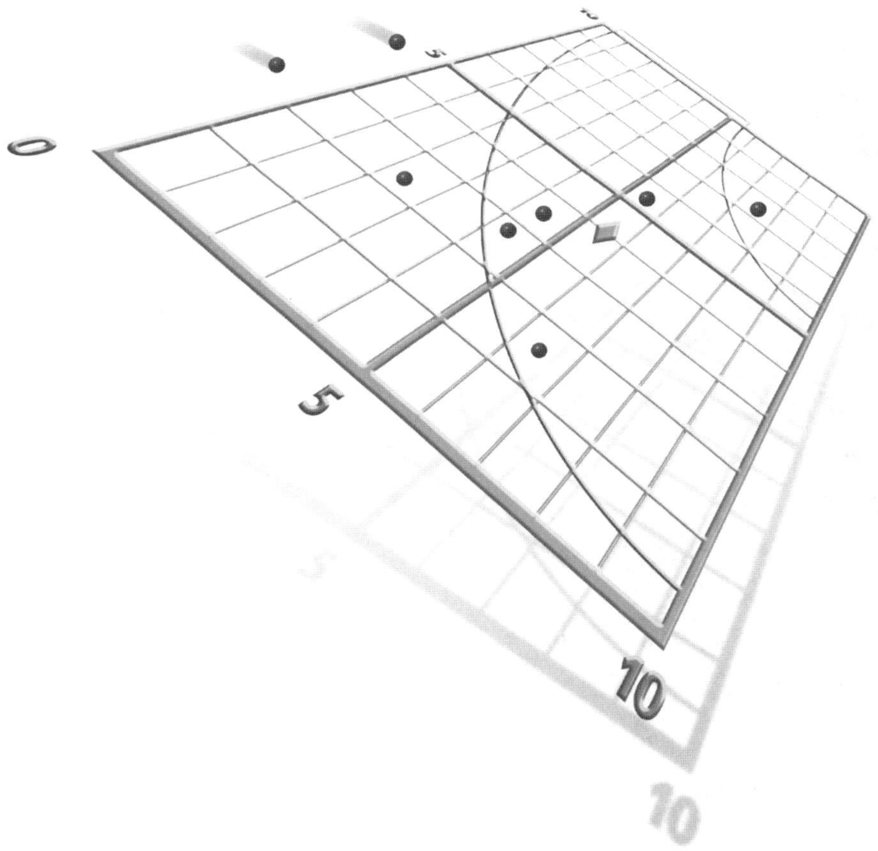

8 Upgrading Research Infrastructure

Ron McCullough, Benchmark-Action Inc.
Clem Bowman, Clement W. Bowman Consulting Inc.

The Infrastructure Problem

A prevalent and long-lasting problem in research organizations, both public and private, has been the maintenance of physical infrastructure. The problem is not only wear and tear over the useful life span of the infrastructure, but the obsolescence that occurs as new processes and new analytical techniques are developed. Organizations and countries must maintain their infrastructure at the leading edge of efficiency and effectiveness if they are to be globally competitive. They must also invest in infrastructure matched to new opportunities at the very forefront of research.

Universities and hospitals in Canada raised Canada's poor record of on-going infrastructure investment as a major concern in the early 1990s. In response, the Canadian Government created in 1997 an independent non-profit organization, the Canada Foundation for Innovation (CFI), to provide funding support for infrastructure for universities and hospitals. It has proven to be an enormous success, with a total budget of $3.65 billion. The CFI funds up to 40% of a project's infrastructure costs, in partnership with eligible institutions and their funding partners from the public, private, and voluntary sectors. The total capital investment by the CFI, the research institutions, and their partners, will exceed $10 billion by 2010.

The Government of Canada set up the CFI to operate outside of government. Investment decisions are made solely by a board of directors, the majority of whom are drawn from the research and academic communities as well as the private sector. Not only is the CFI at arm's length from government, but it is also an unbiased partner in assisting institutions to implement their research plans and priorities. This latter role has been well recognized and appreciated by Canadian research institutions.

Setting the Goals

The CFI's mandate is to strengthen the capacity of Canadian universities, colleges, research hospitals, and non-profit research institutions to carry out world-class research and technology development that benefits Canadians. The original legislation under which the CFI was established set out seven key objectives and these drive all of its operating principles.

- Provide infrastructure to support research in Canadian universities and hospitals.
- Support economic growth and job creation
- Enhance capacity for innovation
- Strengthen training and research careers
- Attract and retain research workers
- Promote networks and collaborations

In 1998, Keith Brimacombe, the CFI's first President and Carmen Charette, Senior Vice-President, had the challenge of establishing an application and evaluation process that would incorporate these objectives, and that could handle the flow of applications expected to be in the many hundreds and, over time, in the thousands. The process also had to respect the time and effort of both applicants and reviewers.

Brimacombe and Charette, aware of a combined application/evaluation decision-assist tool (ProGrid®) that was being used by several of the Ontario Centres of Excellence, decided to determine if this tool would be appropriate for their use. The first step was to convene a management group to identify the values, priorities and expectations of the CFI in a brainstorming session. The group produced the values shown in Table 8.1, shown in the order they were presented.

TABLE 8.1
Brainstorming the Values of CFI

	Priorities, Values and Expectations
1	Develop cutting edge research
2	Increase research capacity
3	Strengthen research capability
4	Enhance HQP through recruitment
5	Put knowledge to practical use
6	Enhance HQP through training
7	Provide state of the art infrastructure to facilitate leading edge research
8	Improve quality of life (environment, health etc.)
9	Promote collaboration, interdisciplinary interactions, networking
10	Create wealth
11	Strengthen the economy
12	Create employment
13	Create a significant science advancement
14	Have a big impact, not a minor step change
15	Sponsor innovative research - research which could not be done in any other way- team approach- think big but not necessarily spend big - have maximum leverage from private sector
16	Develop a portfolio concept- include both small and large endeavours
17	Institutional proposals - demand priority focus - level and coherence of institutional planning
18	Ensure commitment from all partners
19	Ensure continuity, sustainability, and effective management
20	Ensure capability to execute - right people, right choice of tools, choice of infrastructure matches the need, feasibility, solid planning and management from day one
21	Manage risk- stretch versus risk- risk/benefit ratio - shared risk
22	Capture benefits in HQP and technical transfer,
23	Seek wide range of benefits - spin-offs, incremental receptor capacity, new policy and regulations (social, environment etc.), new cures, treatments, reduced costs (health, environment), new processes and services, direct job creation and projects, attract world class researchers, encourage sharing, collaboration and follow-on leverage
24	Develop metrics with ability to track

These 24 "values" were condensed into the nine factors shown in Table 8.2. It seemed appropriate to group these under three broad categories that became the headings of the three columns in the matrix. For the first several years, this matrix provided the framework for the CFI application and evaluation system.

TABLE 8.2
The CFI Evaluation Matrix™ – Original

Quality and Need	Capacity for Innovation	Benefits to Canada
The Research	Highly Qualified Personnel (HQP)	Economic Growth and Job Creation
The Team	Collaboration and Research Partnerships	Quality of Life, Health and Environment
The Infrastructure	Fit with Institutional R&D Plans	Knowledge Interchange

To this day, the CFI still evaluates all proposals under these three broad categories:

- Quality of research and need for infrastructure
- Contribution to strengthening the capacity for innovation
- Potential benefits of the research to Canada

Developing the Metrics and Testing

Language Ladders were formulated representing four levels of performance in each cell of the above matrix. An example for cell A1, The Research, is shown in Table 8.3.

Language Ladders for all nine cells were developed and incorporated into the CFI Application Form. Beta testing was undertaken to ensure that the process was effective and efficient, and that it would provide meaningful separation among applications.

The 10 beta tests shown in Figure 8.1 provided some comfort to Brimacombe and Charette that they had the beginnings of their new system. Figure 8.2 validated that the system would perform in "real time."

TABLE 8.3
Language Ladder™ for "The Research"

Research:	
A	The proposed infrastructure will be used for research that should lead to measurable advances that will be recognized by those active in this field.
B	The proposed infrastructure will be used for research that should lead to major advances that will be recognized at least by the broader research community in Canada.
C	The proposed infrastructure will be used for research that should significantly increase the state of knowledge and be recognized internationally as major milestones.
D	The proposed infrastructure will be used for pioneering research. The initiative has the potential to underpin major breakthroughs

FIGURE 8.1
Beta Test Results

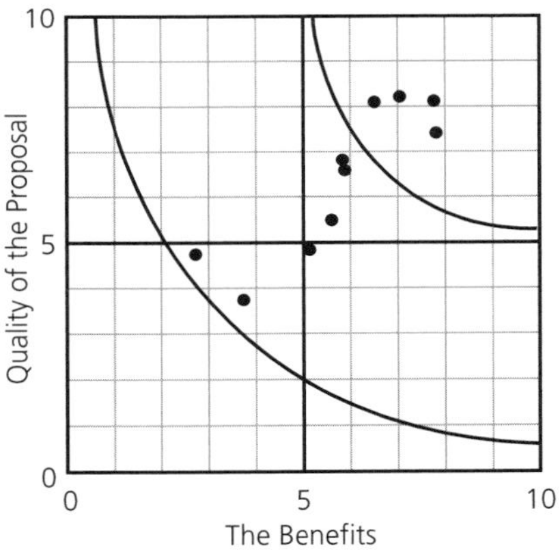

FIGURE 8.2
First Major Competition

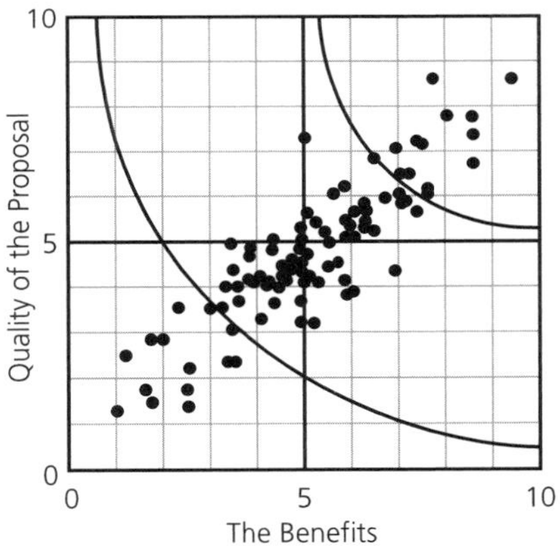

Experience Counts

The CFI has found over time that not all the criteria in the original Evaluation Matrix were equal in their ability to serve as discriminators. The number of criteria has been condensed and reduced to six, as shown in Table 8.4.

TABLE 8.4
The Revised CFI Evaluation Matrix

Quality and Need	Capacity for innovation	Benefits to Canada
The Research	Need for the Infrastructure	Potential Benefits to Canada
The Researchers	Training of HQP	
	Research Collaboration and Partnerships	

The Review Committees at Work

The challenge of reviewing applications for CFI funding has been enormous. The applications are truly multi-disciplinary; any and all fields of research are encouraged. The applications range in scope from a few hundred thousand dollars in value to over $100 million. The research applications can be relatively simple–or can attack the very leading edge of the most complex problems. The number of applications being considered at any one time (most frequently in annual competitions) could range up to 1,000.

The CFI strove to create a process that would not only ensure the applicants had the best chance to excel, but also that each application was fairly and comprehensively reviewed by a team of international experts. Further, they wanted to ensure that the review and recommendation process was focused, timely and resulted in recommendations to the Board that were fair and consistent.

The logistics thus became daunting. Each application was sent to multiple reviewers for assessment–which thus required many thousand assessments to be gathered for each competition session. These assessments then were gathered and the ProGrid outputs were compiled. This stage of the process was enabled by a Web and database interface constructed specifically for the CFI.

Once the initial review data were assembled, the CFI initiated a final review process. This was focused on a number of Multidisciplinary Advisor Committees (MACs) – generally six or seven were established for each competition. Each MAC had a Chair and about 10 (or more) members from around the world who were recognized as experts in their discipline. To ensure that the reviews were truly objective, each MAC was truly "multidisciplinary"; the applications were not grouped according to any "like" themes or topics but were rather distributed among MACs. A MAC could thus have applications in medicine, engineering, biology, or any other discipline and, as well, applications of any scope. A MAC could have over 100 such applications to consider.

The process for each MAC was well-defined and designed to answer one question: "Which of the applications does the MAC consider to be worthy of CFI support?" A MAC was not asked to consider the budget or to select a suite of projects to meet a budget target. They were asked to comment on – if needed – the appropriateness of the requested budget relative to the research objectives.

Each and every application receives a full discussion by the MAC. The results of the ProGrid external review assessments are summarized in special reports provided to the MAC and the Chair then leads a discussion on each application. Specific comments from external reviewers (some of whom may be part of the MAC) are considered and comments and discussion from all MAC members are sought. Conclusions and comments from the discussion are gathered to support recommendations to be made to the CFI Board – and to provide constructive feedback to each applicant.

In the end, an MAC forwards a set of applications that it recommends for CFI support. There are also usually a small number of applications that may have questions that need to be answered, conditions that might apply or strategic considerations beyond the scope of a given MAC. These are clearly documented and passed forward. In most cases, a MAC can review over 100 applications in two days of meeting.

Once each MAC has completed its review, the results from all MACs are combined and a meeting of the Chairs of the MACs is convened. At this meeting, with the assistance of CFI staff, the MAC Chairs are asked to ensure that each of their individual review processes has been consistent with that of the other MACs. The overwhelming consensus has always been that there is virtually no "bias" in the review of individual MACs relative to each other. The consolidated recommendations are then prepared and presented to the Board that makes the final decisions on which applications to support.

The ability to bring many hundreds of applications, thousands of expert reviews, the productive inputs of hundreds of experts in real time and requests for hundreds of millions of dollars in support in as effective a manner as is done at the CFI is probably unique.

The Role of ProGrid

ProGrid did not come unscathed during the implementation of this application and review process. Some unsuccessful applicants attempted to attribute their lack of success to the ProGrid process. Dr. David Strangway, the successor to Dr. Brimacombe, stated publicly at the 1998 Canadian Research Management Association Annual meeting in Ottawa that *"the reason these applicants were not successful was not with the ProGrid process, but with less than satisfactory applications that did not address CFI's priorities."*

The CFI has noted that the process was designed to help:

- applicants to decide whether their project should be pursued further;
- institutions to screen projects according to their plans and priorities;
- the CFI's reviewers and committees to structure their assessment;
- to assess the projects against each of the CFI criteria in a structured way.

CFI also notes that the process does not override the collective wisdom of experts. It actually helps to identify those aspects of a proposal that may require more extensive committee discussion. It is clearly understood that all aspects of the review process are focused on having a committee advise the CFI Board that a project should or should not be funded. Experience with the methodology has shown that the structured process results in better proposals and a more consistent assessment process for all applications.

The Impact of CFI

From 1997 to 2002, CFI's independent Board of Directors, working with hundreds of volunteer experts, has approved and financed 2,300 innovative projects, representing an investment of almost $2 billion in the areas of health, engineering, science, the environment, as well as the social sciences and the humanities at universities, hospitals, colleges, and not-for-profit organizations across the country. Combined with funding from the institutions themselves, as well as other partners, the CFI has triggered an investment of over $4.5 billion in research infrastructure and CFI-infrastructure operating funds.

These investments are having a significant impact on the capacity of the Canadian research community to compete internationally. State-of-the art infrastructure is helping to:

- transform the way research is done
- create a strong and vibrant research environment across Canada;
- attract and retain excellent researchers
- enhance research productivity and the training of highly qualified people
- build new national and international networks and partnerships

The research enabled by this infrastructure is generating benefits for Canadians through the creation of spin-off ventures, the commercialization of discoveries, as well as better health, environment, and public policy.

9 Intergovernmental Collaboration on Infrastructure

Steve Vossos – Director, Alberta Science and Research Investments Program

The Research Infrastructure Challenge in Alberta

As described in Chapter 8, in the early 1990s, universities and research hospitals in Canada were raising concerns over the need to retrofit and enhance the research infrastructure integral to the innovation system. Playing a tangible role in the emerging "knowledge-based economy," meant the nation needed to build the research capacity and capability of its research organizations.

Alberta was acutely aware of the concerns being raised by its research institutions. In 1997, the province proactively decided to introduce a key research funding program—the Intellectual Infrastructure Partnership Program (IIPP). The IIPP was set up to assist Alberta universities and research hospitals to acquire research equipment and facilities that would support strategically important research, enhance the capacity for innovation, and bolster efforts to recruit and retain high-quality researchers and graduate students.

Concurrent with the development and introduction of the IIPP in 1997, the federal Canada Foundation for Innovation (CFI) was set up to provide funding support for national research infrastructure. The introduction of the CFI was seen as a significant opportunity for the IIPP to lever federal funding for Alberta strategic priorities and so, from the outset, both funding mechanisms became involved in cost-shared investments at Alberta's universities and research hospitals.

Between 1997 and 1999, the IIPP operated independent of CFI timelines and review processes. While this "disconnection" did not adversely impact the key federal and provincial investments that were made during this period, the research community was facing an increasing burden with respect to reviewing research funding applications for both programs. In addition, while the IIPP had developed an effective due diligence process for reviewing submissions, it was a substantially different model than the ProGrid® tool that had been developed for the CFI during this period.

Another factor that became a challenge was the timing of awards. It was evident that there would be operational advantages if the IIPP established better coordination of its independent provincial decisions with the federal decisions on research investments. These different review processes and decision timelines, coupled with a growing "reviewer burden" and the duplication of application processes, prompted IIPP staff to consider ways of streamlining the program to ensure overall coordination and collaboration with the CFI. The opportunity to refine the IIPP had arrived.

Program Refinements: A Coordinated and Collaborative Approach

In 2000, the IIPP underwent significant changes and became the Alberta Science and Research Investments Program (ASRIP)—Alberta's key mechanism for building research capacity and capability through strategic investments in research infrastructure. In refining the program, establishing better coordination with CFI processes was paramount, as was the intent to address the above-mentioned reviewer and applicant burden. To achieve coordination, ASRIP adjusted its timelines so that they paralleled those of the CFI's Innovation Fund. To address the issue of reviewer burden, Steve Vossos, program manager, and ASRIP staff worked out a solution with the CFI and ProGrid. The objective was to adopt the ProGrid decision-assist tool for use by ASRIP and thereby incorporate the common peer-review elements that are articulated in the matrix that was earlier developed by ProGrid and the CFI. Importantly, ASRIP also developed Alberta-specific criteria to ensure that independent strategic factors were maintained along with the adoption of common, shared criteria, as shown in Table 9.1.

TABLE 9.1
ASRIP's "Research Infrastructure" Evaluation Matrix™

Quality and Innovation	Process	Strategic Benefits
The Research	Need for the Infrastructure	Potential Benefits of the Research to Canada
The Researchers	Training of Highly Qualified Personnel (HQP)	
	Research Collaboration and Partnerships	
Strategic Alberta Fit *(With Alberta's strategic priorities)*		Capacity for Research Excellence *(Impact on Alberta's infrastructure)*

Along with the development and implementation of the common and Alberta-specific criteria, ASRIP allowed applicants to submit the same application form to its Research Infrastructure program stream that they submitted to the CFI's Innovation Fund. The only addition to the application form was the appended Alberta-specific criteria pages. This accommodation removed the need for applicants to duplicate their submissions and ensured that both programs assessed the same proposal.

The Alberta Science and Research Investments Program (ASRIP) review process encompasses three stages:

- A peer review assessment (using CFI expert reviews, ASRIP Panel and external reviews);
- Review by the ASRIP Scientific Review Panel[i]; and,
- Recommendations by the Alberta Science and Research Authority (ASRA) and final decisions by the Minister of Alberta Innovation and Science.

Sharing Agreement: ASRIP and CFI Synergy

Stemming from the development of a common application form, ASRIP worked with the CFI to establish a sharing agreement for expert reviews, which further streamlined the application and review processes of both programs. The key purpose for enabling ASRIP to use CFI expert reviews for proposals submitted both to the CFI and ASRIP competitions was to reduce the reviewing burden on the university community. The sharing agreement thus streamlined the review process while ensuring that independent decisions were made by both programs.

Specifically, while both the CFI and ASRIP recognized that notwithstanding the common use of expert reviews, both the CFI's Innovation Fund program and ASRIP's Research Infrastructure program should continue to make independent decisions on the proposals submitted to the respective program competitions.

This independence is ensured by the fact that the CFI's Multidisciplinary Committee and ASRIP's Scientific Review Panel tender their advice using their own assessments of the proposals before them, taking into account the advice provided by expert reviews. Each group makes its own recommendations based on the context in which their assessments occur. Although the proposals and reviews are the same for a limited number of proposals, the CFI is national in scope and, as such, assesses in a national context, while ASRIP evaluates proposals using the additional Alberta-specific criteria.

These specific reviewing contexts change the dynamic of competitive assessments and ensure that shared reviews are used in the contextual manner specific to the national and provincial processes. The independent federal and provincial decisions have resulted in a very significant number of strategically important, cost-shared investments in Alberta.

ProGrid: Intangible Tool Enabling Tangible Benefits

An added benefit of streamlining ASRIP and CFI processes is that doing so has significantly helped ASRIP staff to build a collaborative approach with CFI colleagues—a rare and welcome development in the context of Canadian research funding programs. In going forward, both ASRIP and CFI intend to increase collaborative efforts—a goal of importance to both programs. Alberta appreciates the rapport that has been developed with the CFI through these collaborative refinements and ASRIP staff are confident that this complementary approach will not only benefit federal-provincial relationships but, importantly, will benefit the larger research community as we all work together to build research excellence. The development and solidification of this mutually beneficial collaboration is due in no small way to the ProGrid decision-assist tool used by the CFI and ASRIP.

An Example

An application under review is compared with all other submissions in the ASRIP database in Figure 9.1. This permits an assessment of how the current application compares with other opportunities, in terms of Quality & Innovation and Strategic Benefits.

FIGURE 9.1
The ASRIP Research Infrastructure Database

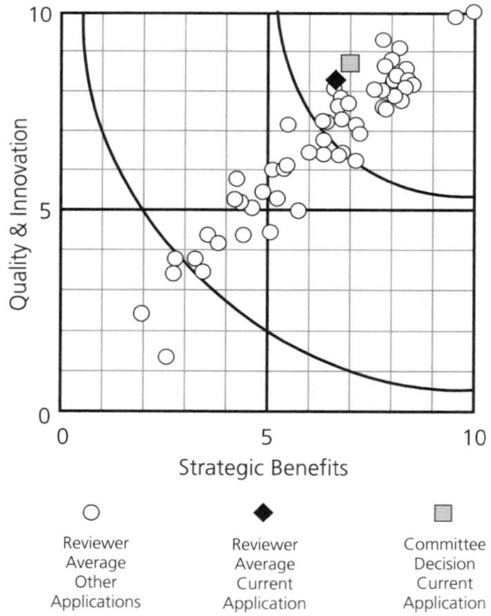

[i] The ASRIP Scientific Review Panel is comprised of senior-level public and private-sector members, and scientists with broad expertise

10 Bridging The University/ Industry Gap

Peter McGeer – former Director of Alcan R&D Centre
Gerald Dyer – former Research Director, DuPont Canada

The Ontario Centres of Excellence Program

The Ontario Government created the Ontario Centres of Excellence Program in 1987. The purpose of the program was to foster increased, and more effective, interactions between Ontario-based industry, and academics in Ontario universities. Peter McGeer, former Director, Kingston Research and Development Centre, ALCAN, and Gerald Dyer, former Research Director, DuPont Canada, were involved in this program from the very beginning. Neither McGeer nor Dyer was initially aware that this engagement would continue on an active basis for 17 years.

On the basis of applications, seven proposals for Centres of Excellence were accepted with a funding envelope of $213 million. This envelope was to be committed over a five-year period and was divided unequally between the seven winning bids. Each of the bids had specified a program in greater or lesser detail, and this determined which initiatives and research projects were to be supported by the Centres. As time passed, additional funds became available, and decisions had to be made with respect to the allocation of these newly available funds.

Those responsible for administering the program had informed the management of each of the Centres that there were two major expectations for the program. The research funded was to be world-class and relevant to Ontario industry. It was specified initially that 80% of the "points' would be awarded for "excellence of the research" and 20% for industrial relevance, but in the later phases of the program, this was to be inverted with 80% of the points awarded for industrial relevance.

Early Performance

Each of the seven Centres developed processes designed to enhance the program while meeting the criteria outlined in the foregoing paragraph. Most faced the problem of allocating percentages of the available funds to specific fields of research, as well as carrying out competitions within their chosen fields and selecting the "most worthy" projects amongst those submitted. For example, the Ontario Centre for Materials Research had six fields of activity; biomaterials, electronic and optoelectronic materials, metals and ceramics, new materials, polymers and plastics, and surfaces and coatings. All newly available money was allocated between the six fields in proportion to that of the original award. Within each of the six fields the selection of the research proposals to be supported was made by a committee, specific to the field, composed of both academic and industrialists active in the field.

Over the first 10 years, it was generally agreed that the process for selecting the "best" projects within a field was satisfactory. However, there was a growing dissatisfaction with the inability to develop a way to reallocate the division of available funds between the fields. This was brought to a head in the 10th year when the Government of Ontario required certain amalgamations in the Centres Program. Specifically the Government required the Ontario Centre for Materials Research, (OCMR), and the Manufacturing Research Corporation of Ontario, (MRCO), to become a single corporation, Materials and Manufacturing Ontario (MMO).

As noted above, OCMR had six fields, and MRCO had a separate set of 11 fields in the area of manufacturing. The issues included how to divide the available funds between materials and manufacturing, as well as between the various fields in each of those technologies. Beyond these specific problems there was also the issue of organizational cultures.

One of the specific but unstated objectives of the Centres Program was to break down barriers between the academic and industrial worlds, and to eliminate stereotypical thinking. The periodic reviews of the Centres Program had shown that this was occurring, though much still remained. The program had done this by demonstrating that the excellence of the research and its industrial impact are not mutually exclusive. There was also a growing recognition that research excellence, as measured by a citation index should not be the dominant criterion, rather advance in engineering or science was a more appropriate measure for the OCE program.

Developing an Approach to Decision Making

Given the need for a system which would allow the comparison of the value to be derived from different technologies, the management of the new MMO sought assistance in developing an unique system, and selected ProGrid® for trial. This selection was based on the familiarity of individuals in MMO with one of the ProGrid tools (ProGrid TA) and on the intimate knowledge that McGeer and Dyer had with the Centres of Excellence Program.

The principals in both OCMR and MRCO had used ProGrid TA to evaluate the readiness of university inventions for commercialization. McGeer had been the Managing Director of OCMR and was now an officer of MMO. Dyer had served on the Board of Directors and evaluation committees for several of the Centres. This shared familiarity and understanding enabled MMO to tackle the problem of comparing "apples and oranges."

The immediate problem that MMO faced was how to select projects for funding that would fall under the guidelines of the program and that would be consistent with the directions provided by MMO's Board of Directors. The program guidelines now required that approximately equal weight be given to two selection criteria, excellence of research and relevance to Ontario industry. These were interpreted by MMO's Board of Directors as advances in engineering or science, and industrial impact. It was also recognized that projects contribute to the development and training of "highly qualified personnel," (HQP), i.e. the next generation of academic researchers, and industry technologists.

MMO's Board decided that, over time, the distribution of the funds available for research should shift from an initial ratio of 64% for enabling research projects and 34% for collaborative research projects to 45% for enabling and 55% for collaborative. Enabling research projects are defined as those that are exploratory in nature, or which could be defined as contributing to a broad knowledge base; in other words projects where it is more difficult to identify the industrial "pay off." Collaborative projects are those where the application of the project outcome can, or will, be applied more immediately by a contributing industrial partner.

The Board directed management to conduct a competition for enabling research projects. The challenge was to develop a system under which applications to the competition could be judged independently of the technology that they supported.

Selecting the Criteria to be Used in Decision Making

ProGrid methodology requires the specification of two overarching objectives for the decisions to be made. The founders of the Centres of Excellence program had selected excellence of research and industrial impact as the prime objectives. These were expressed by MMO, for the purposes of ProGrid analysis, as "Advance in Science and/or Engineering" and "Economic Impact." These are the axes for the grid used to display the results.

The next step was to select the criteria that would embody the objectives given in the preceding paragraph. Seven were selected. They have stood the test of time, as the original seven are still the basis of project selection after seven years of use. The criteria are shown in Table 10.1.

Each of the above seven criteria was assigned in whole or in part to the X axis (Economic Impact) or to the Y axis (Advance in Science and/or Engineering). For example, factor 1, the advance in science or engineering was assigned primarily to the Y axis, while criteria 3, growing the pool of excellently trained scientists and

TABLE 10.1
MMO's "Enabling Projects" Evaluation Matrix™

Advance in Science and Engineering	Enablers	Economic Impact on Ontario
Engineering and/or Science Advance	Enlarging the HQP Pool	Industrial Receptor Capacity
Capability to Execute	Pervasiveness	Market Impact
	Industry Involvement	

engineers, was divided approximately equally between the X and the Y axis since the students involved in the project were conducting the research, and would later, in many cases, become technologists in industry.

The next step in the methodology was to define Language Ladders to serve as the metrics. As an example the Language Ladder™ designed for criterion 6, "Strengthening the Industrial Receptor Capacity" in Ontario is shown in Table 10.2.

TABLE 10.2
Language Ladder for Strengthening Industrial Receptor Capacity

Industrial Receptor Capacity:	
A	It is anticipated that there will be receptor companies in Ontario for the technology but these have not been contacted.
B	Receptor company(ies) with the capacity to exploit the technology in Ontario have been contacted and have expressed in writing (letter attached) commercial interest.
C	Receptor company(ies) with the capacity and market access to exploit the technology in Ontario have expressed in writing (letter attached) a commitment to track the progress of the technology and their intent to identify specific opportunities for commercial use in their Ontario operations.
D	Receptor company(ies) with operations in Ontario who have demonstrated capacity, skills, and market access to aggressively develop and market the technology have expressed in writing (letter attached), their expectation that they will exploit/use the technology in their Ontario operations.

For each of the seven criteria the applicant can score at one of four levels. These scores are apportioned to the two overarching objectives. The X and Y values are then plotted on a grid as shown in Figure 10.1. As this graph shows, not surprisingly for enabling projects, there was a tendency for the projects to score more highly

FIGURE 10.1
Grid Display for an Early Enabling Research Project Competition

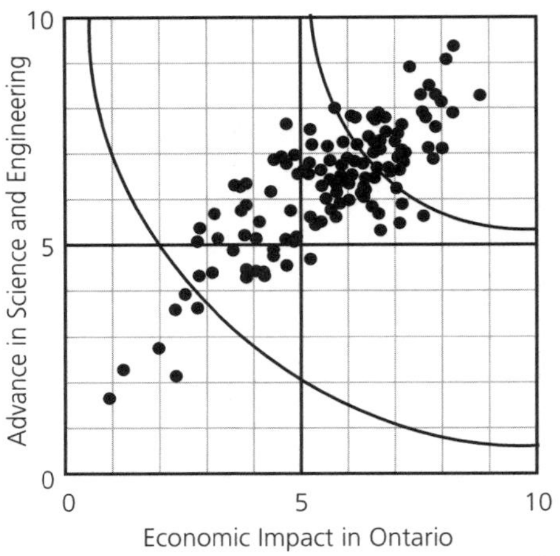

on the Advance in Science and Engineering criteria, but it is clear that projects can have a high achievement for the criteria on both axes.

Using the R-value technique described in Chapter 1, a total score was calculated, such that a D rating for all criteria would represent 100% and a C rating 67%. Similar R-value scores might occur through a high advance in science and engineering but lower in industrial impact, or vice versa.

The Decision-Making Process

While the ProGrid section of the application form provided information as an aid to decision making, the application form contained two other parts providing information of equal importance. The first of these required the applicant to explain the proposed research, including its objectives, milestones and procedures, while the other specified the required financing, including the disposition of all requested funds.

All applications were refereed, both internally by MMO staff, and by selected external referees. At least four external referees were sought, with an approximately equal number from academia and industry. All were selected on the basis of their expertise; for academics based on the field of research and for industry on the basis of familiarity with the market for the product or/and technology to which the research would be applied.

In completing the application, the submitter is asked to rate the application on each of the seven factors used for decision making. This was done through selecting from each Language Ladder (A to D) the most advanced applicable statement. The applicant is then asked to record the reason for the selection made, i.e. to justify the rating selected. Referees are asked to review the application and, based on their own knowledge of the science/engineering being researched, to provide their own rating for each of the seven criteria. The ratings are compiled for discussion by a "project selection committee" comprised of individuals selected for their broad knowledge in the areas of materials and manufacturing.

In reviewing the applications, the project selection committee invariably found the ProGrid methodology to have a very significant value as **a decision-assist tool**. Committee members were able to compare the overall rating, as well as the criterion-by-criterion ratings, given by the applicant with those provided by the external referees, and by MMO staff. Sometimes all parties were in substantial agreement, but frequently there were significant differences. The committee needed to understand how and why these differences arose, and to adjust their perception of the overall value accordingly.

For example, many applicants rated their application more highly than any referee, and it was often obvious that referees were influenced by the overly optimistic rating given by the applicant. In addition, the committee sought to apply a "value for money" criterion by thoughtfully examining the budget. Having evaluated all criteria, the committee then decided whether or not the application should be funded.

In addition to reviewing the R-value score the project selection committee reviewed the relative scores by the submitter and the referees for each of the seven criteria. The ProGrid software generates a table that exhibits these scores, and an example is shown in Table 10.3.

The table illustrates a number of typical issues. First of all, many applicants believe that they deserve the highest rating in almost every category. Second, the applicant's self-rating can overly influence a referee. An example is referee 2. The scores for this referee are higher than any of the other referee's scores, and close to those of the applicant, and this needs to be taken into account in making the final decision. A very important issue is the spread in scores on a given

TABLE 10.3
Language Ladder Scores

	Criterion						
	1	2	3	4	5	6	7
Applicant	D	D	D	D	C	D	D
Referee 1	C	C	D	B	C	C	C
Referee 2	D	D	C	D	C	D	C
Referee 3	C	B	B	C	C	C	C
Referee 4	B	B	C	B	C	B	C
Referee 5	C	C	B	C	C	B	C

criterion. Whenever the referees differ by more than one level on a Language Ladder for a criterion, every attempt should be made to understand why this discrepancy has arisen. Perhaps one referee knows something that others do not, and this needs to be discussed.

These issues illustrate why the ProGrid scores must be treated as an aid to decision-making, rather than being the sole base of the decision. The collective knowledge and wisdom of the reviewers provides the foundation for effective decisions, and the decision makers need to understand referee scores.

Breadth of Applications by MMO

Based on its early experience, and continued satisfaction with the approach, Materials and Manufacturing Ontario uses ProGrid as a major tool to assist in decision making for all six of the research programs it conducts or monitors. These include one each for enabling research, collaborative research, new faculty support, emerging materials research, microelectronics assembly and packaging research and research on industrial applications of gold. For each of these it was necessary to define the overarching objectives, as well as the supporting criteria. The overarching objectives were usually those noted above, or a close variation. However, the criteria could, and did, vary significantly. Usually there were six or seven criteria.

Strengths of the ProGrid Selection Process

The first benefit of the methodology is the discipline it imposes on the process to allocate the research funding. This discipline extends to all the users: the organization (corporation) that is providing the funding, the applicant who is submitting an application for funding, and the referee who is assisting in the evaluation.

It requires the corporation to start by defining two overarching objectives, and then to determine the criteria that contribute to the achievement of these overarching objectives. This contributes to a broader and clearer understanding within the organization of the purpose of its programs, and clarity in its practices. While the overarching objectives should be orthogonal and independent, this is not necessarily true of each criterion. For example for MMO programs one of the criteria is the training of highly qualified personnel (HQP). As a researcher on the project she/he will help achieve an advance in science or engineering (one of MMO's selected overarching objectives). After graduation, he or she may, as an industrial employee, assist industry implement new technologies (industrial impact, the other overarching objective).

The second benefit is that ProGrid conveys to the applicant the values of the corporation. This is done through the criteria selected for the Language Ladders, and by the entries in each step of the Language Ladder. One of MMO's major objectives is to help industry grow through the transfer to industry of academic research outcomes. Completing the application makes it clear to the applicant that MMO places a very high value upon the establishment of a close linkage, insofar as the project is concerned, between the applicant and research team, and a company capable of commercializing whatever results might arise from the research. Thoughtful applicants will recognize what the organization wants and will craft their research and application accordingly. This is particularly valuable for an organization such as MMO where the important outcome is the value to Ontario industry of the research results. This does not mean that all research funded by MMO must, or is expected to, lead to a new or improved product or process. It does mean that the knowledge arising from the project should be important to an Ontario company.

By the same token, the details in the ProGrid form "explain" to the referee the values of the organization that is conducting the competition. This helps the referee put comments on the application into the context of the organization conducting the competition. Even more importantly in the present climate, ProGrid technology is a time saver. It focuses the attention of both applicant and referee on the intended outcomes of the research, rather than solely on the research process itself. The time saving arises because, in both the preparation and refereeing, applicant and referee can focus their attention on the specific criteria of importance to the organization conducting the competition. The referee can focus on how well the application meets the funding organization's objectives, and not on the minute details of how the research will be conducted. MMO has found that, in most cases, referees can evaluate an application in less than an hour, a significant saving of time.

Finally, the use of ProGrid focuses the discussion at the selection committee level. In MMO's experience, the use of ProGrid can reduce by a factor of between three and five the time taken to examine an application and make a decision with respect to funding.

Acceptance by the Community

MMO's community is defined by its title. It includes academics and industrialists in most of the fields defined as natural sciences and engineering. There are significant exceptions, and these are dealt with below. The only complaints/refusals MMO ever had with respect to the use of the ProGrid tool came from individuals who were trained, or carried out research, in fields related to medicine. One of MMO's fields was biomedical materials, such as replacement heart valves, hips, etc. No difficulty was experienced with referees who were on the industrial side of such activity, but a number of the academic referees refused to undertake a review based on an application made with the ProGrid form.

Lessons Learned

MMO found that it was important to periodically review the Language Ladders. This was done to try to tune the "message." In other words to ensure that the values MMO was embedding in the statement sets were those perceived by the applicant and the referees. On occasion MMO also found that it was necessary to provide, at the top of a Language Ladder, a definition of some of the terms used in the ladder. For example, in the criterion related to "enlarging the HQP pool" MMO provided its particular definition of those positions in the academic world that would qualify as being occupied by HQP.

MMO also found it important to define the fields of research in which it planned to be active. For example, while biomedical materials is a field in which MMO supports research, MMO decided that it would not extend its reach to include drugs and pharmaceuticals. By many definitions drugs and pharmaceuticals are materials that do not need to be manufactured. However, these materials were not included in the fields specified at the time of selection for the OCE program, hence the expertise embedded in MMO did not include either of these fields. Furthermore, expanding to include these materials would have incurred an unacceptably high research sponsoring liability.

11 End of Public Procurement Scandals?

Chris Jones, Keith Jones – Forum Decision Systems
Bruce Fountain – Fountain & Associates
John Kramers – ProGrid Ventures Inc.
Ron McCullough – Benchmark-Action Inc.
Clem Bowman – Clement W. Bowman Consulting Inc.

A Troubled History

From the time that kings and their agents and later elected governments and bureaucracies started to collect taxes for war or public works, persons on both sides of the transactions have taken advantage of procurement situations and extracted hidden coinage or other advantages. History ancient and contemporary is bursting with references to abuses of the public procurement system.

Examples abound with major abuses and scandals in building, supplying and maintaining the Royal Navy and Napoleon's army. All jurisdictions have examples of failed bridges and dams as a result of cheating on public contracts. Historians exploring this topic would find many cases in the building of railways and canals.

Public taxpayers were shocked at the waste and suffering and demanded additional improvements to the procurement processes from their elected representatives. It was not until civilian managers, with political support behind them, got control of the standards, procurement and payment processes that controls were established in the public procurement process. The goal was to develop standardized procurement procedures which were more fair and transparent, and where all potential suppliers could enter the game with a prospect of playing on a level playing field.

The consequence was a development of complex bureaucratic centralized purchasing systems or individual departmental systems developed within some centrally-developed guidelines. These represented an improvement but, unfortunately, no purchasing system in itself will guarantee simplicity, efficiency and freedom from abuse.

Troubles occur in public procurement when the process collides with political imperatives that may not share the same values and objectives. Troubles also take place when individuals or organizations fall to the pressures of greed, theft, bribery or fraud. The media are attracted to alleged wasteful expenditures of public money, and let us all be thankful for that preoccupation.

There have been a plethora of examples of headlines such as:

Bureaucrats mismanaged $3-billion

- audit reveals mess in grant-giving process:
  - without submission of an application form
  - approved without any internal or external consultation
  - no evidence of financial monitoring

$150-million federal deal broke rules

- audit finds:
  - contract process was not carried out fairly
  - process lacked transparency
  - incomplete or missing files

A Commission of Inquiry was recently held in Canada, conducted by the Honourable John Howard Gomery, a judge of the Superior Court of Quebec. This Inquiry has arisen as a result of the significant concerns raised in the Report of Sheila Fraser, Auditor General of Canada, with respect to sponsorship and advertising activities of the Government of Canada. According to her Report, there were failures of internal control systems, a lack of appropriate documentation justifying material expenditures of public money, the payment of large sums of money to private parties with no apparent value being received in return, a systematic disregard of the applicable rules including those contained in the government's own *Financial Administration Act,* a lack of competition in the selection of advertising agencies, and a general bypassing of Parliamentary procedure.[i]

Public Procurement is Big Business

Public procurement is a big market. Purchasing by governments and other public bodies in Canada in 2000 at all levels (national, provincial, region/county, and local) including education and health care and other public funded bodies, tops $100 billion annually. This means that some $3,000 for each Canadian citizen is spent annually on public procurement efforts across all levels of government.

The federal government in Canada annually spends $13 billion on goods and services. The United States public procurement is a multiple of the Canadian market size with a larger activity in the areas of national defence. Public sector markets globally are very large and continue to expand both in dollars and in the complexity of the goods and services purchased.

The range and variety of goods and services purchased by public bodies from the private sector suppliers are staggering, extending from simple commodity items to complex technological systems representing the leading edges of technology development.

Most public purchasing decisions are made using a public tender system. In some jurisdictions there are provisions allowing for sole source selection for special situations or budget restricted projects. This may avoid the requirements of a competitive tendering for each purchase, but it might open up questions of transparency and fairness. Sometimes, but not always, these "sole source" procurements are subject to some prior qualification process. The number of purchases in this category is relatively small.

Purchasing requirements are first established by public sector managers and their purchasing agents, then publicly posted or advertised. Potential suppliers of the requested goods or services respond to the request with some form of "proposal" or "quote" by a due date and a decision is made often involving multiple decision makers. Historically the major decision factor is based on price. The concept is simple and for the purchasing of standardized commodity types of products such as gravel and office supplies is probably ideal.

The Increasing Importance of Non-Price Criteria

Over recent years, there has been a marked shift in the mix of public procurement requirements away from "hard" goods to "softer" services. Over the past two decades, the pendulum has swung even further by the practice of outsourcing – the hiring of private and non-profit organizations to undertake work that would otherwise be done by government staff. To some extent, this reflects the growth of the services sector in national economies and the requirement of public bodies to purchase these services. But it also reflects a fundamental change in political direction. Today, outsourcing is not just the preserve of right-of-centre governments, but also of all governments that see the inherent efficiency advantages of a *competitive* outsourcing approach.

Whenever the decision factors move beyond the historic "lowest price wins" format the complexity of the buy is much increased. This is because qualitative and intangible issues tend to take the ascendancy over the quantitative; indeed, the *only* quantitative criterion in services procurement is often the cost.

These qualitative and intangible factors are increasingly incorporated into the public purchasing decision process. However, intangibles do not lend themselves easily to traditional systems of assessment and measurement. How does one measure the experience, reputation, knowledge or IP that the vendor brings to the procurement? These subjective areas are wide open to individual interpretation.

Systems and methods that were used to focus on measuring tangible factors were often extended, with varying degrees of success, into the applications where the intangible factors were actually the most important decision elements.

Public sector purchasing managers often responded to the new requirements by developing the application of subjective scales for use by the proposal reviewers. A good response, except that someone's score of "8" might be someone else's "6," and the reasons for this difference might not be at all explicit. The whole concept was flawed in that vendor selections were not based on consistent standards applied within a robust systemic approach. Further, they were not applied in a consistent way and the creation of a database to enable tracking of decision performance was lacking.

What do Public Sector Practitioners Think?

We undertook a program to understand the challenges and needs of the public sector purchasing market by engaging in more than 40 "conversations" with people regarding the problems with public procurement as it is presently practiced in Canada. These included persons on both the policy and practice side of government procurement. It included four levels of government as well as procurement representatives from government agencies. We also spoke with the supply side – senior managers of vendor organizations whose practices include a high per cent of public sector involvement.

In short, there is frustration on all sides. While there is clear recognition of the problem, there is a general reluctance to seek alternative solutions. Many vendors are unwilling to tackle the existing institutional approaches themselves, and the vendor industry, which is highly fragmented, has not shown the leadership or persistence to attack the systemic problems head on. The crisis was not considered big enough to warrant a full-blown attack on the problem.

Our research also indicated that individual vendors were becoming increasingly frustrated by the huge costs imposed on them by the public sector procurement rules and approaches.

Examples:

- A provincial government organization issued a Request for Qualifications (RFQ) to develop a short list of consultants and consulting firms to meet its needs for the next few years. They expected about 50 responses but they received over 300. The organization could not spare the staff needed to evaluate all the responses according to the method outlined in the RFQ, so they cancelled the whole process. Even at $1,000 cost per proposal, considered low by most industry estimates, the vendor industry invested some $300,000 in a worthless task.

- A provincial government agency sent out RFPs to some 50 vendors that it thought might be interested in a small engagement. Most vendors ignored the RFP because they saw no purpose in bidding against 49 others for such a small contract. The agency received one response, which was not considered qualified.

As part of these conversations, we undertook research on those areas that most professions regard as essential to advancing the "state of the art" of a professional practice area. Those areas included:

- Who and where are the thought leaders?
- Is there a home for capturing best practices?
- How do best practices migrate to practitioners?

In summary, we found the professional associations were balkanized between the private and public sectors. Professional associations represent fewer and fewer of the people whose jobs are in procurement. There appears to be little academic research in the area and limited knowledge transfer.

Our Conclusions from the "Conversations"

Our conversations led to some conclusions about the present practice of public procurement.

The Market

- Contract numbers are increasing in volume and becoming more complex.
- Contracts for services are the fastest growing part of the procurement market and are frequently managed by staff inexperienced in services procurement.

The Suppliers

- The supplier base is expanding in response to the demand for services and the growth of new vendors (many new vendors have arisen as a result of public sector outsourcing and downsizing).

- Preparing responses to proposals is expensive – some shops we spoke with estimated that 20% or more of the total available staff time is devoted to preparing proposals.
- In some situations of multi-year service contracts, firms are prepared to invest from 50 to 75% of the first year's revenues into a proposal effort.
- Paper burden is a concern; both RFPs and proposals are getting thicker without a commensurate improvement to the overall results, largely because of new additional "core" requirements and a lack of explicitness in those requirements.
- Suppliers are frustrated by the lack of feedback when they are not successful – what can we learn for next time?
- Complaints about the time taken in the decision making process.
- Complaints on the "poor quality" of many requests for proposals. Suppliers suspect that the issuers do not know what they really want and use the responses to better define their requirements – in effect obtaining "free consulting."
- "Better" bidders are taking themselves out of the public market because of past frustrations, high preparation costs and low margins.

The Public Sector Procurement Profession

- Many public sector buyers do not have formal procurement training.
- Professional associations are struggling to attract members and there is a growing gap between private and public organizations.
- There are few academic leaders in the public sector procurement field.
- There is little original research on procurement and in particular public sector procurement.
- Best practices are an orphan without an apparent home or a distribution system.

The Problems in Typical Public Procurement Processes

We have examined in detail the practices that governments use to select one or more alternatives from a range of available options. In a vendor selection process using a Request For Proposal (RFP), the government department or agency selects the "best" option from a range of proposals. The choice must be based largely on intangible criteria because the only comparable tangible factor is usually the cost.

In government, the staff responsible for RFPs may be expert in their own fields but they are rarely expert in the procurement of services. Some individuals are able to rely on advice and expertise available from specialists, but many do not have such access. Most purchasers use some form of spreadsheet approach to evaluating proposals, whereby the selection criteria are given weightings and the proposals are evaluated against the criteria.

This frequently leads to a variety of problems, of which the more common are:

- Poorly drafted selection criteria
- Poor linkages between the organization's objectives and the services to be procured
- So-called "requirements" which do not appear in the evaluation criteria
- Unnecessary restrictions on the proposed vendor solutions
- Vendor misunderstandings, leading to wasted vendor effort
- Provision by the vendors of unnecessary and irrelevant information
- Inconsistency in the application of the selection criteria
- Opaque processing of the results
- A poor audit trail
- A challengeable decision

Working Toward an Improved Procurement Process

We have used the methodology outlined in this book as a potential solution to this challenge, recognizing that it has the capability to measure the intangibles involved in vendor proposals: "the values the accountants can't count." The process works by "de-constructing" the decision process and making each of the criteria explicit, rather than implicit. The methodology uses the expert knowledge of the decision makers and applies it in "selecting winners" which best meet the organization's priorities in a rigorous and auditable fashion. A permanent decision support database facilitates a comparison of projects longitudinally over time and between agencies.

The first step, and a critical one, is to prepare the Request for Proposal (RFP) in a form that responds to the requirements of the buyer. The requirements will normally include many intangible factors such as processes, technology, staff, leadership, experience, relevance, relationships, values and special knowledge. Instead of using numerical scores to rate the factors, the ProGrid® methodology relies on written Language Ladders that force explicit assessments of the client needs against the services offered.

The RFP is published with both the Performance Criteria and the Language Ladders so potential suppliers can see exactly what is required. The suppliers are asked to assess their own proposals by checking the Language Ladder™ statements included with the RFP document. In this way the supplier gains a thorough understanding of the review system, responds *only* to the essential requirements of the RFP, and ensures that all requested information (and no more) is supplied. The proposals are submitted to the purchaser in the usual way. The client's review team may be a single individual or a team with each reviewer evaluating the incoming proposals and selecting a Language Ladder statement for each criterion that best represents their view of compliance.

Reporting is one of the methodology's most powerful features. Not only does the purchaser receive a report showing how each proposal matches the Performance Criteria, but each vendor receives a thorough assessment of its own proposal, indicating the strengths and/or weaknesses of the proposal by comparison with the client's specific requirements and the other proposals.

The above approach was used for an RFP to solicit, evaluate and select proposals for the work of management consultants in 16 mainly rural communities. The requirements were set out explicitly in a way that enabled vendors to see immediately whether or not they were likely to meet the mandatory and qualitative criteria. Some 70% of vendors surveyed agreed with the statement: "Government should use this kind of process more often."

The Steps for an Effective Procurement Process

This section describes a generic process for the use of the ProGrid process in procurement. The first step is to construct an Evaluation Matrix™ that comprises the key decision factors of the purchasing organization. A simplified example is shown in Table 11.1 for the situation when a government department is seeking a consultant to perform a stated task. Note that "cost" is not one of the criteria.

TABLE 11.1
Procurement Evaluation Matrix

The Consultant	Enablers	The Results
Credentials	Project Understanding	Delivery
Performance	Work Plan	Quality
Organizational Capacity	Access and Responsiveness	

The next step is to develop the Language Ladders identifying various levels of performance. Those that apply to the Enabling Column in the Evaluation Matrix are shown in Table 11.2.

The ratings of the Supplier and the Reviewers are processed in the supporting software to produce various interpretive charts. The grid chart in Figure 11.1 uses as axes the headings in the first and third columns of the Evaluation Matrix in Table 11.1. These represent the two overarching objectives of the government department, the

TABLE 11.2

Language Ladder for the Enablers

Project Understanding
The understanding of the project's requirements, scope, and objectives.

- ( ) A) The proposal shows a lack of understanding of the project's requirements, scope, and objectives.
- ( ) B) The proposal indicates an incomplete understanding of the project's requirements, scope, and objectives.
- (•) C) The proposal shows a full understanding of the project's requirements, scope, and objectives...
- ( ) D) ...AND demonstrates new, additional insights.

Work Plan
Approach, organization and management of the tasks required completing the project.

- ( ) A) The work plan has significant weaknesses.
- ( ) B) The work plan should result in a satisfactory completion of the project.
- (•) C) The work plan presents a comprehensive management approach to successfully complete the project...
- ( ) D) ...AND includes some innovative ideas which provide additional value without additional risk.

Accessibility & Responsiveness
The geographic proximity or immediate responsiveness appropriate to the project.

- ( ) A) The consultant accessibility and responsiveness does not meet the client's expectations.
- ( ) B) The consultant accessibility and responsiveness meets some of the client's expectations.
- (•) C) The consultant accessibility and responsiveness meets the client's expectations and project requirements.
- ( ) D) The consultant accessibility and responsiveness exceeds the client's expectations and project requirements.

FIGURE 11.1

The Procurement Evaluation Grid

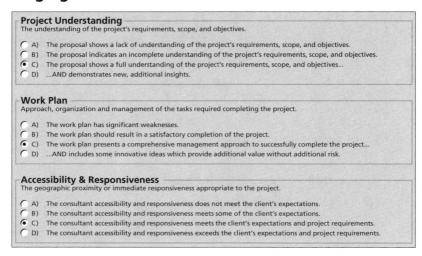

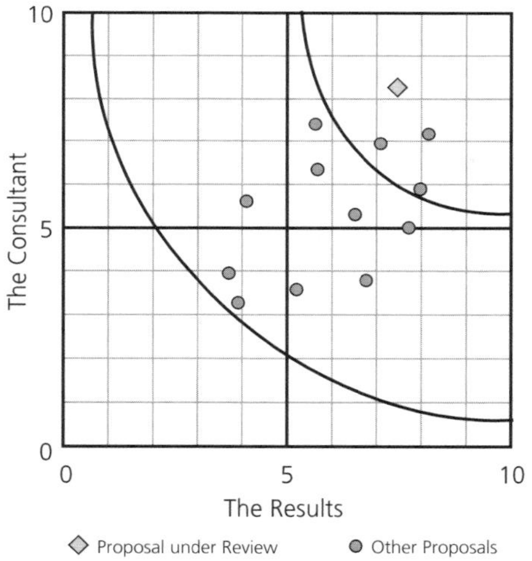

capability of the consultant and the results that the consultant is expected to deliver.

A full test of this methodology was undertaken, with the results shown in Figure 11.1. The data plotted on the grid made it relatively easy to rank the proposals.

The output reports document and demonstrate *in a consistent and graphical form* the ability of any competing proposal to meet the values, priorities and expectations of the procuring agency. The reports provide both an excellent *medium of accountability* and a *permanent audit trail* for future reference, including:

- How each proposal ranks against the client's Performance Criteria
- Ranking of each proposal against all the other proposals
- Profile showing how each proposal rates against each set of performance criteria
- Comparison of the suppliers' rankings with those of the reviewers
- Degree of consensus among the reviewers
- Historical view – comparison of criteria rankings of current applications with those of previous applications

Significant time and cost savings occurred in two areas. Reviewing vendor proposals is one of the most time-consuming elements of the procurement process. The proposal review team found that the consistent ProGrid proposal format enabled the review process to be completed in about a third the time needed for traditionally formatted proposals. The availability of all the proposal review information on the screen at the reviewers' meeting enabled an expected day's meeting to be cut to two hours, even though sixteen "winners" were to be selected, not one.

The Advantages of the ProGrid Public Procurement Process

ProGrid improves the commitment of governments to a more business-like relationship with the private sector. It offers an improved and better process for the management of requests for proposals and provides improved openness, transparency, fairness and accountability. It demonstrates prudent fiscal management by governments by providing consistent scoring and weightings across each response, evidence of which is provided in an automatic paper trail saving on demands for follow-up meetings. A final benefit is the results can be easily integrated into existing government project management systems permitting a project monitoring mechanism for the duration of the project.

At the operational level ProGrid provides benefits to procurement managers and firms participating in a competition. It saves time and money on both sides while shrinking the size of proposals. Indeed, most responses in terms of the core requirements of a proposal can be reduced to no more than 15 pages with all responses taking on a standardized format. This offers advantages to both those firms preparing proposals and to the reviewers of proposals. Historically, reviewers can complete a proposal review within 30 minutes. This means an improved use of reviewers while avoiding reviewer fatigue. With the format and submission being electronic, when reviewers meet, the chaos often experienced is turned into an efficient meeting where all views are on the table in advance.Reviewers can focus not on the areas on which they agree but on the important areas of divergence.

ProGrid provides a rigorous system that can be applied to government procurement decision-making. It provides a decision environment that is open, fair, transparent and accountable. It gets the best out of both the potential vendors and the reviewers while concentrating on the issues that are important to the competition. It is a win/win situation for both sides, offering efficiencies and benefits to the private and public sector while taking advantage of proven automated systems that advance the state of the practice of public procurement.

[i] http://www.gomery.ca/en/index.asp

12 Finding the Pony: The Holy Grail of Venture Capitalists

Ron McCullough – Benchmark-Action Inc.
John Kramers – ProGrid Ventures Inc.
Clem Bowman – Clement W. Bowman Consulting Inc.

Searching for the Home Run

When governments make decisions for grants and awards, values like fairness, transparency, constructive applicant feedback and a sound paper trail come into play. Or at least they should. On the other hand, Venture Capital firms play to a different tune, having usually developed their own evaluation approaches ranging from the "warm feeling in the belly" approach to complex due diligence procedures or the running of various "what-if" scenarios. Whatever their approach, these Venture Capitalists do not talk about "transparencies."

Venture Capital firms expect that nine out of 10 investments will fail, with the one successful project providing a financial return sufficient to pay the freight. But that is not the real prize. They are looking for the one in a hundred that will be the real winner, which will provide the kinds of returns that they dream about. In the words of an old joke, it is the pony buried in the dung that is the real prize.

Venture Capitalists go from tranche to tranche, looking for the entry of longer-term players, such as merchant banks, which then sets the stage for a profitable exit strategy.

Searching for the Indicators of Success

Two early stage Venture Capital groups, using the approaches described in this book, developed their own evaluation matrices as a guide to making their initial series of investments. A team of managers experienced in new technology commercialization further refined these matrices to include criteria that transition into early market trials and customer validation, as shown in Table 12.1.

TABLE 12.1
Evaluation Matrix™ for Early Stage Ventures

The Venture	The Connectors	The Impact
Advance Over Current Commercial Practice	Customer Validation and Acceptance	Market Size and Growth
Competitive Advantage	Business Plan	Market Share
Current Development Status	Business Team Experience and Capacity	Competition
Capability to Complete Technical Development	Investor Support	Financial Returns to the Venture Capital Investor

This Evaluation Matrix includes criteria that are largely intangible and that reflect the experience and commitment of the venture team. But it also includes the precursors for commercial success, such as the validation provided by customers, and a forecast of expected rates of return. These latter two criteria are illustrated by the Language Ladders shown in Tables 12.2 and 12.3.

Results from tests on a range of new ventures are shown in Figures 12.1 and 12.2. The Proponent self-rating is the left set of bars; the average of three Assessors is the right set of bars.

TABLE 12.2
Language Ladder™ for Customer Validation and Acceptance

	The products/processes/services provided by the concept:
A	have not yet been evaluated by potential customers. Preliminary market studies may indicate that a potential market exists.
B	have had limited evaluation by potential customers but they have confirmed the concept has potential value to them.
C	have been fully tested by potential customers who have confirmed their commercial interest and are prepared to place firm orders for the purchase of development quantities.
D	have been accepted for commercial use by two key customers (as identified in their business plans) and these customers are placing repeat orders.

TABLE 12.3
Language Ladder for Financial Returns to the Venture Capital Investor

Commercialization of this concept:	
A	is unlikely to provide minimum acceptable venture capital rates of return.
B	will likely provide acceptable venture capital rates of return of 30% but it is uncertain whether the investor will be able to "realize" that return within 2 years.
C	will likely provide acceptable venture capital rates of return of 30% with the potential that the investor can 'realize' that return within 2 years.
D	has the potential to yield exceptional rates of return of 50% or more with the strong likelihood that the investor can 'realize' that return within 2 years.

The venture in Figure 12.1 is typical of a very early stage venture that is based on a strong technology with a capable technical team. The business plan and people are not yet in place, representing a correctable deficiency. However the market potential and financial returns look weak and may represent fatal flaws. On the other hand, the venture in Figure 12.2 is based on a modest advance, but with encouraging market prospects.

FIGURE 12.1
Profile of Venture Strong on Technology, Weaker on Market

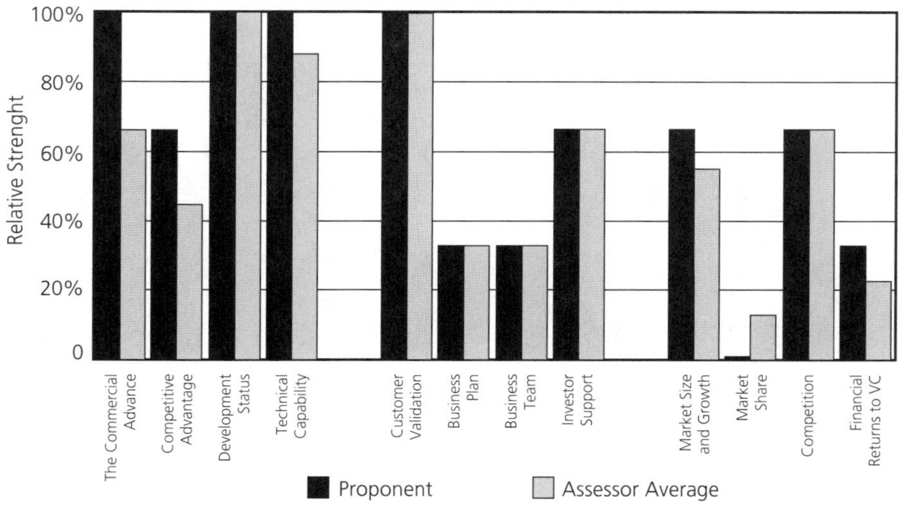

FIGURE 12.2
Profile of Venture with Modest Advance, Encouraging Market

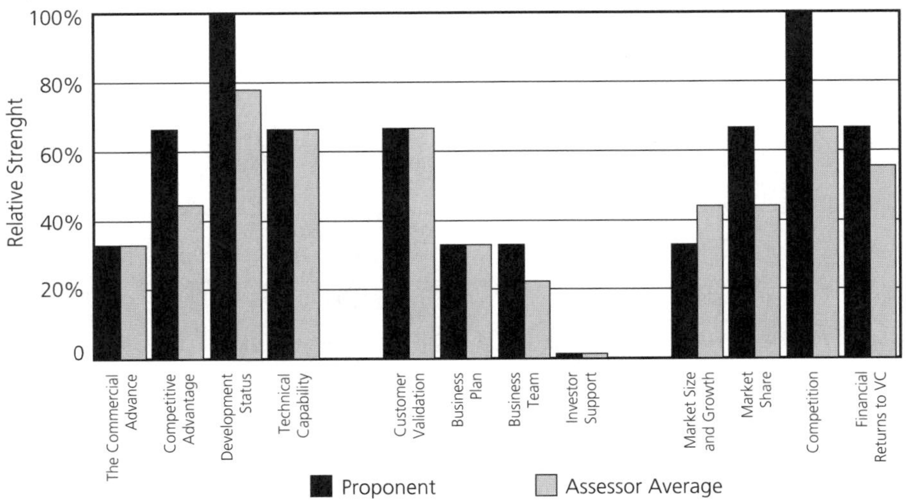

Proceeding to Detailed Due Diligence

Profile charts such as shown in Figures 12.1 and 12.2 provide the foundation for more detailed due diligence. Embedded in the Language Ladders for each cell in the Evaluation Matrix are the prospects for future improvements. For example, the Current Development Status is likely to be a correctable weakness, in that time and resources can be brought to bear to complete the development. Competition on the other hand may not be controllable if the venture faces strong in place competitors who dominate the market.

FIGURE 12.3
Potential for Venture Improvement

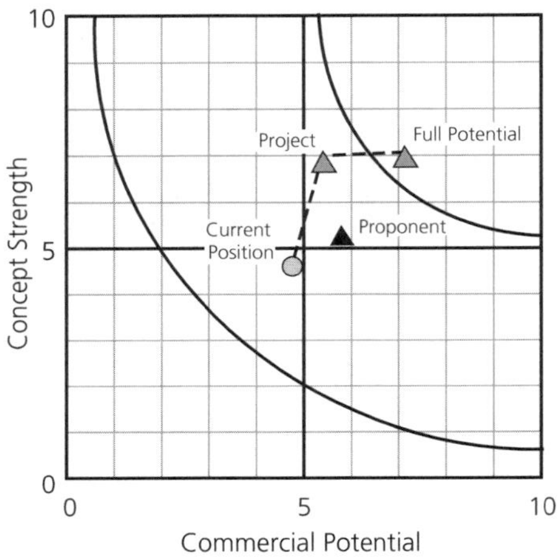

Sensitivity analyses can be developed which estimate the likelihood of future advance, as illustrated in Figure 12.3.

This venture has the potential to improve its grid position by successfully completing those tasks within the capability of the project team (the Project triangle), and by solving some issues related to the business plan and market characteristics (the Full Potential Triangle).

To aid in making these future potential assessments, the following action statements can be formulated to describe what must be done to achieve the two up-sides shown in Figure 12.3. Successful completion of the first four actions would contribute to achieving the Project position in Figure 12.3 and the final three actions would lead to the Full Potential position.

1. Demonstrate that there is a significant and recognizable advance over current commercial practice that will significantly change market dynamics.
2. Finalize testing of the Product/Process/Service under a full range of commercially relevant conditions.
3. Complete the business plan; identify milestones/resources, approved by all key stakeholders, including existing investors.
4. Strengthen the management team with a committed CEO, and an active Board of Directors, who have experience in the business area and markets.
5. Follow through with market validation until two or more key customers are placing repeat orders.
6. Identify market segments that are growing at more than 15% per year and if the opportunity is sufficient to meet business goals, focus on these segments.
7. Identify and implement actions that will increase market share to more than 25% in more than one major market.

Managing the Portfolio

The ventures shown in Figure 12.4 illustrate the spread in ratings for early stage ventures submitted to a Venture Capital Fund. The ventures that rated at or near the upper curved line were usually supported, for at least the first round of financing. Many ventures just below the upper curved line proceeded to more detailed due diligence, such as that provided by the approaches described in Chapter 20. The latter provide a more comprehensive view of the strengths and weaknesses, and a better assessment of future potential.

FIGURE 12.4
Database

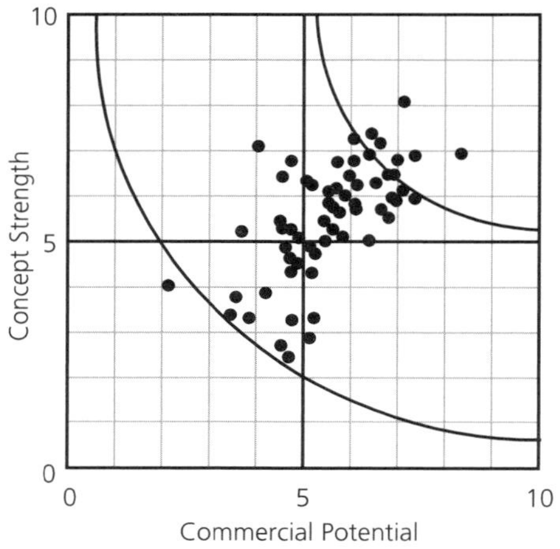

A Venture Capital firm might seek a balance in its portfolio of projects. A few ventures, with strong underlying concepts but with unknown or uncertain markets, might represent opportunities for adding value and future big payoffs. On the other hand, ventures representing more modest technical advances might be closer to commercialization and provide some early winners.

The Next Stages of Financing

Contacting the Venture Capitalist is only one of the steps in what is often a long process. Each step will have its own set of decision criteria and special requirements for evaluation and decision support.

Angel investors (family, friends, wealthy entrepreneurs) foster very early stage ideas prior to the first "formal" capital investment and tend to have very personal goals and criteria. As such they may be less formal in their assessment processes. A set of decision-assist criteria has, however, been used with groups of angels where the tone is "How to assess if you are ready to present your opportunities to a Venture Capitalist?" These criteria serve as a "front end" to those used in this chapter.

Once an idea has made the first big step of getting venture capital, it often faces one or more steps related to second, third, and extended stage financing. At this point, the idea has maintained its initial attractiveness and shown some progress but is still not yet ready for commercialization. The tone becomes "We saw some promises – how are you progressing towards turning them into reality?" There is a greater emphasis on progress than on promise.

Successful ideas eventually reach the end of the Venture Capital investment phase. While a significant number are not yet ready for full-scale commercialization, the pilot operations, initial market introduction and customer satisfaction surveys will have been a success. Full-scale operation may require substantial investments in production facilities, marketing and distribution beyond the scope of the Venture Capitalist. This is the role of the "Merchant Banker" or others who provide mezzanine financing. Decisions at this point require much greater basis in fact, significant due diligence and detailed financial analyses. There will still be a number of largely intangible elements in the decision process and the Merchant Banker may also have to compare numerous opportunities that are very different in type and scope.

And, finally, the idea has come to the point of being fully "ready for prime time." It may proceed to IPO (Initial Public Offering), to a buy-out by a major company, or to financing by a privately-held company; there are many routes. At this stage, well-established financial models drive the decision process. Decision support becomes highly personalized and variants of decision systems such a ProGrid must fit into well-structured processes – and often do.

The progression from an idea to success in the marketplace is a progression from promise to progress to reward. ProGrid decision systems such as illustrated in this chapter are able to meet the needs of effective decision support along this continuum, particularly at the earlier stages. The framework often stays relatively the same but the criteria continually evolve to match the requirements of the "banker."

13 Business Plan Evaluations by University Students

Ted Heidrick – University of Alberta
John Kramers – ProGrid Ventures Inc.

The Importance of Entrepreneurship

The previous chapter describes a process for evaluating early stage technology-based ventures by Venture Capitalists. The original technologies are often developed by university students as part of their science and engineering education. In fact, entrepreneurship education has become increasingly important in Canadian universities. For example, the University of Alberta offers a course on Project Management and Entrepreneurship, taken primarily by senior level Engineering students but open to all students having completed six terms. At the graduate level there is an MBA Specialization in Technology Commercialization that has several relevant courses. Recently, some of the major funders of technically oriented graduate students (Alberta Ingenuity, iCore, Alberta Agriculture Research Institute) sponsored an introductory short course on technology commercialization.

To support formal lectures on a variety of topics (e.g. marketing, financing), a practical methodology is needed that teaches students how to analyze business opportunities that the students have developed in the classroom. The process should be consistent, objective, transparent, user-friendly and use generally-accepted criteria for judging business opportunities. Due to limited class time, a quick and efficient process is needed to evaluate opportunities against these accepted criteria. The methodology for assessing intangibles described in this book has all these attributes.

In order to evaluate the effectiveness of the methodology as a teaching and evaluation tool, the authors used it in both senior undergraduate engineering and MBA level classes at the University of Alberta. A modified ProGrid®-Venture Evaluation Matrix was used and is illustrated in Table 13.1.

TABLE 13.1
ProGrid Venture Evaluation Matrix™

The Venture	The Connectors	Benefits/Impacts
The Advance	Validation	Market size
The Advantage	Business Plan	Market share
Venture Status	Business Team	Competition
The Capability	Investment Offering	Rate of Return

All the criteria definitions and accompanying Language Ladders (the metrics) can be found on the ProGrid Ventures Inc. web site on the demo page (http://www.progrid.ca/demo_frame.html) where a Venture self-assessment demo can be downloaded. Only the *Investment Offering* criterion in the above Evaluation Matrix is different than that used in the demo tool because the student business plan is typically very early stage and as yet there are no investors. Thus *Investment Offering* was substituted for the ProGrid®-Venture *Investors* criterion. The Language Ladder for the *Investment Offering* for this purpose is shown in Table 13.2.

TABLE 13.2
Language Ladder™ for Investment Offering

The Investment Offering includes:	
A	A small number of shares and existing investors include only the company founders, immediate family and friends.
B	A moderate number of shares and investors, other than the company founders, immediate family and friends, are identified.
C	A substantial number of shares with confirmed investment support from other investors for the balance of the shares.
D	A substantial number of shares and the potential for additional shares at a later date with the balance of the shares held by highly credible investors.

Fourth Year Engineering Project Management and Entrepreneurship Class

The methodology was introduced to the approximately 60 members of the fourth year Engineering undergraduate course on Project Management and Entrepreneurship in four different academic terms. The students were put in teams of approximately five students and each team developed a business plan for a technology-based business opportunity. At the three quarters point in each term the teams presented their almost completed plan to the class. The class then undertook a peer review of each plan using the ProGrid methodology. The eight-page feedback report, which included the assessments by the other teams, was given to the students in time for them to improve their final product.

The results of this process are illustrated in Figure 13.1, showing the assessments for all business plans. The results all fell in the lower left quadrant, expected for very early stage ventures.

FIGURE 13.1
Business Plan Comparison Chart

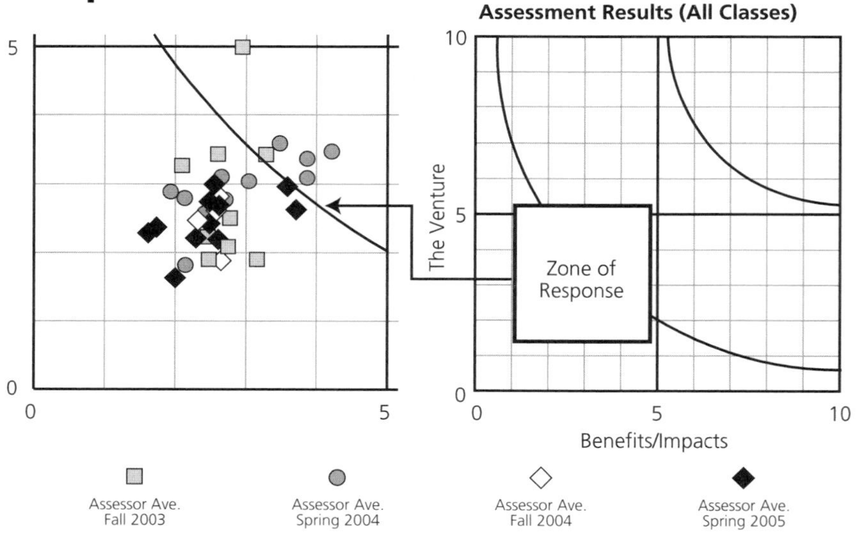

Even with four different populations of 60 students, and approximately 40 different plans, the ProGrid methodology provided consistent results; the evaluation results from the four classes were in

FIGURE 13.2
The Profile Chart – Average for All Classes

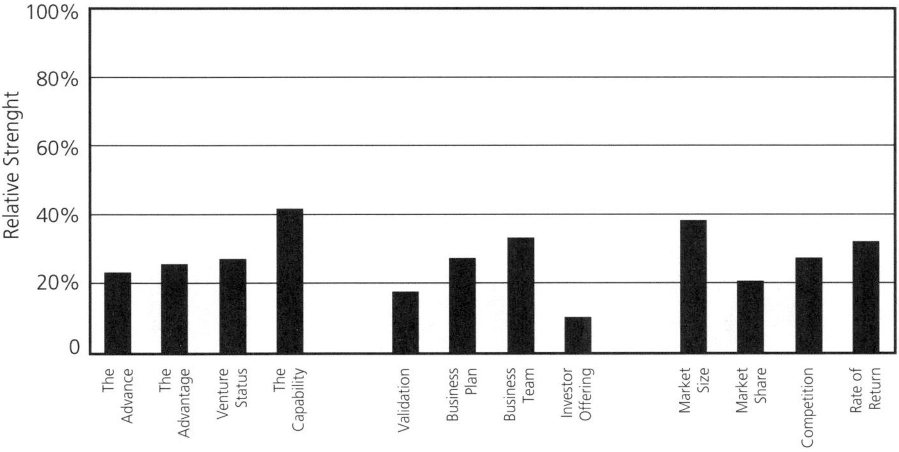

the lower left quadrant of the grid, indicative of early stage ventures. The overall level of the evaluations for the Venture and the Benefits/Impacts are reasonable for the stage of development of the business plans.

The averages for each criterion for all classes are shown in Figure 13.2, with the technical areas stronger (not surprising for Engineering students) and the "connectors" weaker (again not surprising for an embryonic venture).

FIGURE 13.3
Grid Position Comparison

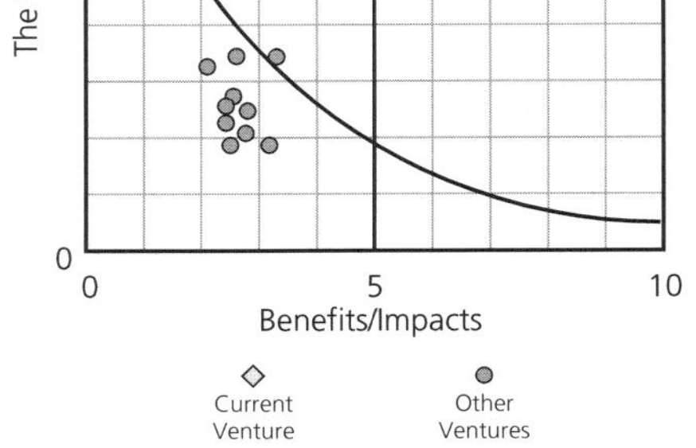

It is also relatively easy to identify the best plan. The plan associated with the diamond (Current Venture) shown in Figure 13.3 was developed by a team lead by Graham Buksa for an opportunity called Rayne Longboards (www.raynelongboards.com) in the spring term of 2003.

FIGURE 13.4
Profile for Rayne Longboards

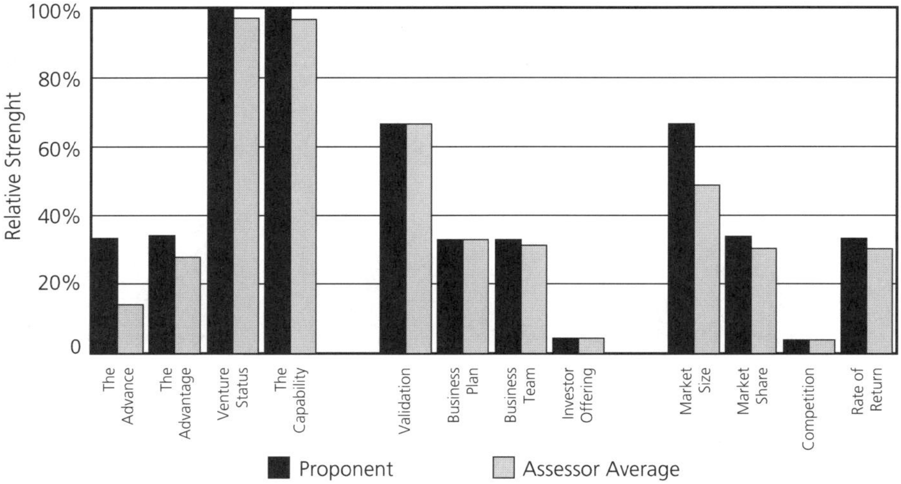

The evaluations of the 11 student teams in the three quarter report are shown in Figure 13.3 for comparison.

FIGURE 13.5
Grid Positions for Final Evaluations

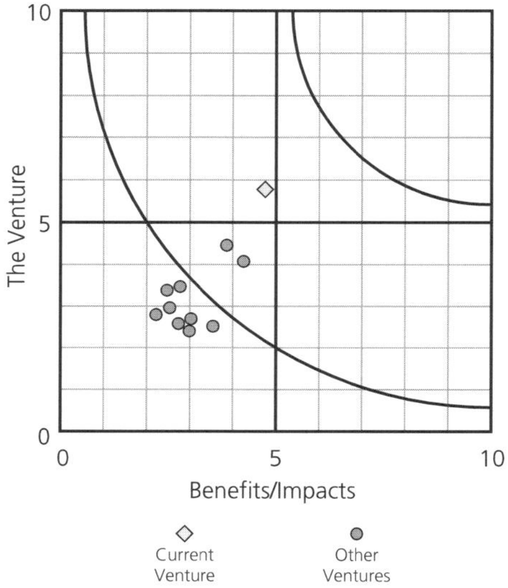

The ratings for each criterion for Rayne Longboards are shown in Figure 13.4. Since Buksa had built several prototypes the capability and venture status were the business plan's strong points.

All final plans were subjected to the same evaluation process. The final ratings improved as shown in Figure 13.5 as compared to those at the three quarter point shown in Figure 13.3. For example, the Rayne Longboards diamond

FIGURE 13.6
Final Profile Chart for Rayne Longboards

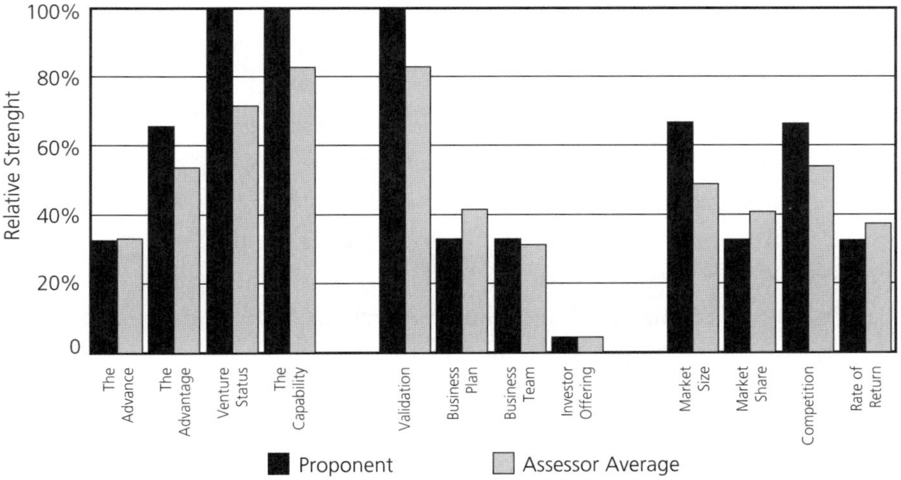

improved to a point 4.7 and 5.8 compared to 3.0 and 5.0 for the preliminary plan evaluation, a shift in both axes.

As shown in Figure 13.6, Buksa and his team made improvements in most criteria.

Subsequent to graduation Buksa and his team entered the Economic Development Edmonton Venture Prize competition. Although they did not make the semi-finals there, Buksa has since moved to Vancouver and entered a British Columbia Business Plan competition with an improved plan and was one of 5 (out of 160) winners in the Small Business category. Buksa and one of the authors have also been recently featured in a short segment on Access TV – Careers TV, highlighting this success. In Buksa's words:

"Using ProGrid was a great experience when taking your class and allowed our group to focus on our weakest points. Making skateboards is not groundbreaking technology and when we were evaluated using ProGrid it was apparent that we needed to focus on creating a unique niche within the skateboard industry. Today the success of Rayne Longboards has been a direct result of studying our competition and differentiating ourselves within the growing longboard market. ProGrid is a great tool for business plan evaluation and has helped us refine our business plan to attract investment."

Student Feedback

In a feedback questionnaire from the fall 2003 class, only one out of 33 students said the evaluation process did not add value to developing their final business plan. A typical comment: *"It gave us a chance to address the weak points of our business plan as seen by the other students in the class. Also, by viewing the information from other groups we could compare the quality of their business plans with ours."* Thirty out of 33 students replying to the feedback survey said the feedback they received in the ProGrid report was helpful in developing their final business plan submission. The comments from the students were consistent from class to class, the evaluation process allowing them to develop a better business plan for submission as their major assignment.

MBA Class – New Venture Management

In order to test the process for use with more experienced students, the same process was followed in a first year MBA class on New Venture Management. The 15 students were put in teams of three and copies of five business plans that had been previously evaluated in a recent Business Plan Prize Competition were provided to all students. Criteria that had been used by the Business Plan Prize screeners were put into the ProGrid format as shown in Table 13.3.

TABLE 13.3
Evaluation Matrix for Business Plan Competition

The Business Plan	Connectors	Benefits/Impacts
Product or Service	Management	Profits (Return on Capital)
Customer Value	The Plan	
Market Size	Marketing Strategy	Market Share
Competition	Risk Management	

Language Ladders were developed for each criterion. For example the Language Ladder for the *"Product or Service"* is shown in Table 13.4.

TABLE 13.4

Language Ladder for "Product or Service"

Products or Service:	
A	The product or service on which the business is based is described vaguely as an idea and a development horizon is not discussed.
B	The product or service on which the business is based is clearly described, its functionality tested and a prototype is being developed.
C	The product or service on which the business is based is clearly defined, a prototype has been completed and/or there is keen interest from a pilot customer.
D	The product or service on which the business is based is completely developed and tested and approved by applicable agencies.

The students were given a presentation on ProGrid methodology. Each team of three was given 20 minutes to read and evaluate each business plan. The evaluations were processed and the results presented to the class in the following lecture.

The very quick class evaluation produced the same rank order as for the Business Plan Competition (Figure 13.7). The competition's semi-finalist was ranked highest of this pool of plans by MBA students. Although it is difficult to draw definitive conclusions (since different parameters were used), it appears that the best plans in the Business Plan competition are rated higher than the Engineering class plans, as would be expected.

FIGURE 13.7

Business Plan Competition Rankings Based on MBA Student Evaluations

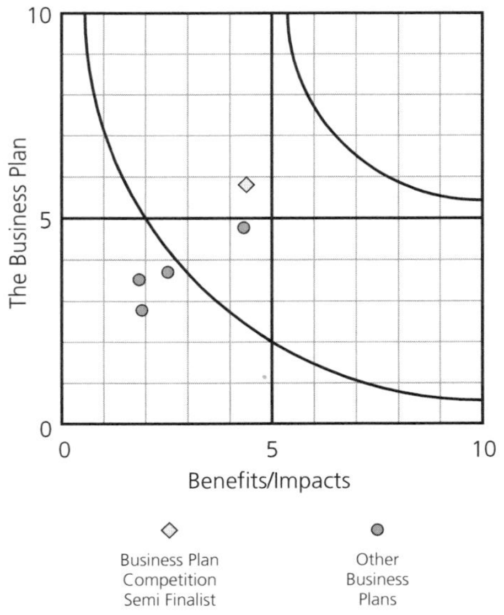

The MBA student's only complaint with the process was that it was too rushed (two hours to read and evaluate six business plans). However, all but one of the respondents to a feedback survey agreed that the process they had gone through added value – *"I like seeing/learning that there can be a somewhat objective way to evaluate the business plan."*

A Final Analysis

Based on the results from four senior engineering student evaluations of their colleagues' business plans and one MBA's class evaluation of businesses plans submitted to a Business Plan Competition, the ProGrid methodology provides:

- A consistent analysis from class to class,
- Feedback which allows student teams to improve their business plans,
- The ability to identify good, better and best opportunities.

The ProGrid methodology provides an interactive process that assists students in learning how to evaluate business opportunities. It also allows students to improve their business plan based on the feedback they receive.

14 Evaluating Students and the Research Training Environment

Jacques Magnan, Richard Thornley, Mark Taylor, and Matthew Spence –
Alberta Heritage Foundation for Medical Research

The Challenge

Formal and informal peer review is used at all stages of the research process to determine the allocation of resources such as funds, time, material, and space. The bedrock of research is the people whose ideas and skills drive the process. These people are frequently reviewed by their peers in the multiple competitions that characterize their careers, and the division and allocation of scarce resources. The graduate training programs of academic institutions (leading to a Masters or a Ph.D. degree) are an integral part of the research enterprise, serving as the principal source of future researchers, and also as a source of person power for research during their formal graduate training. As graduate programs are resource intensive in terms of student time and personal funds, as well as faculty supervisor, faculty time, and university infrastructure, the number of available positions is limited. Accordingly, in most university faculties, there are competitive selection processes for admission to graduate school[i ii], and as a result, the population of graduate students has already been screened for, and score highly for most of the potential attributes of future scientific success. For external funding agencies that support graduate students, picking worthy candidates from this pre-screened, highly competitive pool is a challenging process[iii iv]. In this chapter, we outline the experience of the Alberta Heritage Foundation for Medical Research (AHFMR) with selecting students for graduate awards using a committee-based peer review assisted by the ProGrid software.

AHFMR is an endowment-based Foundation established by the government of Alberta in 1979[v]. Its mandate is to establish and support a balanced, long-term program of health research in the province of Alberta directed to the discovery and application of new knowledge. Most of its activities are in partnership with three Alberta universities and nine regional health authorities, and comprise chiefly the support of faculty-level researchers and approximately 500 researchers-in-training (students at various levels from high school, university undergraduate, university graduate and postdoctoral fellows, collectively known as trainees). Of this trainee group, approximately 200 are registered in graduate degree programs (leading to either a Masters or a Ph.D. degree). This AHFMR-supported cadre is part of an overall population of 10,000 graduate students in the province. It is estimated that those working in health-related fields and possibly eligible to apply to the Foundation number around 2,000.

Any student accepted by an Alberta post-secondary education institution into an approved graduate program leading to a Masters or Ph.D. degree, who is receiving training in a field or topic area relevant to health, and sponsored by their research supervisor and academic department/faculty, may apply for an AHFMR Studentship. The award provides a stipend and a research allowance, and is renewable annually for a total of up to five years. These Studentship awards have been available since the early 1980s. Over the last decade, the Foundation has received between 80 and 150 applications twice a year and, following a thorough review, awards are made to approximately 20-30% of applicants. The absolute number of students supported on an annual basis is determined by the overall budget for the program.

The review process is carried out by a committee of up to 12 established health researchers with faculty-level academic appointments in Alberta institutions. Appointments to the committee have traditionally been for up to three years, which means each committee member reviews applications in up to six competitions. The information for review is prepared by the applicant, guided by a standard form with a format and content designed by the Foundation and its committees to elicit the most helpful information for decision-making. This information consists of:

a. demographic facts and institutional sponsorship agreement
b. academic record
c. research-relevant experience
d. supervisor curriculum vitae
e. brief project description
f. letters of reference.

All applications are sent to a subset of the entire committee, and each member reviews in depth between 15 and 30 applications, assigning a provisional ranking. Prior to the introduction of the ProGrid decision-assist software, the applications were reviewed at a formal committee meeting where each was presented by committee reviewers. Following discussion a final rating/ranking was assigned by the entire committee. The applicants to be supported through Studentships awarded are identified by the Foundation based on this rank order and the number of awards approved depends on the funds available.

The Foundation has always focused a great deal of attention on quality control in peer review, and constantly strives to improve the process. In 1999-2000, we elected to add the ProGrid decision-assist software[vi vii] to the Studentship review process. A number of specific issues and trends led to this decision. First, the number of proposals submitted per competition was gradually increasing, so that the committee was considering as many as 150 applications per competition, as compared to a historical number of 90. At the same time, committee members were reporting increasing concern with the time they could allocate to their individual and collective peer review. To address the latter meant that committee members were faced with extending the durations of their meetings or spending less time reviewing each application, each of which was viewed as potentially decreasing the quality of peer review.

Second, there was increased turnover in the Foundation's review committees, probably part of a wider phenomenon of reviewer fatigue[viii ix], caused by a proliferation of funding agencies and programs, and more requests to individuals to sit on review committees. There was a concern that increased turnover resulted in less consistency in the application of criteria within and between competitions.

Third, there was concern that the pressures of application numbers and limited time could lead to the uneven application of the various review criteria by individual committee members, and that this would not be corrected with the limited amount of time available for the discussion of individual applications. In theory, the overall score awarded to each application represents an integration of all parts of the application; in practice, however, each reviewer's interpretation results in the variable weighting of different criteria. For example, some may attach more importance to academic record; others to the research proposal. Compounded by the turnover among committee members, and the time for discussion, this may lead to some inconsistency in the application of criteria between competitions.

Fourth, the recognition by the potential applicants and their sponsors that the competition was becoming more and more intense had lead to a very high quality application. The committee, as a result, had increasing difficulty in assigning numerical scores that discriminated between applications.

Finally, the Foundation has always believed that peer review should be valuable to both successful and unsuccessful candidates. The large number of high-quality applications meant that little meaningful feedback could be collected and provided on a routine basis without a system of capturing the individual and collective committee opinions in a standard and efficient manner.

Developing the ProGrid® Decision-Assist Tool

In developing ProGrid to advise the AHFMR Studentship review process, the Foundation was guided by its prior experience with a review of Studentship applications, and previous experience with ProGrid in the Technology Commercialization programs of the Foundation, and the experience of other Canadian research organization such as the Canada Foundation for Innovation and the Ontario Centres of Excellence.

Historically, a number of factors have been used by the Foundation's Advisory Committees to predict the performance of trainees in the proposed research environment (Table 14.1).

TABLE 14.1
Trainee Evaluation Matrix™

The Candidate	Linking Factors	The Research Environment
Academic Record	Role of Trainee and Linkage to Supervisor's Research	Supervisor's Research Track Record
Research Experience	Overall Impression of Project	Training Environment
Letters of Reference		

Similar factors have been used by other funding agencies in Canada. For ProGrid, these performance factors were formally attributed to one or both of two independent performance criteria: 1) the characteristics of the candidate; and, 2) the characteristics of the candidate's proposed research environment[x]. These two components of the application package are thought most likely to indicate the future performance of any research trainee. The formal articulation of the performance factors and the independent performance criteria, as well as "linking factors" that might be assigned to both criteria, is shown in Table 14.1.

A Language Ladder™ was constructed for each performance factor in Table 14.1 to allow reviewers to report assessment for each factor on a four-point scale from A to D. In developing the Language Ladder, a major challenge was to obtain experienced reviewer consensus on the actual language describing each rung of the ladder. This is typical in the development of any ProGrid language ladders[vi]. This was done through an iterative process between the Foundation and the reviewers. We have continued to monitor and evolve the language of the ladders over time to provide increasing clarity in the language expressing the values and expectations of the Foundation and the research community. Table 14.2 is an example of a Language Ladder.

TABLE 14.2
"Academic Record" Language Ladder

Academic Record:	
A	Candidate's academic record is adequate for admission to most graduate schools.
B	Candidate has attained above average grades during his/her undergraduate/graduate training and/or candidate has demonstrated steady improvement in his/her grades in the latter stages of training. Candidate has received academic recognition (e.g., Dean's List) or a prize/award
C	Solid, consistently above average academic record throughout the undergraduate/graduate training period and/or candidate has demonstrated significant improvement in his/her academic record in the latter stages of training. Evidence of receipt of several prizes/awards.
D	Outstanding academic record throughout candidate's university level training period. Evidence of receipt of several prizes and awards, some of which are highly competitive, premier prizes/awards.

Applicants and their proposed or actual research supervisors receive a copy of the ProGrid language ladders with the application information, the purpose being to better understand the criteria on which the application will be assessed and to have an opportunity to present the requested information appropriately and completely. With the accumulated experience with the use of ProGrid, the Alberta health research community has also become more knowledgeable generally about presenting the best possible case for the candidate and the research environment.

In a competition, the Committee reviewers are asked to select their ratings for each of the factors in the Trainee Evaluation Matrix, based on the written information provided by the candidates and their supervisors as part of the application (i.e. the application, academic transcripts, letters of reference etc.). Each application is reviewed by three committee reviewers, with assessments sent electronically to AHFMR and entered into the ProGrid software for analysis. The outputs selected are in both chart and text form:

a. graph position of the application with respect to the two major performance criteria (see Figure 14.1),
b. specific comments by the reviewers regarding individual criteria or the application as a whole,

c. comparison of the ratings of each application with the average rating for each performance factor in the overall competition (see Figure 14.2),

d. customized reports for administrators, reviewers and candidates, and

e. a numerical R-value used to rank the application in the competition.

FIGURE 14.1
The Database

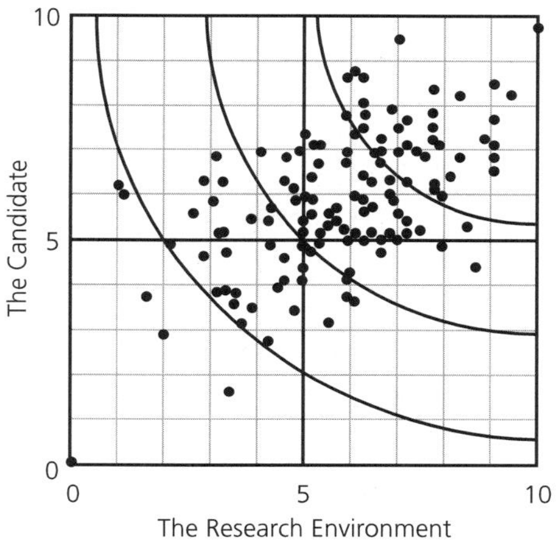

Each single point represents one applicant. The position on the graph is determined by the aggregate score as a candidate, the assessment of the research environment, and the other factors outlined in Table 14.1.

FIGURE 14.2
The Proposal Profile

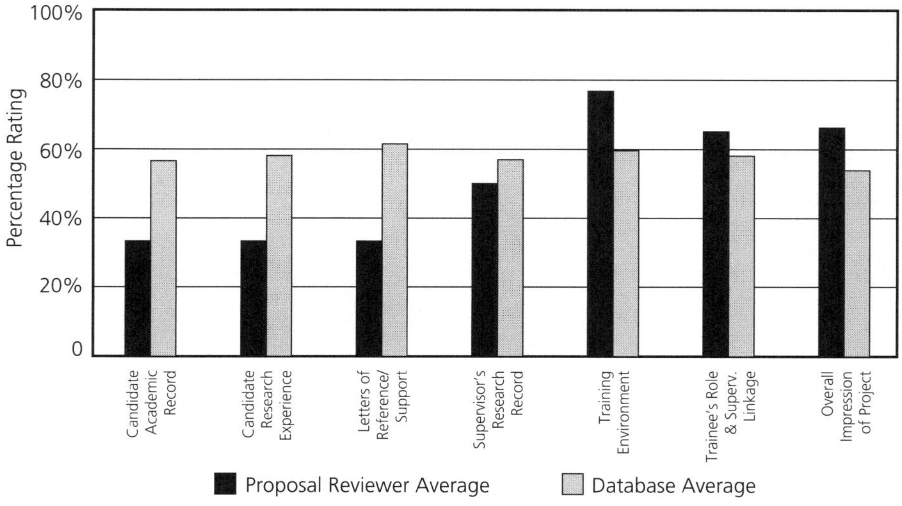

Application in the AHFMR Studentship Competitions

The ProGrid decision-assist tool was introduced as an aid to peer review in the AHFMR studentship competitions in 2000, and has been used subsequently in nine competitions. Unless stated otherwise, we have compared the statistics from the four competitions prior to October 2000 (418 applications), where ProGrid was not used, with the four subsequent competitions (425 applications), assisted by ProGrid. The mean number of applications per competition was slightly lower prior to ProGrid, but was rising, and this is reflected in the wider standard deviation (99 ± 23 versus 106 ± 10 in the ProGrid-assisted group). The number of successful applications was similar (31 ± 4 versus 30 ± 2 in the ProGrid-assisted group). As the total number of applications had increased, the actual success rates were slightly lower, but this should not be attributed to ProGrid but rather to the Foundation's long-range policies and fiscal considerations.

For each competition following the implementation of ProGrid, each application is reviewed by three Committee members who score the application using the ProGrid language ladder for each item in the Trainee Evaluation Matrix[vii]. The scores of the reviewers are collated by Foundation staff. During the developmental stages of the implementation of ProGrid, the Committee was convened (by teleconference or in person) to discuss the applications. While any reviewer could express concerns and initiate discussion about any individual application, there was a rapid consensus that the top- and bottom- ranked groups required no further discussion. Committee attention could then focus on those applications that ranged around applications close to the probable funding cut off-line, where there was substantial discrepancy between the reviewers, or where fewer than three reviewers had considered the application (often due to a real or perceived conflict of interest that was not known to the Foundation at the time the application was assigned to the reviewer). Where there was agreement between reviewers, the Committee consensus was to leave the score unchanged. Disagreement between the reviewers on the score for individual performance criteria was generally quickly resolved, but did not shift the application score more than by a few percentage points (typically less than five per cent). In the experience of the Foundation to date, this did not result in a large enough change in score to shift a single application into or out of the range eligible to be offered funding. Accordingly, in more recent competitions, there has been general agreement that the Committee does not need to be assembled and the scores obtained independently from the reviewers have served as the basis for the analysis of the competition results and the funding decisions.

The distribution of scores has been consistently wider using the ProGrid tool as compared to the previous Committee scores (Figure 14.3). The performance factors appearing to contribute to this wider distribution include those related to the supervisor, the training environment, and the project, as well as the research experience of the student. As a result, the application of ProGrid has led to slightly higher success rates for students who are further along in their graduate studies, and who have been able to demonstrate some initial success at research (Table 14.3). The success rate is also higher for students advised by senior members of faculty who generally have a strong, recognized research record (Table 14.4).

FIGURE 14.3
Distribution of Applicant Ratings

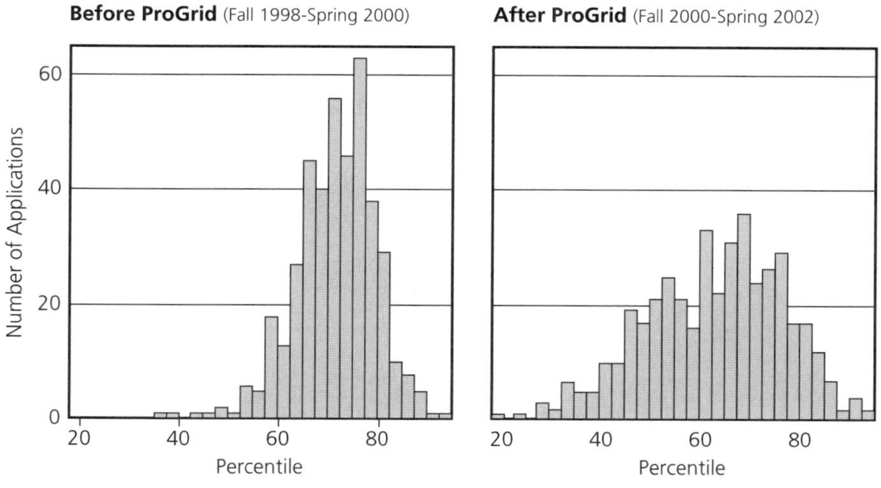

TABLE 14.3

Effect of Graduate Student Experience

		Applied		Approved	
		# of Proposals	% Total	# of Proposals	% Total
Without ProGrid	Bachelor (level 0)	97	24.6%	33	26.8%
	Bachelor (level 1-2)	153	38.7%	36	29.3%
	Bachelor (level 3)/Masters	145	36.7%	54	43.9%
	Totals	**395**	**100%**	**123**	**100%**
		# of Proposals	% Total	# of Proposals	% Total
With ProGrid	Bachelor (level 0)	89	21.1%	19	16.1%
	Bachelor (level 1-2)	157	37.2%	44	37.3%
	Bachelor (level 3)/Masters	176	41.7%	55	46.6%
	Totals	**422**	**100%**	**118**	**100%**

Level 0 applying prior to receipt of Batchelor's degree, or within first year after receipt.

Level 1-2 applying within 12-24 months after receipt of Batchelor's degree.

Level 3 > 2 years after receipt of Batchelor's degree and/or completion of Master's degree

TABLE 14.4

Effect of Supervisor Academic Rank

		Applied		Approved		Success Rate
		# of Proposals	% Total	# of Proposals	% Total	
Without ProGrid	Assistant Prof.	86	20.4%	11	9.3%	12.8%
	Associate Prof.	94	22.3%	30	25.4%	31.9%
	Professor	242	57.3%	77	65.3%	31.8%
	Totals	**422**	**100%**	**118**	**100%**	
		# of Proposals	% Total	# of Proposals	% Total	
With ProGrid	Assistant Prof.	56	14.2%	12	9.8%	21.4%
	Associate Prof.	102	25.8%	35	28.5%	34.3%
	Professor	237	60.0%	76	61.8%	32.1%
	Totals	**395**	**100%**	**123**	**100%**	

Discussion

The Foundation's collective experience with peer review of the Studentship applications spans a range of 50 competitions, the last nine of which having been advised by ProGrid. We offer the following initial observations on the use of this tool.

First, the tool is only as good as its components, and the development and testing of the Language Ladder is an important step. The primary challenge was to develop reviewer consensus on the definitions of each rung of the ladder, and to make these as distinguishable and as uniformly separated as possible[vi]. These statements continue to be the subject of discussion by the committee members, and their consensus has periodically led to modest but important modifications in the language.

Second, there is a learning curve for the applicants, supervisors, and committee members with respect to the use of ProGrid. While much of the Alberta scientific community was peripherally aware of ProGrid through its use by the Canada Foundation for Innovation and the AHFMR Technology Commercialization program, its use in the Studentship program required additional discussion and advice from the Foundation, and from experienced committee members. In general, the initial perceptions of the tool were lukewarm at best, but most committee members have come to appreciate its advantages, and support its continued use.

Third, a major object of the Foundation in developing and applying the ProGrid tool for the Studentship competition was to ensure a thorough, effective, well-defined, fair, transparent, timely and responsive review in the face of increasing application numbers and time pressures. In general, committee members report that the review of these applications continues to be time-consuming; the advantage is having more time devoted to the actual review of the applications and less to the logistics and formal consultations of face-to-face committee meetings. While some recognize these advantages, others miss the education and scientific camaraderie that is an invaluable part of peer review. To address these latter concerns, the Foundation has continued to periodically assemble the committee members by telephone or in person. In addition, feedback of the continuing analysis of the ProGrid data from each competition will be helpful as an additional educational tool for both new and experienced members.

That the committee reviewers must formally assign a language ladder ranking on several performance criteria helps to ensure that each of these has been considered for every application, and at each competition. This also occurred without the use of ProGrid, but with limited committee time for the formal discussion of each application, it was always possible that some factors may not have been adequately considered, or were over-emphasized. Further, the availability of the individual scoring of each committee member should theoretically allow Foundation staff to point out to committee members, individually and collectively, any consistent trends that depart from the majority decision. This may provide the individual committee member with additional information on which to base future scoring, but may also result in modifications to the committee application of the Language Ladder. Insofar as consistency between competitions is concerned, the committee members continue to apply the same Language Ladder informing the same performance factors.

A major addition to the Studentship peer review process has been the provision of consistent feedback to all applicants with their individual score identified in graphs similar to Figures 14.1 and 14.2. While most of the scientific community welcomes the feedback, there are some disagreements by both students and supervisors with the committee's ranking. It is particularly troublesome to supervisors who may feel that their track record and the training environment that they provide should rank higher. Further, since supervisors may be sponsoring more than one Studentship application, and hence receive feedback from different committee reviewers, there is some inconsistency in the reviewer perception of the strength of the supervisor and the training environment. The Foundation continues to examine ways to improve this aspect of the review. On balance, however, the potential of this feedback to improve the training environment in the Alberta scientific community and the peer review system has been viewed positively.

The Foundation finds the new process timely, and possibly slightly more cost-effective, with fewer and shorter committee meetings. The latter generally concern preparation for the review of applications, discussion of a limited number of proposals, and matters related to the Language Ladders. The ProGrid tool also has the potential to aid in program evaluation and review at the Foundation. Our preliminary experience indicates we can make comparisons between competitions, groups of reviewers, and subgroups of applicants. Such information has the potential to inform and improve the peer review system and the entire research process that it advises.

i Brink, W. J. (1999) *Journal of Higher Education* 70, 517-523

ii Dunlap, K.M., Fraser, M.W., and Henley, H.C., Jr. *Journal of Social Work Education.* v34 n3 p455-62 Fall 1998.

iii O'Brecht, M. and And, O. (1989) Research in Higher Education 30, 647-664

iv O'Brecht, M. and Pihl, R.O. Canadian *Journal of Higher Education*.v21 n3 p47-58 1991.

v Alberta Heritage Foundation for Medical Research Website, 2004, Ref. Type: Electronic Citation

vi Bowman, C.W. (2001) *Canadian Chemical News* 53, 30-32

vii Thornley, R., Spence, M.W., Taylor, M., and Magnan, J. *Journal of Research Administration.* v33 n2-3 p49-56 2002.

viii Brzustowski, T. (2000) NSERC Contact 25, 1-2

ix Brzustowski, T. (2000) NSERC Contact 25, 1-2

x Krulwich, T.A. and Friedman, P.J. (1993) Acad.Med. 68, S14-S18

15 Launching Early Stage Health Innovation

Linda A. Humphreys, Christina Blake, and Matthew W. Spence – Alberta Heritage Foundation for Medical Research

Introduction

Throughout recorded history, fundamental research has been supported by patrons ranging from individual philanthropists to corporations to governments[i]. While most have recognized the value of knowledge for its own sake, and that new knowledge derives from previous knowledge, part of the motivation has been to see the research applied for the benefit of the patron and the collective community. Fundamental biological and clinical research is no exception, and the knowledge gained from even the most fundamental studies of single-cell organisms can have potential for application in the promotion of human health and the prevention of disease[ii]. Society has developed a wide variety of tools to help with the application of research, including publication, education, and patenting, supported by both the public and private sectors. Where knowledge is applied by the latter sector, it has been described as "technology commercialization."

The private sector obtains its research knowledge from information available in the public domain, and from its own research. The latter may be conducted by the private sector itself, or contracted in academic and/or health care institutions. The process of acquiring knowledge can be either a "pull" from the private sector (identifying knowledge with potential commercial application and "extracting" it from the general pool of knowledge) or a "push" (the recognition of potential commercial application of a fundamental discovery by the inventor, and the appropriate presentation of that discovery to potential commercial backers). While both processes are clearly commercialization of technology, the "push" process has achieved increasing importance with the rapid recent increases in new knowledge, the development of technology transfer and commercialization organizations and offices as part of the academic landscape, as well as the adoption of innovation as a means to prosperity by most Western governments. The "push" process requires that the academic enterprise and its associated agencies and organizations develop the knowledge, skills, mechanisms and tools to advance technology to the point where it can be adapted and adopted by the commercial sector. A continuing challenge for both "push" and "pull" mechanisms (and to combinations thereof), is to identify those pieces of knowledge and/or technologies that may be successfully commercialized. In this chapter, we describe an approach to this challenge by the Alberta Heritage Foundation for Medical Research (AHFMR).

AHFMR, established by the Province of Alberta, has a mandate to develop and support a balanced, long-term program of health research in the province directed to the discovery of new knowledge, and the application of that knowledge to improve health and the quality of health services in Alberta[iii]. Its portfolio of funding activities spans the range of health research including fundamental biomedical investigation, clinical research, health services research, and population health research. Foundation funding flows through three research-intensive universities, nine regional health authorities, and some province-wide boards and services, all of whom are the hosts of various research activities. From the beginning, the trustees at the Foundation recognized the importance of commercialization and the private sector in the application of knowledge to improve health and treat disease, and in the mid-1980s, approved the launch of an AHFMR Technology Commercialization program.

AHFMR Technology Commercialization Program

The goal of the Foundation's Technology Commercialization Program is to assist Alberta innovators with the transfer of new health-related ideas and scientific findings into successful commercial products and services. In particular, the Technology Commercialization Program and its strategy have focused on the earliest stages of commercial development: identifying opportunities, supporting the people behind the ideas, and gearing technology development toward market readiness. Structured to promote research/industry/business collaboration, the program is not intended to further basic research. Accordingly, the Foundation's Technology Commercialization program will not consider projects judged to be eligible for funding through the operating grant programs of research agencies, or where other sources of capital such as equity or bank financing are deemed more appropriate. Historically, most of the applications have originated from individuals or spin-off companies associated with Alberta-based universities, hospitals, and affiliated institutions.

The program has evolved over the years, and the description that follows is of the current program, advised by the ProGrid® process-support software[iv].

To be eligible for consideration, proposals to the program must meet the following criteria: 1) show promise for real commercial success; 2) be Alberta-based; 3) be health-related; and 4) have a unique scientific/engineering/intellectual contribution. The program has three distinct phases, each with different requirements and expected results. Applications may be made for any phase of funding; however, most expected results from the previous phase should be present at the start of the phase being applied for, regardless of whether or not the previous phase was supported by the Foundation. Phase 1 (maximum award $35,000) is to assess and strengthen the technical aspects of a scientifically sound project, to verify its uniqueness, and to explore the potential for commercialization. Phase 2 (maximum award $150,000) is to strengthen the business and marketing aspects of the project, including continued work on prototypes, intellectual property protection, clinical trials, and development of a detailed business plan. Phase 3 (maximum award $500,000) is to finalize the strategy to take a product or process to market, to complete market surveys and detailed business plans, and to continue commercial development of the project.

Applicants apply using an application form designed to elicit the information required to assist an Advisory Committee in making an informed recommendation. The application process is highly iterative, and applicants have the opportunity to respond to reviewers' comments, and provide supplemental information. The Advisory Committee meets four times a year to review the applications and the supporting documentation available, and makes recommendations to the Foundation. The decision of the Foundation is final, but unsuccessful applicants may apply again, taking the comments of the reviewers and the Foundation into consideration.

In the late 1990s, the Foundation decided to develop and test a ProGrid-based process-support system as an aid to the peer review of the Technology Commercialization Applications, to the Advisory Committees and to the Foundation. The decision to do so was based on the following considerations:

First, the accumulating experience of the committee and the Foundation, as well as that of other organizations concerned with commercialization, had demonstrated the complexity and varied nature of the commercialization process[v]. There was a perceived need for some systematic process supporting the peer review, which ensured that all of the factors bearing on successful commercialization were considered and given appropriate weight.

Second, the increasing interest in commercialization was leading to proposals from many sectors of the health community, requiring an increasingly diverse range of external reviewers. Some process to better and more uniformly capture their opinion of the various aspects of commercialization was needed.

Third, with turnover of the Technology Commercialization Advisory Committee over the years, there was a perceived need for some sort of structure/process that would help to ensure an even application of standards and criteria for the program over time.

Fourth, the Foundation has always believed that peer review should be valuable to both successful and unsuccessful applicants; a process which supported some uniformity and comprehensiveness in the feedback would be useful.

Fifth, with the passage of time, more proposals were coming back for later stages of funding, and the committee sought additional information in a relatively standardized form about the peer review of the application at the earlier phase.

Finally, the use of a relatively standardized process-support tool might be used by the Foundation and others to study the process of technology commercialization from the point of view of a funding agency, and lead to improvements in the process[vi].

Development of the ProGrid Process-Support Tool

The ProGrid approach requires those developing the tool to articulate explicit criteria upon which decisions will be based[iv]. In the case of the AHFMR Technology Commercialization program, a number of factors had already been identified that were thought to be predictive of the likely success in commercialization (Table 15.1). These factors could be attributed to one or both of two relatively-independent performance criteria: the technology itself, and factors bearing on it; and the commercialization plan, support, and potential.

TABLE 15.1
Factors Predictive of Likely Commercial Success

Commercial Impact	The Technology	The Connectors
Market Fit	The Project	Business Skills
Health Impact	The Project Team	Technical Collaboration
Alberta Impact	Technology Protection	Commercial Partnerships
		Proof of Concept

A Language Ladder was developed for each of the factors in Table 15.1. The ladder allows the user to report their assessment of a factor on a scale of A to D (see an illustrative example in Table 15.2). The primary challenge for Language Ladder™ construction and revision has been developing reviewer consensus on the definitions of each rung in the ladder and making the rungs as distinguishable and as uniformly separated as possible. Developing this "ladder" is an iterative process between the Foundation and the reviewers, and there has been some change in the language over time to reflect the increasing experience and changing expectations of the Foundation and its stakeholders.

Applicants provide a self-assessment of the 10 areas identified in Table 15.1 with supporting evidence to substantiate their rankings.

TABLE 15.2
Language Ladder for "The Project"

The Project:	
A	The project may contribute scientific or technological information to the field of investigation.
B	The project has clear and recognizable scientific or technological merit, and will measurably extend the boundary of knowledge or application.
C	The project is innovative, has considerable scientific or technological merit and has been recognized for materially extending the boundary of knowledge or application.
D	The project is highly innovative, has exceptional scientific or technological merit, and has already achieved a recognized advance of "breakthrough" stature.

The reviewers of each application are asked to select their ratings for each of these factors based on information provided in the application and any additional information resulting from the due diligence process. The applicants' and reviewers' assessments are then entered into the ProGrid software for analysis. The output record, in either chart or text form, includes the following components: 1) the graph position of each reviewer, the applicant, and the reviewer average; 2) a tabular analysis of the reviewer's ranking, flagging those were variation is unusually high; 3) a graph of the project profile based on the applicant and the reviewer average rankings for each of the criteria; 4) a comparison of the ranking of the current application with others for the same Phase (Figure 15.1); 5) a sensitivity analysis, illustrated in Figure 15.5; and 6) a list of the reviewer comments.

FIGURE 15.1
Ranking of Applications

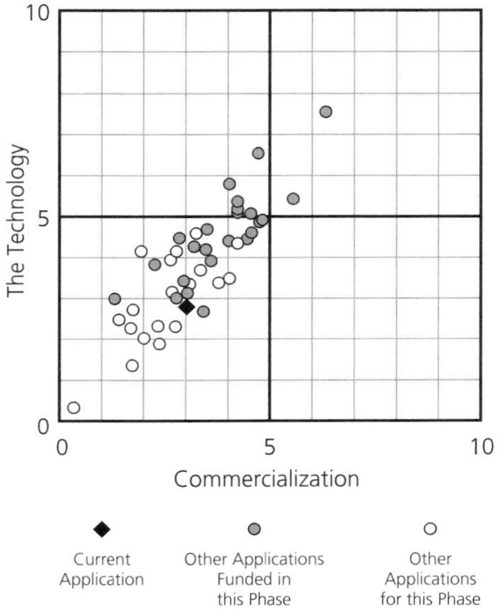

Application to the AHFMR Technology Commercialization Program

The ProGrid process-assist software was used to advise decision-making for the last 99 applications processed (Table 15.3). The ProGrid report for the application under consideration is carefully reviewed by the committee, and forms one part of the overall discussion of the application, its strengths, weaknesses and potential. A representative example of a Project Chart is shown in Figure 15.2. Where there is a wide divergence in reviewer scores, the committee discusses the reasons for the different opinions, which can be based on a reviewer's expertise or additional knowledge of a specific area such as intellectual property, the science, the industry or the market. The aggregated reviewer ratings for each of the 10 performance factors (Figure 15.3) focuses attention on any areas of significant strength or weakness, and helps to ensure a uniform evaluation of each proposal.

TABLE 15.3
Three Phases of the AHFMR Technology Commercialization Program

Phase	Applications processed	Applications Approved	Success Rate	Final Review
1	45	26	57.8%	10
2	37	16	43.2%	9
3	17	5	29.4%	1
Total	99	47	100%	20

The applicants' opinion of their position on the Language Ladder for each of the factors is helpful to further due diligence and to committee members' discussion and ranking. Where there is a perceived discrepancy between the applicant's opinion and the documented evidence, further information supporting the ranking is requested. Realistic perceptions of potential strengths and weaknesses are noted by the committee, whereas unrealistic perceptions and unsupported claims result in differences between the committee opinion and ranking and that of the applicant. In some cases, the applicants ranking of their positions on the Language Ladder appear

FIGURE 15.2
Sample Project Grid

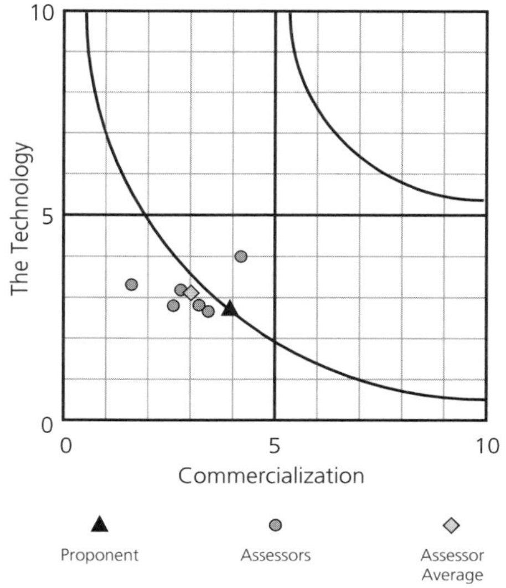

to reflect their perception of where they would like the project to be at the end of the support from the Technology Commercialization program of the Foundation, rather than a realistic appraisal of the current status.

While a relatively high ranking with respect to both technology and commercialization performance factors tends to be a feature of applications that are recommended for funding (Figure 15.1), this is not always the case, and applications that rank lower with respect to both axes have also been recommended for funding. The more highly-ranked unsuccessful applications generally had a very serious flaw or risk factor that was identified by expert

FIGURE 15.3
Sample Project Profile

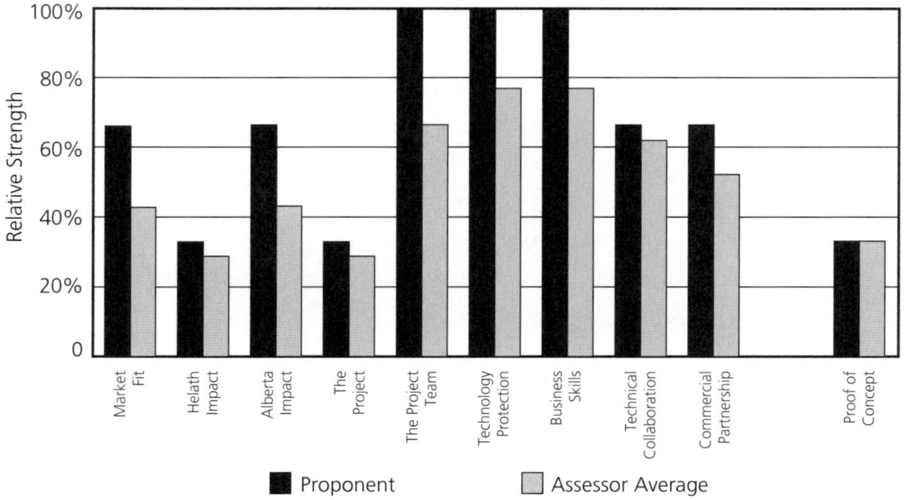

reviews, committee members or additional due diligence provided to the committee at the end of the process. Examples of such serious flaws may include concerns about the scientific foundation of the technology, the unlikely ability to secure intellectual property protection, the lack of access to appropriate skilled personnel, and inadequate or unrealistic assessments of market potential. In such circumstances, the committee may decide not to recommend the proposal for funding, despite a relatively high ranking. Similarly, if the flaws noted in less highly ranked applications are deemed by the committee to be readily correctable, they may recommend conditional approval. Thus, the ProGrid tool helps to ensure that the high risk areas are identified during the peer review, to the advantage of project proponents.

As noted earlier, the AHFMR Technology Commercialization Program provides three phases of support, with increasing expectations for the degree of development for both the technology and potential for commercialization at each phase. Since we are using the same ProGrid performance factors and Language Ladders for each phase, one might expect that the collective scores, and the rankings for each individual score, would be higher for successful applications in a Phase 3 level as compared to Phase 2 and to Phase 1.

While an aggregate database graph for successful applications in all three phases (Figure 15.4) demonstrates a trend in this direction, it is clear that there is substantial overlap between the phases, likely due to several factors that include:

- a higher expectation by the reviewers for each rung of the Language Ladder for the more complex and expensive proposals that make up the applications for the more mature phases
- a recognition in the review of some proposals of great technological and commercial possibilities and/or a great project team, and/or substantial potential health and economic impact, even at the earliest phases
- that the database has been accumulated over time, and there has been a gradual shifting standard and expectation, reflecting the increase in commercialization skills and resources within the province

A feature of the ProGrid software for the AHFMR Technology Commercialization Program has been the generation of a report for each project entitled a "Sensitivity Analysis" (Figure 15.5). This report tries to predict some possible upsides and downsides based on the current position of the project with respect to technology and commercialization, and experience with similar projects at this stage. In all cases, there is an expectation that the position could either improve (upside) or get worse (downside).

Some of the improvements or problems are largely within the control of the applicant, and would be important to address in the continuing commercialization. Other factors are largely outside the control of the applicant and reflect external conditions related to the market and the competitive environment. This Sensitivity Analysis graph and supporting statements has been used to varying extents in the committee discussions, but has also been helpful in framing the appropriate funding milestones for successful projects.

FIGURE 15.4
Comparison of Phases

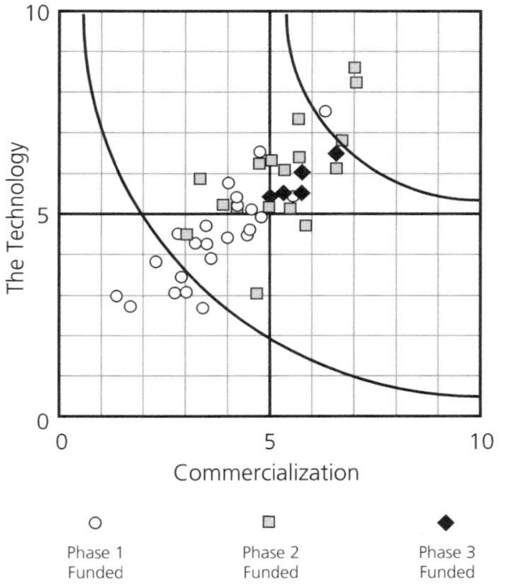

FIGURE 15.5
Sensitivity Analysis

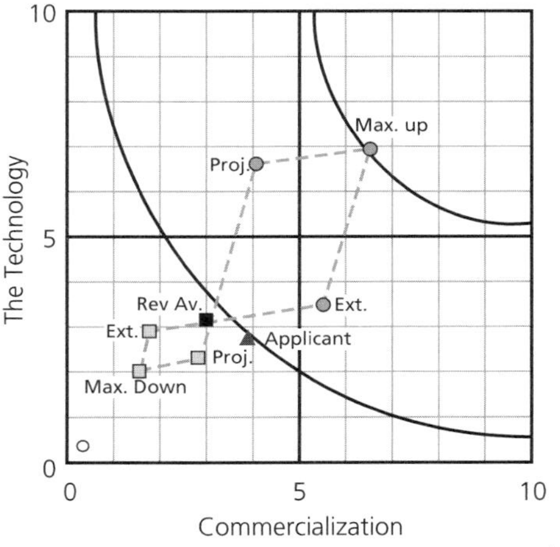

We have recently run a pilot project on the use of the "Sensitivity Analysis" to evaluate the impact of AHFMR Technology Commercialization funding on the progress of the project towards commercialization. Final reports are provided to the Foundation for every funded project. A sample of these final reports (Table 15.3) was studied by two independent reviewers, and their scoring of the project was fed into the Sensitivity Analysis. As a result, we could determine whether in the opinion of these independent reviewers, the position of the project with respect to the upside and downside had improved, remained unchanged, or become worse (Table 15.4). As might be expected, all but one of those projects that were sufficiently mature to be considered for funding at a Phase 2 or 3 level had improved their current and potential positions. Also as expected, the Phase 1 projects presented a more varied picture, with six of 10 showing no change or improvement, and four getting worse. Since this is the earliest stage of commercialization, one would expect the higher risk shown in this

TABLE 15.4
Post Approval Analysis

		Number of Applications		
		Phase 1	**Phase 2**	**Phase 3**
Current Position	Better	3	6	1
	No Change	3	1	0
	Worse	4	1	0
Upside	Better	4	7	1
	No Change	1	0	0
	Worse	5	1	0
Downside	Better	4	7	1
	No Change	3	0	0
	Worse	3	1	0
Proof of concept	Better	5	7	1
	No Change	5	0	0
	Worse	0	1	0

pilot project. Further studies of the use of ProGrid to track these projects are planned.

Discussion

In the view of those administering the program, and the committee members with continuing experience with the use of ProGrid, its introduction has led to greater attention by applicants to the multiple factors that contribute to successful technology commercialization. The requirement of an applicant to self-rank on the Language Ladder makes it difficult for him or her to ignore some of the essential prerequisites and processes required to bring a discovery to market. For many, this forms part of an education process concerning commercialization that is an important objective of the Foundation's program.

The introduction of ProGrid has also furthered the Foundation's objective of ensuring that the review of each application appropriately considers all the relevant factors that predict successful commercialization, and appropriately apply standards to multiple widely differing proposals, and in multiple meetings, over time. It is also been helpful to new committee members in contributing early and effectively to the review process.

We have called ProGrid a process-support tool for technology commercialization rather than a decision-support tool. It starts to inform the process as soon as the application with the applicant's rankings on the Language Ladders is received. The review process is iterative; as such the information is being requested, received and evaluated right up to the time of final consideration of the application by the Technology Commercialization committee. The ProGrid assessments and other opinions on the application are incorporated and received at various times in this iterative process, and so some reviewers may be basing their opinions on information that can be updated subsequently. This temporal and information difference contributes to the variation in reviewer opinion shown graphically in Figure 15.2.

However, it is clear from the relative positions of the successful and unsuccessful applications on the database graphs (Figure 15.1) that the ProGrid ranking is not the only information affecting the final recommendation of the committee. Rather, the committee is using expert opinion from external reviewers and their own personal expertise in determining that certain features of the application are either extremely promising and balance other perceived weaknesses, or that some deficiencies are virtually fatal flaws that are not overcome by other strong features of the application. Thus, the committee is selectively weighting the relative importance of some rungs of the Language Ladder against other factors in order to arrive at the final recommendation. Because this selectively is so heavily dependent on other factors related to the technology and commercialization potential (and the fact that these factors vary from application to application) the weighting does not lend itself to an adjustment in the software or a mathematical formula.

Our initial pilot studies of ProGrid to assess the final reports from funded proposals show some promise as an evaluation-support tool. It is not surprising that the Phase 1 projects show such a mixed result. These projects are at the stage where the least is known, and the risk is highest, and so one might anticipate the varied outcomes documented in the ProGrid assessment. Variation in the progress of the Phase 2 and 3 projects would also be expected.

Our experience with ProGrid in the Technology Commercialization program has demonstrated its usefulness as a process-support tool. It is more than a complex checklist; its ability to graphically display in a semi-quantitative fashion the opinions of the applicants, the individual reviewers, and the collective committee opinion, helps with the informed planning and conduct of due diligence, the development of creative funding agreements, and provides constructive feedback to the applicants.

i Weaver W. (1967) *Philanthropic Foundations: Their History, Structure, Management, and Record.* Harper Collins, New York.

ii La Montagne J.R. (2001) *Biotechnology and research: promise and problems.* Lancet 358, 1723-1724.

iii Alberta Heritage Foundation for Medical Research Website . 2004, Ref Type: Electronic Citation

iv Bowman C.W. (2001) *Evaluating intellectual capital--III. Evaluating investment opportunities.* Canadian Chemical News 53, 30-32.

v Keller J.B. and Plath P.B. (1999) *Financing biotechnology projects: lender due diligence requirements and the role of independent technical consultants.* Appl.Biochem.Biotechnol. 77-79, 641-648.

vi Luukkonen-Gronow T. (1987) *Scientific research evaluation: A review of methods and various contexts of their application.* R&D Management 17, 207-221.

16 Climbing the Agriculture Value-Added Mountain

Keith Jones – President, AVAC Ltd.
John Kramers – ProGrid Ventures Inc.
Clem Bowman – Clement W. Bowman Consulting Inc.

The Challenge

Adding value to resource-based products is a monumental task in any of the resource industries, but in agriculture it flies in the face of tradition and an entrenched production and marketing system. This has not diminished the commitment of AVAC Chairman Aaron Falkenberg or CEO Keith Jones in meeting Alberta's goal of $20 billion of agrivalue revenue by 2010.

Alberta companies need help in bridging the "commercialization gap," according to Jones, and this is where AVAC is bringing its resources of money and its knowledge of the industry and its people. Already AVAC has contributed $32 million to support entrepreneurial activity in this area, attracting additional investments of over $180 million.

Value-added in the agriculture industry is not just a matter of an incremental increase in upgrading existing products dominated by grains and unprocessed meat. It includes capturing advances in biotechnology, biopolymers, nutraceuticals and a host of high value consumer products based on new ideas developed by Alberta researchers and entrepreneurs. One project supported by AVAC involves the production of polymers from oilseeds such as canola. This is a remarkable objective for a province with one of the world's largest non-renewable source of polymers – oil. How about a beta glucan concentrate from barley with up to 13 times the dietary fibre of oat bran? Or using transgenic plants to produce healthy cosmetic or as pharmaceutical factories, thus reducing the cost of drugs such as insulin by 70% or more?

The demand and need for financial capital at the early stages of innovation is one of the single most important factors in business success or failure, according to AVAC. But it is not simply a shortage of capital. It is a shortage of seasoned managers with a track record of moving good ideas to commercial success. Many of the ventures that AVAC sees do not meet the financing hurdle rates of either debt or equity investors; they nevertheless have strong potential for economic viability and commercial success.

Although the ultimate $20 billion value-added target is clearly tangible and quantifiable, the routes to the target involve a host of intangible factors. The intermediate goals set by AVAC's management team include:

- Increase agrivalue project quality and quantity
- Move client projects towards commercial success
- Attract financial capital and human resources to agrivalue
- Establish and grow an agrivalue network
- Connect entrepreneurs with the knowledge necessary for success
- Increase access to research capacity for agrivalue
- Build Alberta's technology commercialization capability

In considering where to apply its financial and managerial resources to best catalyze new ventures to drive value-added growth, AVAC realized that three types of capital were required by new ventures to become economically viable:

- Financial capital
- Managerial capital
- Intellectual capital

AVAC's challenge is how to assess which ventures to assist, and then how to best assist those ventures in achieving commercial success by helping the selected ventures attract and build all three types of capital.

Bridging the Commercial Gap

It became clear to AVAC in the review of early proposals that few projects had the capacity to take a new idea and bring it into commercial practice in one step. Early stage projects did not yet meet the criteria that most venture capital financiers establish as their thresholds for support. Nevertheless, some of these projects have the potential for major technological advances and the potential for new products, processes or services. The ultimate challenge for AVAC was to develop a process to assess the business intangibles for an idea which did not yet have a business case.

AVAC, based on ProGrid® methodology, used a "disciplined creativity" approach to establish two separate application and assessment processes, the first for early stage research projects, the second for ventures closer to commercial start-up.

Research and Strategic Initiatives

Nine criteria were established in the application form for research and strategic projects, as shown in the Evaluation Matrix™ in Table 16.1.

TABLE 16.1
Evaluation Matrix for Research and Strategic Proposals

Importance of the Advance	Enablers	Technological Outlook
Knowledge Advance	The Project Team	Technological Contribution
Uniqueness	The Networks	Market Knowledge Contribution
	Facilities	Competitive Position
		Alberta Impact

AVAC was seeking projects that have the potential for a significant technological advance, as evidenced by the Language Ladder™ for Knowledge Advance (Table 16.2). Recognition for the Project Team was provided in the Language Ladder shown in Figure 16.3.

TABLE 16.2
Language Ladder for Knowledge Advance

The project will:	
A	provide new information that will strengthen the knowledge base in the field.
B	provide new information that will significantly extend the boundary of knowledge in the field.
C	provide important new scientific insight that will revise in a major way the state of knowledge in the field.
D	open up a new and potentially important field of investigation.

TABLE 16.3
Language Ladder for The Project Team

The Project Team Members ...	
A	have an established research and/or development record among their colleagues or are new team members who show promise.
B	have established a national record of innovative research and/or development or are new team members with an initial record of accomplishments.
C	are recognized internationally for being innovative leaders in their fields with good linkages to industry or are emerging researchers who have demonstrated early excellence and the ability to be leaders in their field.
D	are recognized internationally for being innovative leaders in their fields with good linkages to industry. Plans are in place to add additional recognized researchers or a significant number of promising new researchers to augment the team.

Pre-Commercial and Entrepreneurial Projects

For later stage projects that are closer to commercial application, emphasis shifts towards venture validation, the current team and development plan, and the business outlook. Eight criteria representing the key elements necessary to drive economic viability and commercial success are included in the assessment, as shown in the Evaluation Matrix in Table 16.4.

TABLE 16.4
Evaluation Matrix for Pre-Commercial and Entrepreneurial Proposals

The Venture	Enablers	Business Outlook
Stage of Development	Senior Management Team	Commercial Opportunity
External Validation	Business Plan	Market Acceptance
	Regulatory Environment	Competitive Situation

As an example, the Language Ladder for Stage of Development is shown in Table 16.5. Ventures at this stage should have a well-defined business plan and clear evidence of likely market acceptance, as reflected in the Language Ladder for Market Acceptance (Table 16.6).

TABLE 16.5
Stage of Development

Stage of Development:	
A	The concept behind the commercial opportunity has had a limited level of testing.
B	Key elements of the concept behind the commercial opportunity have been confirmed but an integrated system, model or prototype has not yet been developed.
C	An integrated system, model or prototype has been developed and tested under limited controlled conditions.
D	An integrated system, model or prototype has been developed and successfully tested under a full range of commercially relevant conditions.

TABLE 16.6
Language Ladder for Market Acceptance

Market Acceptance: With respect to the products/processes/services that are involved in this commercial opportunity:	
A	there is no evidence at this time of customer acceptance.
B	preliminary market studies indicate positive customer acceptance.
C	specific customers have been identified who have indicated their intention to place orders.
D	current or new customers have provided firm orders.

Leveraging Previous Experience: The Database

AVAC's programs in support of Alberta's value-added goals have been well received by researchers, entrepreneurs, and both small and large companies. An example of the response to the initial call for proposals is shown in Figure 16.1; subsequently, AVAC has assessed over 700 project proposals and has invested in more than 160 projects supporting value-added agriculture growth in Alberta.

FIGURE 16.1
Database for Pre-Commercial and Entrepreneurial Proposals

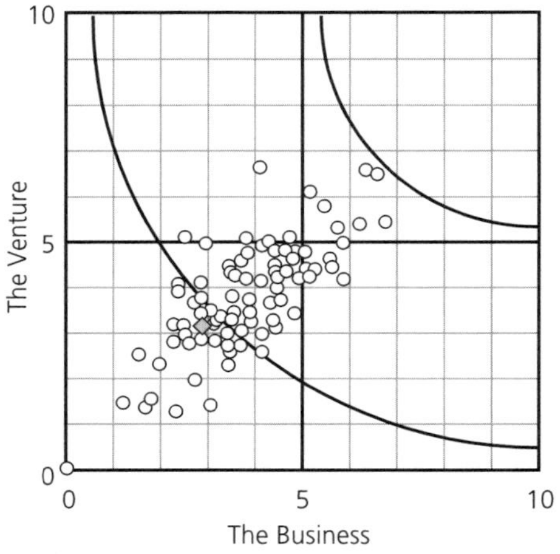

The criteria for this assessment involved factors that could only be fully obtained once the first steps of commercialization had been successfully achieved. Therefore it is not surprising that the rating of the majority of the proposals after review are found in the lower left hand quadrant. The higher ranked proposals did pass the 5, 5 mid-point and were in reach of the upper curve, representing the zone of full commercial success. Projects assessed above and to the right of the first curve were priority projects for AVAC investment. This process established a clear baseline for all proposals against which future progress and later stage funding could be assessed.

The Importance of Networks

In addition to funding for specific projects, AVAC provides its own "value-added" for the community of researchers, entrepreneurs, start-up companies and major operating companies active in the pursuit of new value-added agricultural products. AVAC puts major emphasis on establishing networks to share information and to help, in the words of Geoffrey Moore[i], in *"Crossing the Chasm."*

Examples include:

- New and enhanced food products network
- Wellness products network (including functional foods and nutraceuticals)
- Industrial and non-food applications (bioproducts) network
- Enabling technologies network

AVAC's networks help bridge the commercialization gap by providing coaching, knowledge, contacts, financial resources and business management expertise to guide a product from concept to commercialization. The networks include scientific, business, finance and technical expertise which AVAC clients can access as they develop their concepts towards commercial success. This is all about dealing with intangibles, as affirmed by Debra Amidon[ii], "Gaining knowledge is a human process dealing with mental objects, requiring awareness and intuition, and is transferable through learning." AVAC's experience showed that the most value the networks can provide is moving beyond sharing data, information or knowledge to the sharing of "wisdom." In this context, wisdom refers to specific, relevant knowledge applied to the specific next challenge faced by the venture at each stage of development. To achieve this, AVAC uses its assessment process to first identify the specific challenge facing the new venture, then identify an expert resource or partner within its network who may have the "wisdom" to help its client address this challenge.

AVAC uses each of its four networks to strengthen and grow investment capabilities and knowledge base in its sectors. While the formalization of these networks is in its early stages, AVAC is rapidly becoming recognized as the "partner to work with" for those interested in investing in, or developing, value-added agriculture ventures.

Collaboration: "The Secret Weapon"

Jones says that financing technology commercialization is not simply a matter of more venture capital, more angel investment and more government support. "*What we need to do is focus on the sectors where Alberta and Canada can have the most success and create stronger partnerships to support those sectors.*" This requires increasing collaboration to build new ventures while respecting competition between new and established firms in the same "community of interest." Plus, both start-up and established ventures need mechanisms to provide management expertise, marketing skills and funding options for innovative ideas to move them from concept to success. Jones feels that Canadians have an advantage in this regard in the global marketplace; their respect for cultural and social diversity, plus their global perspective, combined with their participation in a fiercely-competitive North American marketplace, helps Canadians identify and pursue opportunities to collaborate first, and compete second. Jones observes: *"Perhaps this is why you see a disproportionate number of Canadians as the heads of very successful multi-national and global corporations and institutions."*

Exemplifying this collaborative approach, AVAC helped form an alliance (the Agricultural Funding Consortium, www.fundingconsortium.ca). Initially five members, the group has grown to 13 provincial and national funding organizations providing a one-window research and development application process (also see Chapter 17, "One-Window Approach to Agriculture R&D Support"). This approach was designed to give individual projects more exposure to a greater number of potential funding organizations, and to share assessment, due diligence and coaching expertise. In doing so, a greater coverage of the research and development continuum is achieved to help fund priority projects. The Agriculture Funding Consortium uses a common assessment tool for evaluating project intangibles in a manner very similar to AVAC's Research and Strategic investment process.

As a result, the overall quality of research and development project proposals is dramatically improving, and is becoming more oriented towards the common strategic goals of the various funding organizations. The Agricultural Funding Consortium co-operatively publishes a quarterly magazine, "Reach and Discover," which profiles new, on-going and completed projects and illustrates the opportunities for further development on a collaborative basis. Another benefit of this collaborative approach is increased confidence in the effective investment of public funds in early stage discovery and research activities. For example, the Province of Alberta recently committed an additional $72 million to agricultural research and innovation in Alberta, to be delivered by several of the Agricultural Funding Consortium partners. This approach has also been instrumental in encouraging the research performers to work more closely together and collaborate on the development of outstanding research initiatives. As a result, the Institute for Food and Agricultural Sciences Alberta was recently established to formalize collaboration between the researchers.

The Results: Value-Added Agriculture Growth in Alberta

So is it working? Are these novel approaches to assessing intangibles, fostering shared learning and enhancing collaboration driving commercial success?

Since joining AVAC in 2000, Jones feels the AVAC approach is starting to demonstrate its potential. Agriculture is not usually the first place equity investors think of investing; AVAC's clients, however, have attracted over $85 million in new equity investment to their value-added agriculture ventures (in addition to the $14 million committed by AVAC). AVAC's new venture clients have attracted 90 partners to their projects. There are over 60 industry-science partnership projects currently underway in Alberta, which is where AVAC believes true technology commercialization takes place–when science and business jointly pursue a tangible opportunity. Client success is beginning to pay off in financial terms as well; client royalties to AVAC based on their commercial success are growing dramatically. At the same time, the Alberta government is encouraged by AVAC's progress, demonstrated by announcements of an additional $34 million being provided to AVAC for research and early stage pre-commercial initiatives.

Ultimately, AVAC's success in evaluating intangibles, leading to investment and coaching of early stage ventures, is best indicated in client success. The initial indications are very encouraging. AVAC has had 18 of its clients achieve revenue stage with their new venture projects. One of the first of those, CV Technologies Inc. of Edmonton, has achieved remarkable success with its first commercial product Cold-FX. With year over year sales growth in excess of 400%, CV Technologies Inc. has been transformed from a university spin-off technology company from the University of Alberta, to a publicly traded venture with a market capitalization in excess of $300 million. Another AVAC success story, SemBioSys Genetics Inc., was acclaimed as Canada's biotechnology Company of the Year by BIOTECanada, an industry association It recently completed what has been referred to as *"Canada's most successful biotechnology IPO of 2004,"* launching on the TSX under the symbol "SBS" in December of that year.

At the most recent SemBioSys Genetics Annual General Meeting, President Andrew Baum discussed the company's potential to use its technology to produce the world's supply of insulin on 10,000 acres of Canadian cropland by 2010. In an October 2004 article in Alberta Venture magazine, Baum referenced the helpfulness of the AVAC program. *"It allowed us to make investments in two programs that have turned out to be core but were relatively risky when we first started ... these equity matching programs such as AVAC's initiatives will be really, really worthwhile."*

AVAC's use of "disciplined creativity" in assessing intangibles on a collaborative basis is successfully stimulating innovation in what is seen by many as a very traditional industry.

[i] *Crossing the Chasm,* Geoffrey A. Moore, 1991, Harper-Business, ISBN 0-06662-002-3

[ii] Debra M. Amidon, *Innovation Strategy for the Knowledge Economy: The Ken Awakening.*

17 One-Window Approach for Agriculture R&D Support

Freda Molenkamp and Joan Unger – Alberta Agricultural Research Institute
John Kramers – ProGrid Ventures Inc.

The Challenge

As noted in Chapter 16, Alberta has identified the development of a value-added agriculture industry with an increasing percentage of revenue from value added products, processes and services as a key priority. There are numerous value-added opportunities within the agricultural industry and it is recognized that R&D is a critical component of capitalizing on these opportunities. Alberta is home to numerous R&D funding agencies that traditionally have had a multiplicity of funding application routes and forms. This has resulted in a very unwieldy and cumbersome system.

Dr. Ralph Christian, Executive Director of Alberta Agricultural Research Institute (AARI), who committed to improve the agricultural R&D funding process, first adopted the ProGrid methodology as a process for AARI to evaluate and assist in deciding which applications to fund. Through a process of consultation with stakeholders, AARI developed a list of Values, Priorities and Expectations for agricultural R&D funding for Alberta. This is shown in Table 17.1.

These attributes were then grouped and the Value-added Agriculture Evaluation Matrix™ was developed (Table 17.2).

Based on attributes in each of the Evaluation Matrix cells preliminary Language Ladders were developed and agreed to by all stakeholders. An example is shown in Table 17.3.

This information was presented to the AARI Board of Directors for final approval and implementation for the next round of funding in October 3, 2000. After a long discussion, led by Dr. Roger Palmer, the Board Co-chair and Deputy Minister of Alberta Innovation and

TABLE 17.1

Goals of Funding Organizations

Priorities, Values and Expectations		Priorities, Values and Expectations	
1	Need for work	28	Critical Mass
2	Understand science	29	Quality of team
3	Review of literature	30	Extension capability of scientist
4	How does proposal address need	31	Technology transfer plan
5	Clearly stated objective	32	History of plan
6	Hypothesis for research design	33	Visionary proposal
7	Strategic fit to program	34	Champion/leader
8	Defined economic benefit	35	Champion track record
9	Importance for Alberta Agri-food business	36	Availability and commitment
10	Breakthrough/advances in S&T applied to Alberta	37	Collaboration and networks
11	Adds to knowledge pool	38	Related research
12	Validity of research design (project plan)	39	Redundancy- Uniqueness
13	Statistical validity	40	Institution organization
14	Methods accepted by peers	41	Project management
15	Progressiveness of idea	42	Track record on projects of similar scope
16	Design related to hypothesis	43	Adequate facilities and organization
17	Yearly goals for project	44	Access to other facilities
18	Description of deliverables	45	Capital facilities
19	Goals achieved to date	46	Land
20	Milestones/Progress reports	47	Laboratory
21	Milestones achieved compared to deliverables/goals	48	Meets all regulatory requirements (animal care and environment impact
22	Redesign of project design/goals	49	Will be effected by regulatory requirements
23	Valid budget	50	Will lead regulatory requirement
24	Reasonable estimate of budget	51	Scope for improvements
25	Manpower requirements	52	Receptor capacity
26	Educational background	53	Potential for commercial advance
27	Publication/track record		

TABLE 17.2
Value-added Agriculture Evaluation Matrix

The Proposal	The Connectors	The Benefits
Background and Objectives 1, 2, 3, 4, 5,17, 33, 38, 39,	Research Design, Methodology & Analysis 6, 12, 13, 14, 16,	Contributions to Advancement of Agri-food Knowledge 10, 11,
Qualifications of Researcher(s) 26, 27, 28, 29, 30, 32, 34, 35, 36, 37,	Ability to Complete Project 18, 19, 20, 21, 22, 40, 41, 42,	Benefits to Alberta's Agri-food Industry 8, 9, 31, 52, 53
Relationship to the Research Priorities 7, 51, 15	Budget Estimate and Manpower Needs 24, 25, 43, 44, 45, 46, 47,	Regulatory Impact 48,49, 50,

TABLE 17.3
Language Ladder™ for Background and Objectives

The scientific background and objectives are:	
A	not adequately described. The reference to existing literature and related research is limited.
B	described, but there are gaps and unanswered questions. The reference to existing literature and related research is not comprehensive.
C	sound and clearly presented. Existing literature and related research are well described.
D	comprehensively described, with visionary objectives. There is a comprehensive description of existing literature and related research

Science, it was decided that the columns of the Evaluation Matrix were in the wrong order and that the Benefits should be in the first column, followed by the Proposal column and then the Connectors column. To the Board, it was imperative that sponsored research provides benefit to the industry. Thus the Evaluation Matrix columns were transposed.

The "One-Window" Approach

At about the same time that AARI was developing the AARI ProGrid® process, the Provincial Government created three industry development funds: the Alberta Crop Industry Development Fund

(ACIDF), the Alberta Livestock Industry Development Fund (ALIDF), and the Diversified Livestock Fund of Alberta (DLFOA).

Under the leadership of AARI, the industry development funds and AARI met to determine how best to work together in funding agricultural R&D. Out of these discussions, the funding consortium model was developed, Table 17.4. This model created a one-window approach to funding agricultural R&D. A standard application form was created by the four funding agencies using the criteria in the Evaluation Matrix developed for AARI. All applications received on this form were shared amongst all the funding agencies. This expedited the application writing process and also streamlined the due diligence process for reviewing all the applications.

TABLE 17.4
Founding Members of the Agriculture Funding Consortium

• Alberta Agricultural Research Institute (AARI)
• Alberta Crop Industry Development Fund Ltd. (ACIDF)
• Alberta Diversified Livestock Industry Development Fund (ADLIDF)
• Alberta Livestock Industry Development Fund Ltd. (ALIDF)
• AVAC Ltd.
• Agriculture and Food Council (AGFC)

AARI was responsible for processing all applications for the Consortium using the ProGrid system. An enhanced due diligence process was developed and, using ProGrid, the reviewers' feedback was captured and presented to the boards of the members of the Consortium. Each individual board made their funding decisions and then the Consortium met to determine if there were any opportunities for joint funding. This resulted in multiple jointly funded projects that in turn resulted in an increased leverage ratio for the funders.

Several years have passed since the above ideas were introduced. The current application form for the Agriculture Funding Consortium is based on the Evaluation Matrix shown in Table 17.5. Two criteria, Innovation and Uniqueness and Knowledge/Technology Transfer and Commercialization Plan, have been added, but the other seven cells are essentially as originally conceived. The original cell on

Regulatory Impact has been replaced by other information in the application form on regulatory compliance. The evolution of the evaluation criteria and their Language Ladders is an important aspect, in that as circumstances for a funding program change, the criteria, Evaluation Matrix and Language Ladders should evolve along with those changes.

TABLE 17.5
2004/2005 Evaluation Matrix

The Benefits	The Proposal	The Connectors
Contribution to Advancement of Agriculture and Agri-food Knowledge	Background and Objectives	Knowledge/Technology Transfer and Commercialization Plan
Benefits to Alberta's Agri-food Industry	Innovation and Uniqueness	Project Team
	Research Design, Methodology, Analysis and Plan	Ability to Complete Project
		Funding Contribution

The Funding Consortium adopted a two-stage process for applications (Pre-proposals and Full Proposals) to lighten the load on both applicants and reviewers. In the fall of 2001, 380 Pre-Proposals were submitted that resulted in 110 Full Proposals. Of these Full Proposals, 33 were funded and a further 37 were combined into nine other funded projects. In the fall of 2004, 165 Pre-Proposals were received that resulted in 102-invited Full Proposals. Of these Full Proposals, 35 were funded.

By the fall of 2004, the Funding Consortium has grown to include seven full Members and eight Affiliate Members, as shown in Figure 17.1. The Consortium has also begun to work with some of the larger provincial and national funding agencies, including Alberta Ingenuity Fund (AIF), NSERC, Canada Foundation for Innovation (CFI), ASRIP and others.

FIGURE 17.1
2004 Funding Consortium Members

Evaluation Procedure and Experience

Pre-Proposals are submitted to the Consortium website where they are processed and then posted for all members of the Consortium to review. The evaluation of the Pre-Proposals is done individually by the boards of the consortium members and is based on strategic fit. The Consortium then meets as a whole to discuss the Pre-Proposals and a finalized list of invited proposals is developed.

Successful applicants of the Pre-Proposal round are invited to submit a Full Proposal. Once the Full Proposals are received, AARI staff enters them into the ProGrid database and the proposals are divided into either the Crop or Livestock Sciences Review Committee. The Review Committees are made up of technical and industrial experts and each Review Committee Member is requested to review approximately five proposals. Each proposal is also sent to a minimum of two international peer reviewers. The results of all the reviews are then processed into a reviewer report that serves the basis of the two-day Review Committee Meetings. Each proposal is addressed

FIGURE 17.2
Database of Proposals Submitted to a Consortium Committee

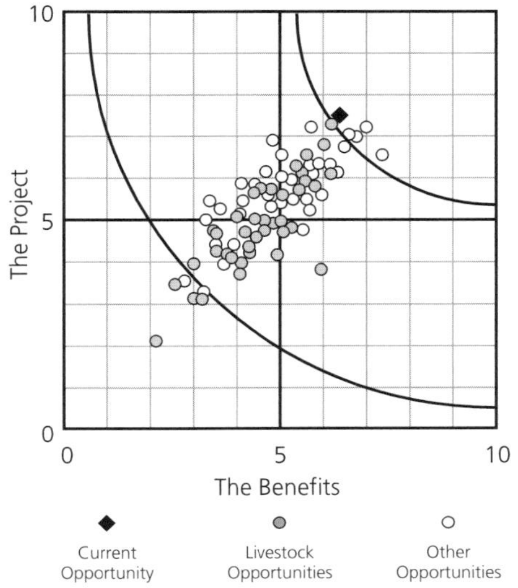

in the meeting and a Committee Consensus rating is created for each proposal. All of this information is then presented to the boards of the Funding Consortium members.

Evaluation Results

The boards receive all the technical review comments and the ratings for each project that is reviewed. The results also show how each proposal ranked in comparison to the other proposals submitted. For example, Figure 17.2 illustrates the results of the Livestock Review Committee's ratings for 2004.

The Consensus of Stakeholders

Working together as a Consortium has been a key factor in ensuring that progress is being made toward our 2010 vision. Areas of growth toward the 2010 goal have been identified and the members of the Consortium have taken on the challenge to ensure that the R&D required to capitalize on these areas of growth is undertaken. Utilizing ProGrid in the due diligence process was a key component to making this happen. The stakeholders valued the ProGrid methodology in that it provided a consistent, transparent mechanism for evaluating the proposals and that information could then be used in the informed decision-making process.

Researchers have also recognized that in order to achieve growth in key areas, they need to be involved in strategic R&D that supports the growth areas for the province. The one-window approach helps to ensure that the researchers receive the required funding to move ahead in the right areas of focus.

It is truly innovative and rewarding to see government, industry, researchers and academia working together to further the R&D agenda in Alberta. The whole truly is greater than the sum of the parts.

18 Stimulating Innovation Within Government

Darren Hutton – Alberta Innovation and Science

The Government of Alberta Innovation Program

Future success in both the public and private sectors increasingly depends on the ability to innovate. An innovative initiative often cannot be pursued without an initial, supportive investment. The Innovation Program is designed to support Government of Alberta efforts to develop and implement innovative ideas and initiatives that improve service delivery to Albertans and that stimulate innovation in Alberta. The Innovation Program accomplishes its objectives by promoting innovation within the Government of Alberta and by providing "seed funding" support for projects that meet established requirements and criteria.

The overall intent of the program is to support incremental initiatives that align with the Alberta Government's strategic plan, entitled *"Today's Opportunities, Tomorrow's Promises."* This plan lays out a course for the Alberta government for the next 20 years (2004-2024) with a vision for the future: *"A vibrant and prosperous province where Albertans enjoy a superior quality of life and are confident about the future for themselves and their children."*

Program Format

The Innovation Program is comprised of two streams: Service Excellence and Unleashing Innovation. The Service Excellence stream supports strategic initiatives that accelerate improvements to provincial government service delivery and fosters overall service excellence. The projects are seen as improving the accessibility or efficiency of government services and produce fiscal benefits for the Alberta government. The Unleashing Innovation stream supports initiatives that foster innovation and the application of new knowledge. Desired outcomes include increasing the rate of innovation and technology creation, creating economic benefits for Albertans, and fostering a culture of innovation. The program has a value of $33 million and is designed to operate for three years with a limit of two years of funding for successful projects. Proponents are expected to make a substantive financial contribution (equal to or greater than 50% of the total project cost) and demonstrate a clear "exit strategy" and/or viable plans for the continuation of the initiative after Innovation Program funding ceases.

All Government of Alberta departments, agencies, boards, commissions and Crown corporations are eligible to apply for Innovation Program funding support. Other organizations are encouraged to partner with eligible Alberta Government organizations in the undertaking of projects. Funding for both program streams is transitional (i.e. one-time grants within the program's three-year budget).

The Innovation Program is intended to provide term-limited funding support for projects that are deemed, through a competitive process, to closely align with the program criteria. The program is not designed to provide long-term development or operational funding. The evaluation process encompasses three stages that begin with reviews and assessments by Government of Alberta employees, followed by a review and assessment by a panel comprised predominantly of external stakeholders, and concludes with decisions by the Minister of Alberta Innovation and Science.

Use of ProGrid®

The main challenge identified during development of the Innovation Program was the establishment of an objective, transparent and reliable methodology for assessing a relatively large volume of diverse project applications. It was speculated that the majority of applications received would possess significant intangible attributes. This considered, the ProGrid methodology was selected as the foundation of the review process.

An exercise was conducted to develop criteria and Language Ladders for both Innovation Program streams. It was established that the streams would share six criteria (the Project criteria and the Enabling criteria) and have three "Benefits/Impacts" criteria that are specifically tailored to their respective focuses. The criteria for the Service Excellence stream is illustrated in Table 18.1, with an example Language Ladder™ for the "Strategic Fit" criterion in Table 18.2. The Unleashing Innovation stream is shown in Table 18.3, with an example Language Ladder for the "Innovation Adoption" criterion in Table 18.4.

TABLE 18.1
Service Excellence Stream Evaluation Matrix™

The Project	The Enablers	Benefits/Impacts
The Initiative	Project Plan	Service Accessibility
The Project Team	Collaboration	Service Functionality
Strategic Fit	Long-Term Viability	Fiscal Benefits

TABLE 18.2
Sample Language Ladder for Service Excellence Stream – "Strategic Fit"

The activities to be undertaken in implementing this innovation will:	
A	make an indirect contribution to one of the pillars of Alberta's 20 year Strategic Plan;
B	make a direct contribution to one of the pillars of Alberta's 20 year Strategic Plan;
C	respond to an identified need, with the potential to make a significant and recognizable contribution to achieving one of the pillars in Alberta's 20 year Strategic Plan …
D	… and have high potential to significantly impact other pillars of Alberta's 20 year Strategic Plan.

TABLE 18.3
Unleashing Innovation Stream Evaluation Matrix

The Project	The Enablers	Benefits/Impact
The Initiative	Project Plan	Societal Benefits
The Project Team	Collaboration	Culture of Innovation
Strategic Fit	Long-Term Viability	Innovation Adoption
		Economic Benefits

TABLE 18.4

Table 18.4 Sample Language Ladder for Unleashing Innovation Stream – "Innovation Adoption"

	Innovation is the process through which new economic and social benefits are extracted from knowledge. **The proposed innovation will lead to:**
A	the adoption of a new innovative practice, process, model, product or technology by the sponsoring organization;
B	the adoption of a new innovative practice, process, model, product or technology by at least one other stakeholder and/or client group;
C	the pervasive use of a new innovative practice, process, model, product or technology by a large number of stakeholders and/or client groups within and/or outside the Alberta Government ...
D	...**with** a high potential for the adoption of the new innovation in other provinces or countries

Competitions

The ProGrid methodology was instrumental in the success of the first Innovation Program competition. The criteria and Language Ladders effectively guided project proponents in the completion of their applications. The ProGrid assessment tool enabled peer reviewers to efficiently assess the project applications, which primarily involved topics in which the assigned reviewers did not possess full technical expertise. Consequently, the well-defined Language Ladders were beneficial.

The review results were compiled and presented to the Innovation Program Review Panel. The ProGrid assessment reports augmented the application information. The reports clearly and concisely illustrated the peer reviewer perspectives and listed all projects by the resulting R-values. This format reduced the burden on panel members (who maintain demanding schedules) in arriving at funding recommendations. A database grid plot for the proposals received for the first round of the Unleashing Innovation stream is shown in Figure 18.1. An application (Current Opportunity) under review is compared with all other submissions in the Unleashing Innovation stream database. This permits an assessment of how the current application compares with other opportunities, in terms of the project's quality and innovation and the expected benefits and impacts.

FIGURE 18.1
Database Plot for the Unleashing Innovation Stream

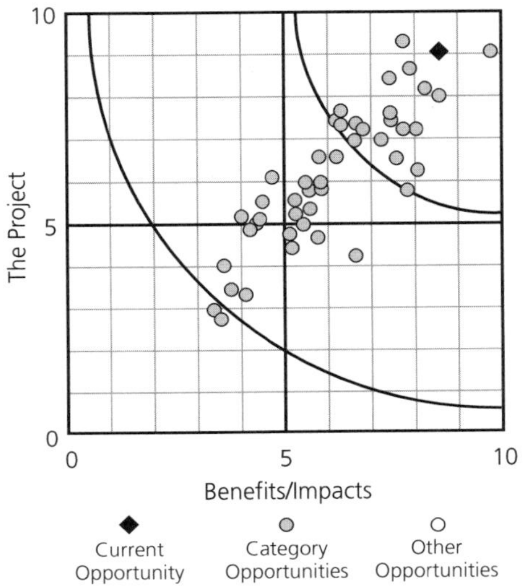

The large number of projects near the upper right hand corner of the grid is a testament to the high quality of the proposals that were received.

Project Diversity

An exciting aspect of the Innovation Program is that it attracts a diversity of project applications. They varied in project technical nature, complexity, magnitude, structure, approach, and collaboration. This creates a challenge in that vastly dissimilar projects need to be assessed, rated, and arranged relative to each other so that the limited funding budget can be awarded. By incorporating intangible and tangible factors, the ProGrid methodology made this objective possible.

19 Evaluating Individual Performance

Ron McCullough – Benchmark-Action Inc.
Clem Bowman – Clement W. Bowman Consulting Inc.

The Challenge

The challenge of matching achievements with rewards such as pay and promotion exists in all aspects of human endeavour, and is a significant factor in research. How do you distinguish between the rewards granted to scientists who pioneer singular advances that lead to a new industry, such as Wallace Carothers (who discovered Nylon[i]), and the researcher who year after year achieves the new product improvements that his company needs to stay in business? How do you separate these accomplishments from those of a group of researchers who toil diligently on a major technological problem for years before achieving success? How do you reward and motivate research staff who have diverse roles–such as pure research and technology transfer—each of which is strategic to an organization? Not very well in the opinion of many observers.

A major study carried out by Imperial Oil's John Tiedje, reported in a paper presented to the Canadian Research Management Association (CRMA)[ii], compared the impact of new products developed to meet defined business needs with major technological advances developed in advance of any defined market opportunity. Both categories made substantial contributions to the company, but the really big pay-offs came from the research concepts that started with an idea of a champion and often took years to bring to fruition.

Tiedje and his team examined the characteristics of researchers that excelled at the two different challenges of meeting defined business needs and undertaking innovative exploratory research.

Experience and an in-depth understanding of petroleum technology were key attributes for meeting the objectives of a sponsoring client, whereas exploratory research was best tackled by young PhDs with the latest scientific knowledge and skills. Some researchers had the capability to carry out both mission-oriented and exploratory research and would migrate between these functions during the span of their careers.

A team approach is sometimes the best solution for blending talents. The Imperial Oil experience indicated that the development and commercialization of new technology required:

- An initiator with the vision to see the opportunity
- A dedicated and persistent researcher
- A supportive and patient management
- An optimistic sponsor with faith
- A first user with guts

A follow-up study was undertaken by Imperial Oil to identify the key attributes of staff members who were the champions for the major advances. At that time, the company had instituted a decile performance ranking system, in which every staff member was rated by management in a 10-step seriatim. The top 10% were in decile D1 and the bottom 10% in decile D10. Staff members involved with each of the advances described in the CRMA paper were correlated with their decile standing. For previous researchers who had not been rated using the new system, there was sufficient information in the personnel files to estimate where they would have ranked. The conclusions were remarkable. D1 and D9 researchers made the majority of the advances. In fact the advances with the highest financial impact were made by the D9s. Perhaps one should not extrapolate too far based on one study, but it clearly shows the fallacy of a linear one-dimensional system for evaluating people. The decile seriatim system did not survive long in the company!

Aligning Organizational and Personal Goals

James Baker et al[iii] from the Ontario Ministry of Natural Resources set out to tackle the age-old problem of aligning the goals of an organization with the personal career plans of the people who are responsible for achieving those goals. Using the ProGrid® evaluation methodology described in this book, they first established the corporate criteria for research proposals, as shown in Table 19.1. Based on this matrix, the organization rated a set of proposals as shown in Figure 19.1.

TABLE 19.1
Forest Science Project Performance Criteria

Relevance	Quality	Impact
Fit to Strategic Priorities	Project Design and Methodologies	Technology and Knowledge Transfer
Supporting Legal Obligations	Effective and Efficient use of Resources	Building Capacity and Profile
Reducing Uncertainty in Resource Management Decisions	The Team	Building Sector Capacity
Advance on Prior Science and/or Technology Transfer	Partnerships and Collaboration	Ecological, Economic, and Social Impact

With this framework, Baker and his team were able to balance what had previously been seen as two opposing (and, to some researchers, incompatible) strategic objectives within their organization:

- The need to conduct scientific research of the highest quality
- The need to put the science in a form used by practitioners in the field and to get it to them in an effective way (often called technology transfer)

The framework was used to not only select a portfolio of projects that best delivered the full range of strategic expectations, but also to evaluate every project annually and at its completion to enable an end-to-end portfolio management approach.

FIGURE 19.1
Ratings of Forest Science Proposals

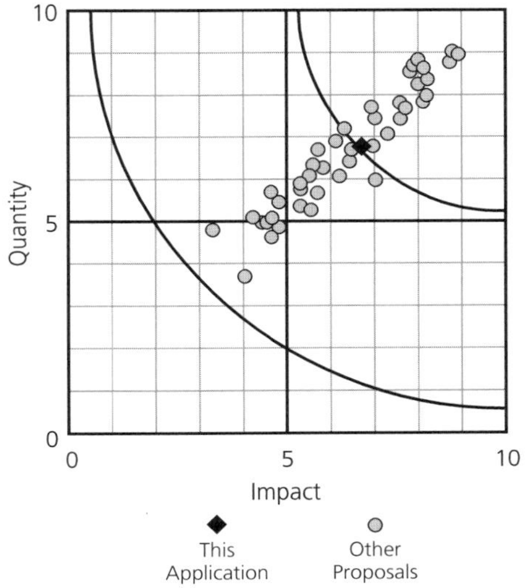

The Baker team then set out to make the connection with the personal career goals of the staff. The challenge was to ensure that high performance of research staff in meeting corporate objectives was directly linked to performance and promotion–in exactly the same context as research project selection. Projects selected must not only be good strategically for the organization but research staff must be able to see clear benefits for each of them in carrying out the research projects.

The team, with significant inputs from human resource experts, developed a similar approach to evaluate research personnel for their annual performance, to promote career development, and to assess readiness for advancement opportunities. The Evaluation Matrix and the resulting staff evaluation grid are shown in Table 19.2 and Figure 19.2 respectively.

TABLE 19.2
Scientist Personnel Evaluation Matrix™

Research	Professional Development	Transfer
Research Planning and Development	Productivity	The Transfer Plan
Relevance	Recognition	Transfer Effectiveness
Advance on Prior Science	Program Management	Transfer Impact

Staff members in three categories are evaluated in Figure 19.2. The triangles represent staff in the Lower RS3 category, the circles represent staff in the Middle RS4 category and the diamonds represent staff in the Top RS5 category.

FIGURE 19.2
Staff Evaluations

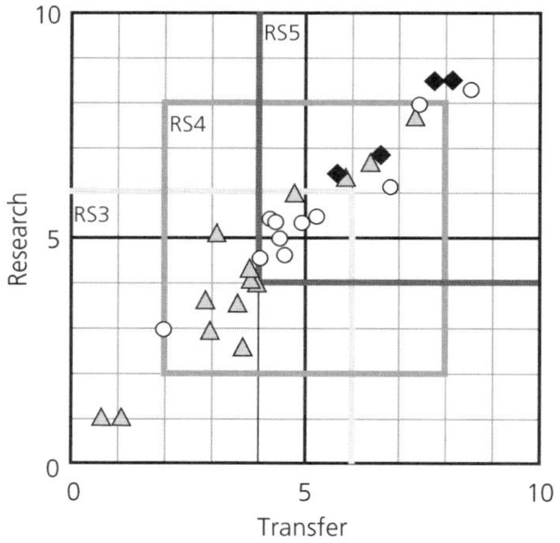

As individual staff members improve in their research and technology transfer accomplishments, merit and promotion decisions become evident and justifiable.

Using these criteria, staff can be evaluated as part of their annual performance review in relation to their current job classification and strengths and weaknesses identified. Further, objectives for progression can be identified and (of significant benefit to both the researcher and organizations) these can be matched to the type of research projects on which the researcher could work. In addition, when a researcher feels they are ready to be promoted to a higher classification, the system can be used to assess whether the training, accomplishments and scope of the researcher's capabilities are sufficient to warrant promotion. If there are gaps, the researcher and the supervisor can identify clear actions for filling these gaps.

Baker believes that the process ensures that this process is consistent with "fourth generation R&D," which in addition to ensuring that the portfolio of projects is closely aligned with business plan objectives, also engages all partners in a relationship that addresses the social, economic, political and environmental issues. (Fourth generation R&D, as he described it, is essentially equivalent to the fourth phase outlined in Chapter 21.)

Baker notes: "*The use of the personnel performance system... is extremely helpful in enabling a scientist to plan annual activities to address deficiencies that might hinder timely career advancement.*"

Application to a Team of Professionals

In a similar vein, professionals in most disciplines are hired to, and are committed to, building value in their organizations. Aligning day-to-day activities with the long-term impact on the organization is difficult enough. Going a step further and linking to rewards such as promotion, pay and participation in profits is very challenging, indeed. Ron McCullough and Jeff Parr[iv] developed a process that can be used to assess the contribution of professionals in a joint practice, thought to be applicable to groups of engineers and lawyers and similar disciplines. The Evaluation Matrix they used in a trial for one group is shown in Table 19.3.

TABLE 19.3
Professional Team Evaluation Matrix

Tools	Support	Impact
Acquired Expertise	Administrative Support	New Business Secured
Development of New Tools	General Marketing Support	Participation in Projects
Knowledge Integration	Client Support	Strategic Impact

Language Ladders for two of the cells in this matrix are shown in Tables 19.4 and 19.5, illustrating the breadth of coverage.

TABLE 19.4
Language Ladder for Administrative Support

During the assessment period, the staff member has:	
A	Performed no administrative functions other than those related directly to the submission of invoices and the management of customer accounts.
B	Undertaken the responsibility for routine administrative tasks in the organization and has performed these to a fully satisfactory level.
C	Undertaken the responsibility for a major administrative function in the organization and has performed this to a high level.
D	Undertaken a major multifunctional administrative role in the organization and has met or exceeded all expectations in this role.

TABLE 19.5

Language Ladder for Strategic Impact

During the assessment period, the participant has:	
A	Had little or no impact in formulating strategies or achieving key strategic objectives.
B	Had some involvement in formulating strategies and has supported some aspects of achieving key strategic objectives.
C	Been active in and has made significant contributions to certain aspects of strategy formulation and the achievement of key strategic objectives.
D	Been a leader in both the formulation of strategies and in achieving key strategic objectives.

FIGURE 19.3

Contributions of Staff

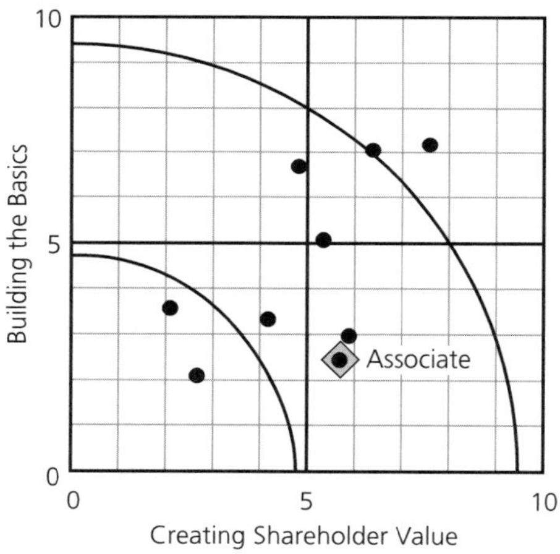

Each staff member carried out a self-assessment that was validated by colleagues and associates, with comparative results shown in Figure 19.3. The overarching objectives were Building the Basics of the organization and Creating Shareholder Value. Some of these staff members were part time.

In this example, the curves are drawn concentric with the point 0,0, using R_0 as a measure of chart progress (as defined in Chapter 1). This approach does not penalize a staff member who makes a contribution on one axis only.

It was recognized that in a complex organization, individual staff would not be expected to make major contributions in all of the defined criteria. Excellent performance in one or two criteria, often referred to as "spikes," could easily be recognized and rewarded, as illustrated in Figure 19.4.

The organization can also look at the overall composite results in each of the performance areas to identify organizational strengths and weaknesses and take steps to reinforce strength and correct weaknesses.

FIGURE 19.4
Example of Performance Profile

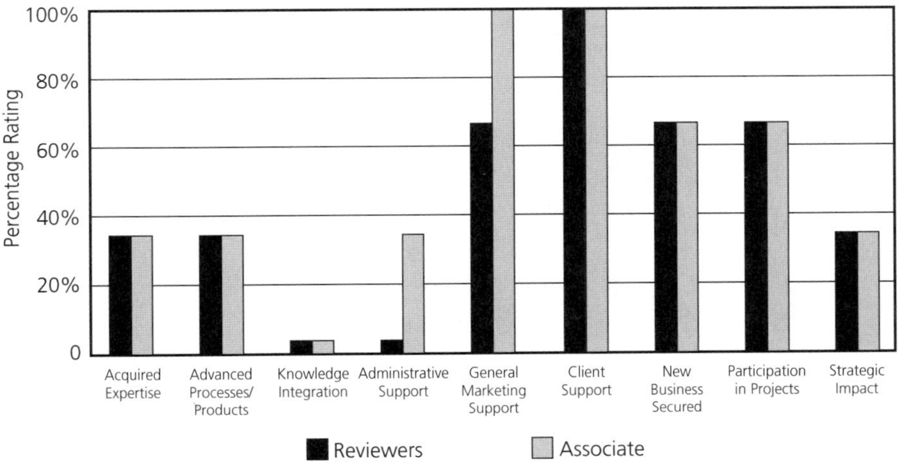

Conclusions

The performance of an organization and the individual performance of its staff are inextricably linked. As more organizations become knowledge based and move into new paradigms (such as "fourth generation R&D"), the problems of relating these two elements of performance become more complex and dominated by "intangibles." Productivity and performance can no longer be measured by tables and metrics related to piecework production methods. New frameworks such as those described above are needed to enable the strategic objectives of the organization to work in harmony with the personal objectives of its staff. The key in these frameworks is to create a process to define and measure the personal "intangibles" which contribute to the strategic success of the organization.

i http://www.chemheritage.org/EducationalServices/chemach/pop/whc.html

ii *Research at Esso – Sixty Years of Practice-Organizing for the Future,* C.W. Bowman, Canadian Research Management Association, September, 1985

iii James A. Baker, David Deyoe, Des McKee, Michael L. Willick, *The Forest Chronicle,* January/February 2002, Vol. 78, No. 1

iv President of the Clairvest Group, Toronto, Canada

20 Technologies – From Conception to Commercialization

Gerald Dyer – former Research Manager, DuPont Canada Ltd.
Clem Bowman – Clement W. Bowman Consulting Inc.

Identifying the Winners

New ideas are fragile and can be easily destroyed if not given a chance to grow and develop into viable technical concepts. At some stage, however, they must face increasingly more rigorous technical and market hurdles as they proceed through various stages of scale-up and market trials. Venture capital companies put major emphasis on being able to identify winners early in their development in order to realize the maximum gain in their investment.

During a series of evaluations of the best practices of research organizations, some research managers, perhaps frustrated by the number of benchmarking and re-engineering processes that they had endured, indicated that it was not the organization that needed to be evaluated, but their new ideas and emerging technologies. Clients and stakeholders were putting increasing pressure on their portfolio of programs, seeking a better forecast of potential market impacts.

This led to an intensive effort to develop a method for identifying potential winners, and tracking progress. Initial testing was carried out on four projects in the Joint Research Venture program of the Alberta Research Council, and on several projects undertaken for Ortech International. Extensive testing was done for Environment Canada for evaluating the possible import of environmental technologies into Canada as part of a consulting contract with the Ottawa office of KPMG. Several technologies were also evaluated for DuPont Canada and Manufacturing Research Corporation Ontario. An effective Evaluation Matrix™ and set of Language Ladders was developed through these various tests and used over the next five years to establish a database against which new technologies could be appraised. The methodology was known as ProGrid-TA®.

The Evaluation Matrix

The results of these initial tests led to the Evaluation Matrix shown in Table 20.1.

TABLE 20.1
Evaluation Matrix for Emerging Technologies

Technical Strength	Enabling Strengths	Commercial Strength
Technical Framework	Commercial Readiness	Market Characteristics
Level of Verification	Proprietary Strength	Margin and Profit Potential
Excellence of Project Team	Technological Durability	Commercialization Channels

The factors in the first column define the technical advance, the degree to which the advance has been verified, and the strength of the people behind the development. The factors in the third column establish the commercial outlook, the nature of the market, expected financial drivers and the route to the market. The middle column includes some key enablers that support the venture enterprise, evidence of commercial readiness, strength of the intellectual property and the durability of the technology over its expected life span.

This matrix recognizes the two overarching objectives that venture capitalists would value, high technical strength and high commercial strength, clearly orthogonal and indicative of a successful and sustainable venture. These are candidate axes for the positioning grid.

A Language Ladder™ has been developed for each cell in this matrix to provide metrics needed for an initial analysis of a new technology (see TA-Basic, Table 26.3, Chapter 26). However, the complexity in bringing technologies to the market requires a finer grain of criteria. This was accomplished by defining additional criteria in each cell, as shown in Table 20.2, each of which has its own set of Language Ladders.

TABLE 20.2
Thirty-Seven Criteria for Technical and Market Readiness

Technical Strength	Enabling Strengths	Commercial Strength
Technical Framework • scientific basis • advance on prior art • uniqueness • pervasiveness	Commercial Readiness • current stage of development • level of development required • complexity of scale-up	Market Characteristics • market acceptance • competitor's strength • regulatory compliance • regulatory leadership • market impact • geographic reach
Level of Verification • proof of concept • system integration • external validation	Proprietary Strength • patent/copyright position • competitive IP • trademark strengths • know-how requirement • scope for improvement	Margin and Profit Potential • cost reduction opportunities • competitor's price sensitivity • speed of commercialization • price-margins
Project Team • technical credentials • technical networks • understanding market needs	Technological Durability • avoidance • dependence on other products • duplication • robustness • obsolescence	Commercialization Channels • investment availability • market trials • partners • marketing networks

Defining the Language Ladders

Two examples of Language Ladder statement sets that provide the metrics for the evaluation are shown in Tables 20.3 and 20.4.

TABLE 20.3
Advance on Prior Art

The Concept represents:	
A	a relatively small advance on the prior art that would not be apparent to most users.
B	a definable and measurable extension of the prior art that will be discerned by discriminating users.
C	a significant and readily recognizable improvement over the prior art, but the basic scientific and technical principles are similar.
D	a major advance on the prior art and embodies significantly different principles.

TABLE 20.4
Market Acceptance

With respect to the products/processes/services provided by this concept:	
A	there is no evidence at this time of customer acceptance.
B	preliminary market studies indicate positive customer acceptance.
C	specific customers have been identified who have indicated their intention to place orders.
D	current or new customers have given firm orders today.

The Positioning Grid

Once a technical asset has been evaluated using this methodology, its position can be represented on the following grid, depending on its state of technical and commercial readiness. The data in Figure 20.1 represent technologies that were evaluated during the initial series of tests.

FIGURE 20.1
Positioning Grid

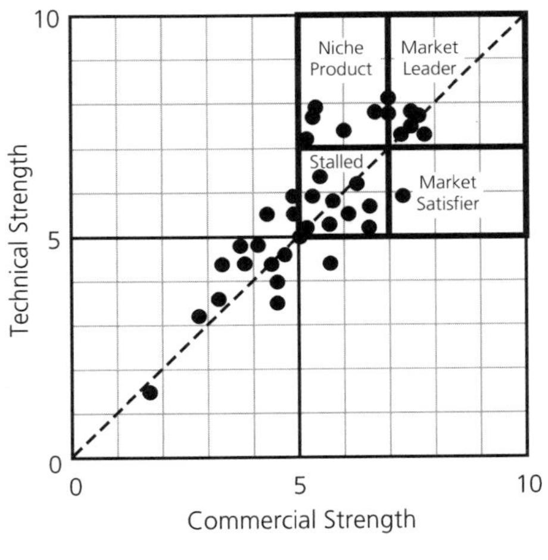

At the inception of a new idea, its location on this grid will likely be close to the origin. As the idea matures into a bona fide technology, it will follow a specific trajectory. If the technical and market developments proceed in parallel, the trajectory will follow a 45 degree diagonal. If the market develops faster than the technology, or if the technical content is relatively low, the trajectory will lie closer to the x-axis. Conversely, if technical progress proceeds faster than market development, or if the technical content is very high, the trajectory will lie closer to the y-axis. Where the trajectory ends will determine the overall merits of the technology.

FIGURE 20.2
Positioning Grid

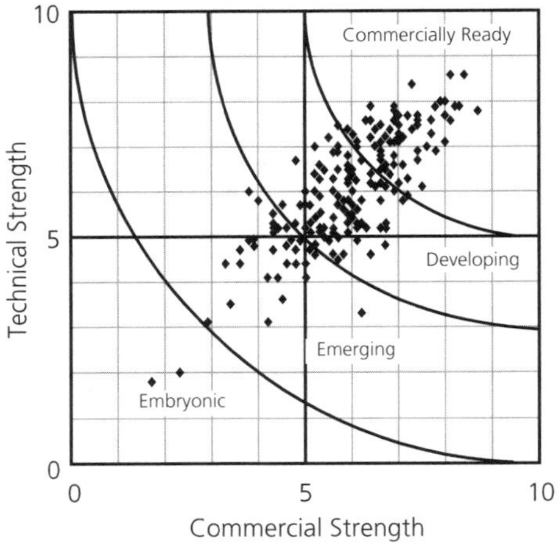

The division of the upper right hand quadrant into four zones illustrates the characteristics of technologies that fall within those zones. The nature of technologies that lie in the stalled zone will be discussed later; the characteristics of the other zones are self-explanatory.

The four-quadrant grid is useful for obtaining an overall view of the status of a technology. An alternative display of the status is shown in Figure 20.2, in which the four-quadrant boundaries are replaced by three curves that are concentric with the point 10,10. Points that lie on one of these curves have different combinations of technical and commercial strength but have the same distance to "travel" to reach the upper right hand corner of the grid. With this display, zones between the curves can be described as "Embryonic," "Emerging," "Developing," and "Commercially Ready."

Technology Profile

An equally-important chart is the profile of strengths and weaknesses based on the ratings for the individual cells in the Evaluation Matrix. With experience these can be recognized for their "DNA-like" characteristics with descriptive names such as Technology Push, Market-Pull, Stalled. Examples are shown in Figures 20.3, 20.4 and 20.5.

Two of top three bars in Figure 20.3 are very strong, indicative of a Technology Push project. The Level of Verification and Commercial Readiness and Commercialization Channels are weak. There is moderate strength in the balance of profile suggesting that the project is worthy of some additional work.

FIGURE 20.3
Technology Push

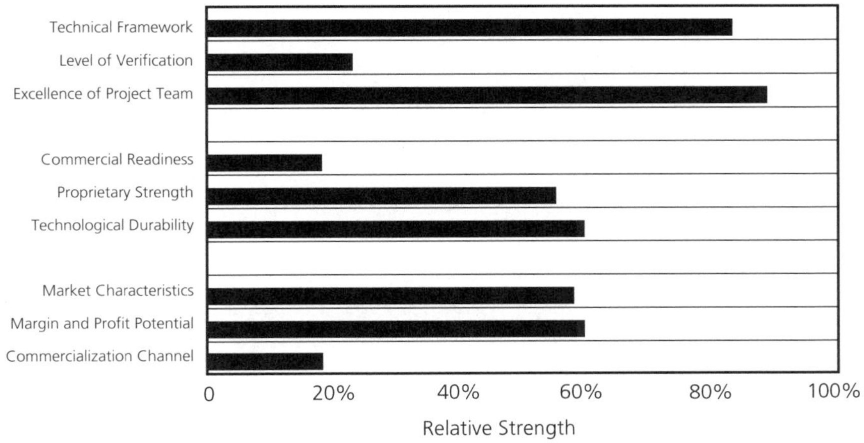

FIGURE 20.4
Market Pull

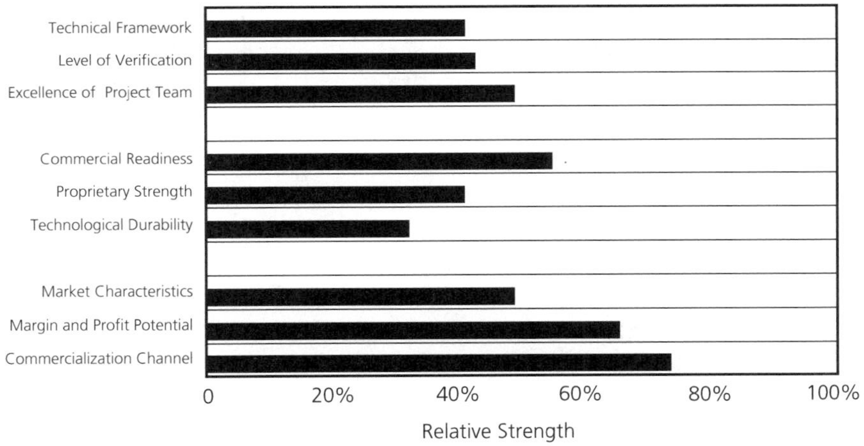

The project shown in Figure 20.4, with modest technical strength, has strong profit potential with clearly defined channels to the market place, indicative of a Market Pull project.

The project shown in Figure 20.5 has a very flat profile. This is typical of a mature technology that has been involved in several commercial launch attempts where the obvious weaknesses have been corrected but no outstanding strengths have emerged. This project would fall in the stalled zone in Figure 20.1.

FIGURE 20.5
A Stalled Project

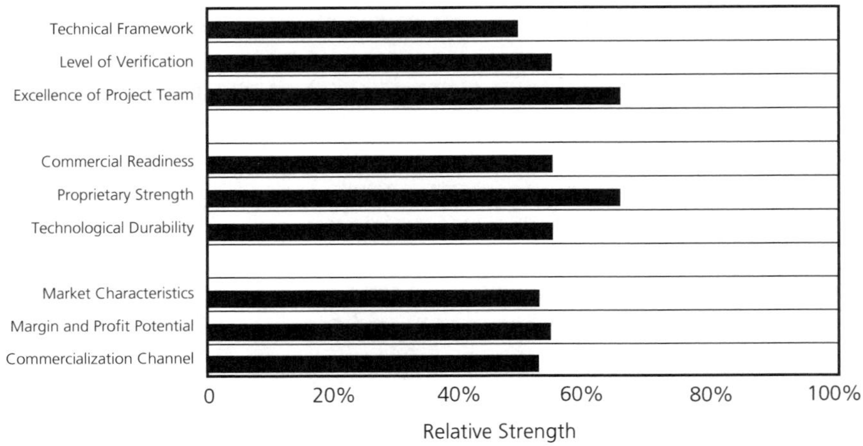

R-Factor Comparison

The R factor, as defined in Chapter 1, can be used to rank a set of technologies as shown in Table 20.5. Ten technologies that have different X, Y values and therefore different R-values are compared and sorted.

TABLE 20.5
R-Value Rating Table

Tech. #	X	Y	R
7	7.4	7.6	75.0%
10	6.9	7.9	73.5%
8	6.4	7.6	69.4%
3	7.2	5.9	64.9%
9	5.2	7.0	60.0%
1	6.7	5.3	59.4%
6	6.7	5.2	58.8%
4	6.0	5.5	57.4%
2	4.8	4.4	46.0%
5	2.9	3.1	30.0%

Predicting the Future

The profile charts shown above raise the possibility of assessing the likelihood that weaknesses can be corrected through further research and development. For example the proprietary position could be strengthened with the granting of a patent. The successful completion of a scale-up test or a market trial would similarly improve prospects. However, a weak market position or presence of cutthroat competition operating with low margins is likely to represent fatal uncorrectable flaws. This leads to the feasibility of introducing an expert system to predict future grid travel and to serve as a trajectory for tracking performance.

Possible future rating values can be determined by the following relationship:

Future value = Current value (A, B, or C) + increment (x, y or z)

The values x, y z can be determined by those with experience in the development and commercialization of technology. Once determined, the x, y, z values are kept constant until experience shows a change is appropriate.

Similarly, it is feasible to estimate what downsides might occur if certain events do not work out as expected.

Future value = Current value (B, C, or D) – increment (u, v or w)

The individual criteria in the Evaluation Matrix can be grouped into various categories, such as those that affect the technical development program, project fundamentals, competitive position and market confirmation. Applying the sensitivity analysis to each category results in a trajectory, as shown in Figure 20.6. The expert system can be constructed to produce a list of actions required to achieve the upsides and a list of areas to address to protect against the downsides.

FIGURE 20.6
Predicting the Future

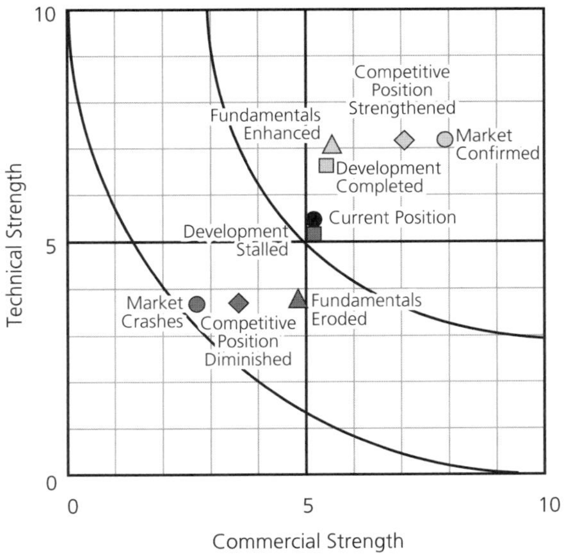

Undertaking the ProGrid® assessment at periodic intervals will show the level of progress that has been made.

The Assessment Process

The technology assessment procedure, best carried out by a small panel knowledgeable about the technology and the market to be assessed, will normally include individuals representing the technology developers, the commercialization team, and preferably one or two individuals who are not part of these two groups but whose participation will add credibility.

A trained facilitator adds considerable value to the assessment by ensuring that the assessment decisions are consistent and well-supported. It is essential that agreement is reached regarding the specifics of the technology being assessed and the markets to be served. The assessor also makes sure that no one person dominates the discussion and that all players have the chance to add their point of view. The discussion and comments are as valuable to the technology developers as the actual assessment results–grid positions and the identification of strengths and weaknesses. The discussions put the flesh on the evaluation results, which are available immediately at the end of the session. In several cases, the developers rewrote their business plans after the assessment session and are now heading up successful companies.

21 Benchmarking Research Performance

Clem Bowman – Clement W. Bowman Consulting Inc.
Ron McCullough – Benchmark-Action Inc.

Intellectual Capital is the Currency

Intellectual capital is the currency of research organizations. If they fail to both generate and use it wisely, they are doomed for the rubbish heap, subject to the wrath of stakeholders.

Assessing the performance of their research has been always been one of the highest priorities of research managers, and was a major reason for the establishment, in 1963, of the Canadian Research Management Association. Best practices in assessing the impact of research were shared among members at every annual meeting. One example of the experience of one of the charter members, Imperial Oil Limited, was presented in 1985, covering the previous 60 years[i]. The origin of many of the projects that had the highest payout for the company "was primarily in the minds of one or more individuals who perceived a technical opportunity, frequently in advance of a business need." These ideas were clearly intangible, and often fragile in the early stage, but led to the generation of important intellectual capital.

Let's first take a look at what intellectual capital is all about. The factors shown in Table 21.1 are generally considered to be the major components, and are largely intangible. Intellectual property was once assumed to be the underpinning of intellectual capital, and for many start-up companies based on a single technological advance, this remains true. But as organizations mature, their codified knowledge, systems and processes and the talents of their people become of increasing importance.

TABLE 21.1
Components of Intellectual Capital

Intellectual Capital			
Structural Capital			
Intellectual Assets		Systems Processes Relationships Innovation	Human Capital
Intellectual Property	Codified Knowledge		

A Historical Perspective

The management of intellectual capital in research organizations has changed dramatically during the past 40 years. This evolution has not been linear and has involved a number of different relationships between R&D organizations and the stakeholders served. The concept of performance measurement has changed from the time when scientific excellence was the only criterion for success.

It is useful to define two "bookend" types of organizations to illustrate the changing relationships.

Type X Organizations (Market Pull) – Organizations whose mandate is determined solely by the current business interests of clients and who hire staff and select and monitor projects on this basis. Deliverables are closely-defined and the technology is transferred under contractual relationships within a corporate envelope. Although effective at meeting the needs of clients, these organizations frequently have difficulty adding to their intellectual capital.

Type Y Organizations (Technology Push) – Organizations whose mandate is defined by a scientific charter and who hire staff and select and monitor projects based on meeting the objectives of this charter. Specific deliverables are generally not defined and technical information is made available through publications to the broad scientific network. Although effective at creating intellectual capital, these organizations are usually not involved in the commercial use of this capital.

Many research organizations displayed blends of Type X and Type Y behaviour, which evolved over time in response to the business environment. This evolution took several phases, as illustrated in Figure 21.1.

FIGURE 21.1
Evolution of Research Organizations

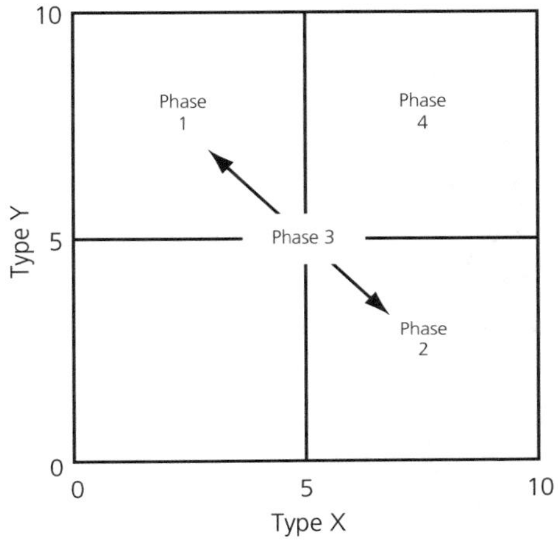

Organizations in Phase 1 had dominant Type Y characteristics and received essentially all their funding as a core "grant" from the owner, with only a general statement of expected deliverables. "Good science," supported by access to the world pool of science and technological information, was the driver for R&D programs. These organizations were generally successful in generating new intellectual capital, which frequently resulted in new processes, products or services having significant technological impact. However, the transfer of technology to clients tended to be sporadic and dependent on the personal relationships developed by senior R&D management with counterparts in the business units. Central corporate research laboratories during the 1960s had strong Type Y characteristics.

Many owners became dissatisfied with the impact of their research investment and were instrumental in the change to a Type X arrangement, whereby R&D contracts were provided directly from the business cost centres. The programs were approved by and in many cases almost entirely defined by these centres. R&D projects were short-term and responded to the current needs of the business, with limited attention to global technology developments. The benefits of R&D were determined through periodic audits of successful projects. These organizations, although effective at technology transfer, were less effective at replacing their depleting intellectual capacity. This Phase 2 behaviour was prevalent with many industrial research organizations during the 1970s.

Owners generally felt more comfortable with Phase 2 results, but were concerned that there were opportunities and threats not being addressed by this focus on the short-term needs of the business units. Some owners reinstated a modest level of corporate funding for longer-term R&D, with the selection of projects largely residing with the R&D organization for that component of the total budget. The business lines still provided the majority of the funding for the organization. This dual mission approach (Phase 3) involved a non-integrated blend of Type X and Type Y characteristics. The effectiveness is debatable. It did provide research management with some discretion to initiate exploratory programs, but the capacity to expand these when successful was limited. A number of industrial research organizations adopted this strategy in the 1980s.

Most companies realized in the late 1980s that they were entering a new fiercely-competitive global economy in which technology would become a key strategic weapon. It became imperative that technology be fully integrated into the corporate strategic plan. It was necessary to involve senior levels of both business and research management in this process and to focus on both the short and long-term technology needs of the corporation (Phase 4). An aggressive R&D management unit was needed to energize this process. Achieving this level of integration was a goal pursued through

FIGURE 21.2
Achieving Full Integration

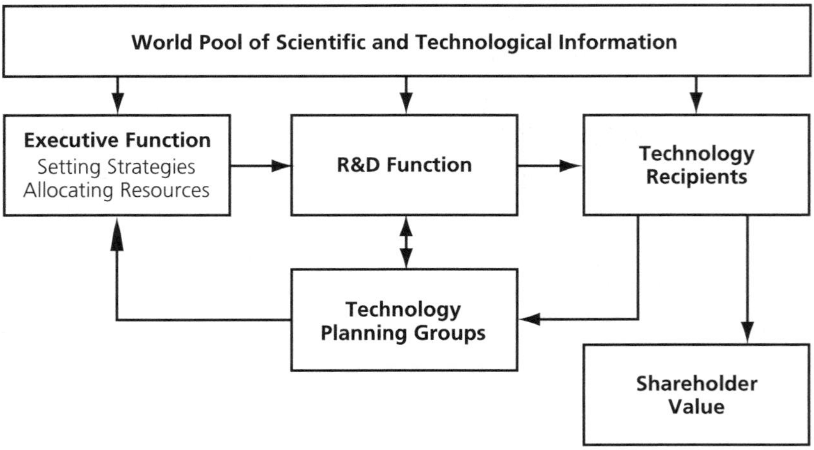

the 1990s and continues to this time. It depends on the interactions of many stakeholders, as illustrated in Figure 21.2.

Establishing the Performance Criteria

With intellectual capital as the currency and a wide range of stakeholders involved in the research enterprise, the measurement of performance can become very complex. The ProGrid® methodology for measuring intangibles that is the basis of this book was found to be a logical place to start.

Two of the key objectives for R&D managers, as identified in numerous surveys, are the need to balance the short- and long-term technology goals for the parent organizations. These are clearly connected to Type X and Type Y characteristics and in turn to the deployment and generation of intellectual capital respectively. Several international benchmarking projects were undertaken during the 1990s that used the latter terms as the measurement indices, and as the axes of the performance grid. The challenge in these projects was to define the Evaluation Matrix™ and corresponding Language Ladders.

Several variations of the Evaluation Matrix were tested, but the one shown in Table 21.2 was able to span the scope of most research organizations. Public sector organizations tend to have mandates that impact on societal issues such as the creation of new enterprises and training. The areas of impact of private sector organizations tend to be more internal to the corporation. Some R&D organizations have limited internal capability and contract out much of their activity.

TABLE 21.2
Matrix for Measuring R&D Performance

R&D Inputs	The Connectors	Benefits/Impact
Vision/Mission	Business Alignment	Corporate Impact
Program Management	Technology Transfer	Industry Impact
Human Resources	Performance Measurement	Social Impact

Nevertheless, they all can be measured by how well they fulfill the short and long term expectations of their owners and key stakeholders.

The next step was to decide on the performance criteria in each cell of this matrix. An early version of the methodology used 96 criteria, which proved to be unwieldy and tried the patience of some evaluators. This was condensed to about 50 key criteria. It was soon recognized that some of the criteria were not performance related but derived from different mandates, essentially describing Type X and Type Y characteristics. This led to the development of two assessment modules, the first defining the slope of the trajectory on the performance grid, the second establishing the level of performance along that trajectory.

Module 1: The criteria that govern the slope of the trajectory are shown in Table 21.3. An example of the Language Ladder™ for

TABLE 21.3
Mandate-related Criteria

Organization mandate	Monitoring R&D Projects
Budget Sources	Staff Deliverables
Hiring Strategy	Technology Transfer
Selecting R&D Projects	Networking

TABLE 21.4
Language Ladder For Budget Sources

Budget Sources:	
A	The annual budget is established almost exclusively through a renewable grant from the owner for work related to the mandate of the organization.
B	The annual budget of the organization is established mainly through a renewable grant or appropriation from the owner, supplemented by support from clients for specific projects.
C	The annual budget of the organization is established roughly equally through a renewable grant or appropriation from the owner and support from clients for specific projects.
D	The annual budget of the organization is established mainly through support from clients for specific projects, supplemented by a renewable grant or appropriation from the owner.
E	The annual budget is established almost exclusively through support from clients for specific projects.

Budget Sources is provided in Table 21.4, which sets the principle that whoever pays the piper calls the tune.

FIGURE 21.3
Establishing Current and Future Position

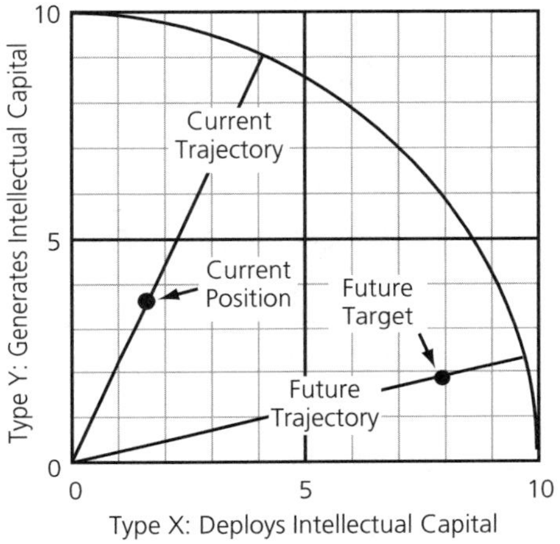

These criteria enable an organization, either through self-assessment or with the aid of an external evaluator, to establish a current and desired future X/Y trajectory, as shown in Figure 21.3. This defines the balance the organization has chosen between building and deploying intellectual capital. This is a real case where the organization currently had dominant Type Y characteristics but planned to become a strong Type X organization.

Module 2: Once the trajectories are established, the remaining criteria can be used to define current and future performance levels along these trajectories, using appropriate Language Ladder

TABLE 21.5
Developing R&D Objectives

R&D Objectives:	
A	The R&D objectives been developed with general reference to the needs of the key clients.
B	Consideration of the needs of the key clients has been taken into account in developing the R&D objectives. The objectives are reviewed with the clients to obtain comments and suggestions.
C	The R&D objectives have been developed collaboratively with the key clients and are well aligned with their business needs.
D	The R&D objectives are fully integrated into the business objectives of the owner and key clients and represent key components of the overall corporate strategic plan.

statements. Table 21.5 shows an example of Language Ladder statements for one of the criteria in the Business Alignment cell.

Through aggregation of all criteria, the current and future grid positions can be established. The example shown in Figure 21.3 indicates that this organization has identified the need to make major changes in its performance. Having defined the Language Ladder statements for each criterion, the actions needed to move from one level to another are apparent and form the basis for the ongoing operational plan.

Benchmarking a Group of Organizations

The above performance evaluation methodology was used in various benchmarking projects involving 30 R&D organizations, grouped as follows:

- Private Sector – Single Company
- Private Sector – Consortia
- Government Laboratories – Industrial Sector Related
- Government Laboratories – General Industrial Support
- Government Laboratories – Science/ Technology Focused

FIGURE 21.4
Current and Future Grid Positions

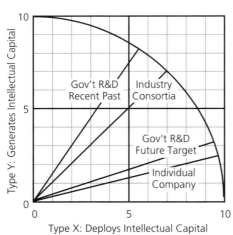

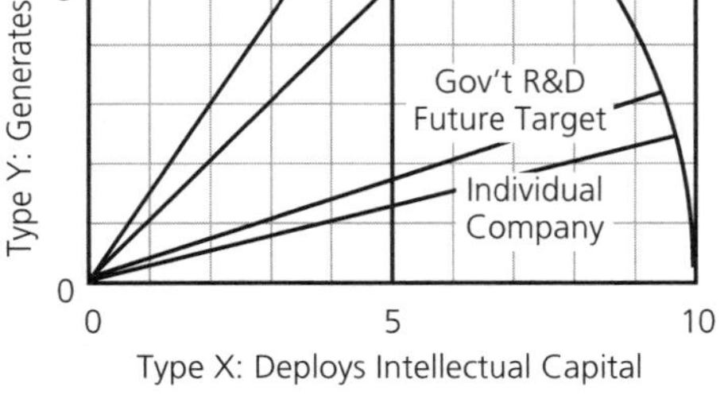

Although the results are proprietary to the specific organizations involved, one major conclusion was reached that can be more-broadly shared. This is illustrated in Figure 21.4. Many government R&D organizations position themselves in a zone where they put more emphasis on the generation of intellectual capital than on its use. Individual companies place themselves more strongly in a zone where the deployment of intellectual capital is the more dominant focus.

Neither of these is entirely satisfied with its current position. Many companies have coalesced around R&D consortia in order to achieve a better balance in short and long term activities, as shown by the Industry Consortia position. Government laboratories on the other hand are attempting to become more responsive to the needs of clients and to identify as a target a position closer to the current position of individual companies. It is unlikely that government laboratories can put in place the necessary tight linkages among a broad range of clients to achieve this position. More importantly it raises the question as to whether they will so weaken their position for generating intellectual capital that they will cease to perform the mission for which they were established.

What Do These Findings Mean?

Since these studies were carried out, several of the government R&D organizations who were most aggressive in shifting to a Type X organization have been shut down. At least one of the industrial R&D organizations in the study that stayed too close to the X-axis has also been terminated. This suggests that if a research organization only does what its sponsor says it wants today, it may find that it is no longer called on for service.

The methodology can be employed in a number of different ways:

- by an owner organization to set the stage for a major change in R&D strategy
- by an owner organization to compare different R&D units within its corporate structure
- by R&D management to prepare the baseline for an ongoing organization improvement program
- by an R&D organization to strengthen its interactions with key clients
- by an R&D organization to assess the extent of buy-in of its strategic plans and processes throughout the organization

The uniqueness of the method its that it defines the standards for performance, measures the organization against these standards, and then converts these into comparable metrics. The metrics can be translated back into the actions needed to move from a current to a future state, and to track progress.

[i] C.W. Bowman, *Research at Esso: 60 Years of Practice-Organizing for the Future*, 23rd Conference of the Canadian Research Management Association, Jasper, Alberta, Sept 22-25, 1985

22 Aligning Strategies Within Government Organizations

Ron Dyck and Ray Bassett, Assistant Deputy Ministers, Alberta Department of Innovation and Science
John Kramers – ProGrid Ventures Inc.
Clem Bowman – Clement W. Bowman Consulting Inc.

The Challenge

Managing multiple research units within a single organization creates major challenges, as we found in the operations of the Alberta Department of Innovation and Science. If the future states defined by the department could be achieved, huge economic, environmental and social benefits would be realized in the energy, agriculture, forestry and health sectors, and related knowledge-intensive industries, with major reductions in greenhouse gas emissions and water use.

Entities reporting to the Department of Innovation and Science include:

- Alberta Heritage Foundation for Medical Research
- Alberta Ingenuity Fund
- Alberta Science and Research Authority comprised of:
  - Alberta Energy Research Institute
  - Alberta Agricultural Research Institute
  - Alberta Forestry Research Institute
  - Alberta Research Council
  - Informatics Circle of Research Excellence (iCORE)

Each of these entities has their own governing structures, and strategic plans. The department committed to ensure that these strategies were well aligned and focused on the long term goals of the Alberta Government. The vision was a close interaction between the strategies of the Government and the reporting organizations, as illustrated in Figure 22.1.

FIGURE 22.1
Linking Strategies

The Alberta Evaluation Matrix™

The "engine" for the task is the Alberta Evaluation Matrix, linking inputs to outputs through enablers (Table 22.1).

The concept behind this matrix is that the Strategies defined in the first column result in R&D Capacities in the second column, that lead to short and long-term Outputs identified in the third column. In research and development, it is well known that many of the "outputs" are very long-term and hard to quantify during the course of the R&D program. Some of these are identified in the right hand column as Outcomes, and in large measure reflect the "People, Prosperity and Preservation" strategies of the Alberta Government. The detailed analysis described in this chapter was confined to the first three columns and included Language Ladder™ statements, that provided the metrics for the calculations.

Cascading Matrices

The concept of cascading matrices, based on ProGrid® methodology, had been developed for measuring the alignment of divisions in a private sector company, and was adopted for the purposes of our current challenge. The subset of organization unit included in the study is shown in Table 22.2.

Each of these units developed their own Evaluation Matrix and Language Ladders that can be considered as a set of linked cascading matrices, as illustrated in Figure 22.2. Using appropriate Language

TABLE 22.1
The Alberta Evaluation Matrix

Inputs Strategies	Enablers Increased R&D Capacity	Outputs Economic and Social Value	Outcomes People Prosperity Preservation
Energy Research Strategy	People	Energy Processes, Products and Services	• Effective environmental stewardship • Value added economic activity • Prosperous rural communities • Alberta made strategy for reduction of greenhouse gases • Skilled labour force (attract, educate and retain) • Economic prosperity • World class infrastructure • Attract, establish and retrain businesses • Healthy population • Unleashing innovation • Industrial sustainability • Knowledge-based economy
Life Sciences Research Strategy	Infrastructure	Agri - Processes, Products and Services	
ICT Research Strategy	Strategic Project	Forestry Processes, Products and Services	
Tech. Comm. Strategy	Technology Adoption and Commercialization	Health Processes, Products and Services	
	Innovation Facilitating Mechanisms	ICT Processes, Products and Services	

TABLE 22.2
Organization Participants

<table>
<tr><th colspan="3">Department of Innovation and Science (INNSCI)</th></tr>
<tr><td rowspan="2">Alberta Energy Research Institute (AERI)</td><td colspan="2">Life Sciences</td></tr>
<tr><td>Alberta Agriculture Research Institute (AARI)</td><td>Alberta Forestry Research Institute (AFRI)</td></tr>
<tr><td colspan="3">Alberta Science and Research Investment Program (ASRIP)</td></tr>
<tr><td colspan="3">Technology Commercialization Program (Tech Comm)</td></tr>
</table>

Ladders, positioning grids and profile charts can be established comparing the current position and two desired future states.

This enables senior management of the Department of Innovation and Science to compare their current and desired future positions (Level One) with an aggregated assessment of the views of the five reporting entities. This results in an

FIGURE 22.2
Alberta Cascading Matrices

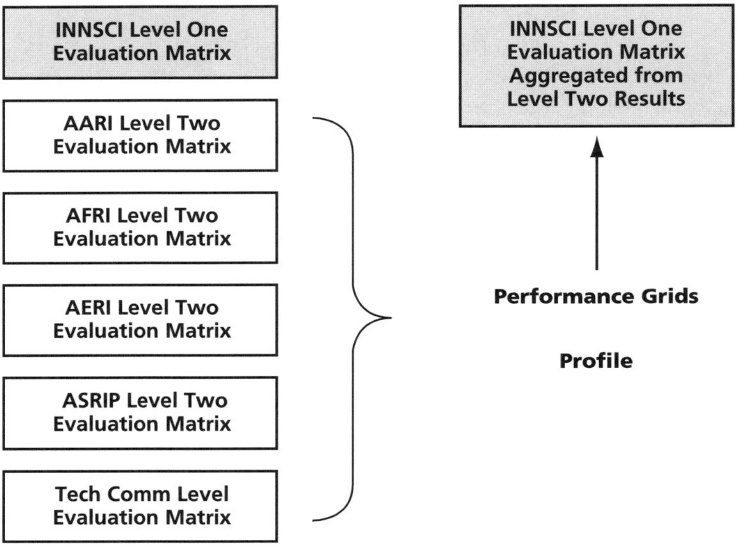

assessment of the degree of alignment between the current and desired future positions as seen at various organization levels.

Alignment Study Results

FIGURE 22.3
Grid Positions

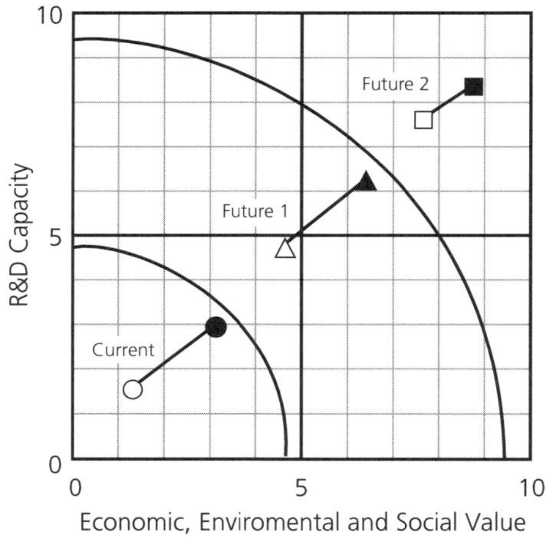

As shown in Figure 22.3, there is a solid consensus on the challenges and opportunities with respect to establishing R&D Capacity and achieving Economic, Environmental and Social Value. There is a difference in the grid positions in the Level One analysis (dark symbols) and the Level Two analysis (white symbols).

Future 1 is the desired position in 2012 and Figure 2 the preferred state in 2020. The Current position is the starting point in 2003.

Senior management believe that they are further along with respect to chart travel compared to the views of the Institutes but the differences between the current and future positions are similar.

The expected progress in each cell of the Evaluation Matrix is shown in Figure 22.4.

FIGURE 22.4
Profile of Individual Matrix Cells (Level One)

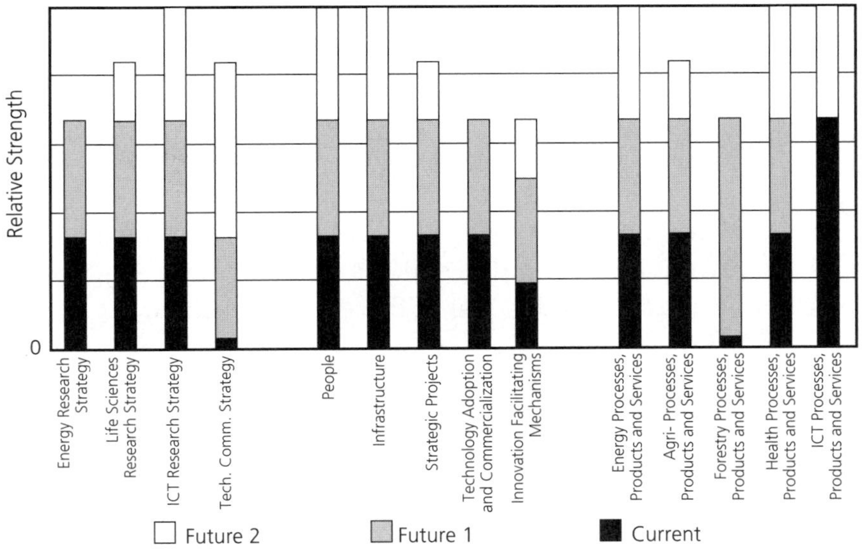

The Current grid positions of the three Institutes and two programs that participated in the study are shown in the lower left corner of Figure 22.5. It should be stressed that each entity used their own judgment in their assessment of their current position; the position was not arrived at by reference to an external benchmark. The average Future 1 and Future 2 positions provide a trajectory for tracking performance.

FIGURE 22.5
Comparison of Institutes/Programs

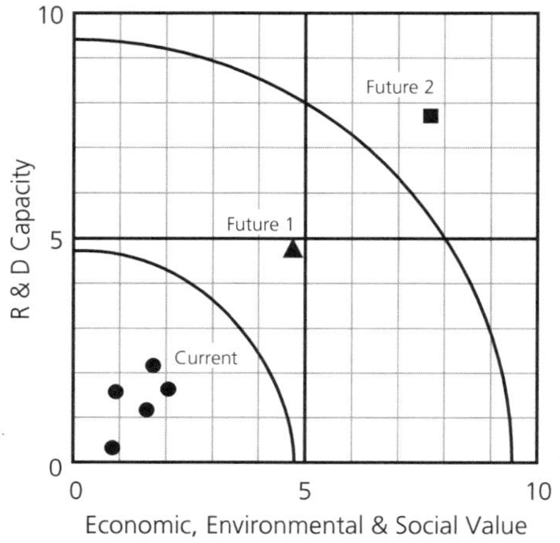

What Have We Learned?

The most important result from this analysis is that the Alberta Department of Innovation and Science and the entities reporting to it, have established ambitious targets for the future of the Province in a wide range of economic, social and environmental areas. They also see that they are at a very early stage of delivering on this "promise."

The methodology developed in this study will be used to measure performance toward the 2012 and 2020 targets, and to develop the necessary action plans. These measurements will clearly demonstrate the difference between activities and progress. Activities do not necessarily contribute to chart travel.

The differences between the perspective of senior management and the Institutes/Programs raise some important questions. The differences in grid position in Figure 22.3 indicate that areas of non-alignment do exist. The Level One Matrix results aggregated from the Level Two matrices (not shown in this chapter) identify the specific areas where alignment needs to be improved.

Has senior management built in some of their expectations into their ratings of the current position? Do the Institutes/Programs have a more realistic understanding of the technological problems that they face? Interviews with those "closest to the trenches" suggest that their ratings reflect in part their worries concerning the availability of the necessary resources and funding.

Building on these findings, the Alberta Energy Research Institute has completed a more detailed study of the enormous opportunities and challenges facing the energy sector, and this has taken it well beyond provincial boundaries, as described in Chapter 23.

23 The Energy Challenge: Meeting Future Goals

Eddy Isaacs, Surindar Singh, Duke Du Plessis – Alberta Energy Research Institute
John Kramers – ProGrid Ventures Inc.
Clem Bowman – Clement W. Bowman Consulting Inc.

Technology Oil

When oil was first produced in commercial quantities in the United States and Canada[i], you only had to scratch the surface of the ground and oil would flow. Now, 150 years later, oil is still being discovered and produced but now requires advanced technologies for economically and environmentally sound recovery.

Hydrocarbon resources occur in many forms in the earth's crust. Deeply buried methane, methyl hydrates and coal bed methane are examples of lighter hydrocarbons; the oil sands and heavy oil deposits in Canada and Venezuela are examples of heavy and more viscous materials. For example, there are in the order of 8-9 trillion barrels of heavy oil and bitumen in place worldwide, of which 900 billion barrels are potentially recoverable, if the right technologies are available. If coal deposits are included, the total resource of hydrocarbons increases by many times.

It was popular to predict during the latter part of the last century that in a short time, in the order of 10 years, we would "run out of oil." Hydrocarbon fuels are now expected to supply over 90% of global incremental energy demand through at least 2030[ii]. Much of this resource can be considered to be "technology oil," oil that will not be produced unless new technologies are made available.

The Canadian Energy Picture

Canada has one of the largest supplies of hydrocarbons in the world, which combined with hydroelectric, wind, solar, biomass, geothermal and nuclear energy sources, makes it the largest per capita energy source in the world. Currently, it is the fifth largest energy producer, and a net exporter of energy. Aggressive public and private investments in research and development and field trials have led to many new recovery and processing technologies and an array of enabling technologies such as horizontal drilling, instrumentation, automation, reservoir simulations and 3-D seismic surveys. However, more investments and new technologies are needed if Canada is to achieve the full potential of its abundant energy resources.

With current recovery technologies, almost 40% of natural gas, 70% of conventional oil and 90% of the *in situ* oil sand resources will be left in the ground. There is a growing recognition that solutions to the energy challenges will emerge when the energy industry is seen as one large interconnected system, whereby key issues such as hydrogen requirements for upgrading, water reuse, and greenhouse gas emission are addressed through effective integration.

The Alberta Energy Research Institute (AERI) has taken a lead role in developing an energy innovation strategy to ensure that the right technologies are available as the new energy challenges are faced and met.

It is a collaborative and integrative strategy, which can be summarized by the following statement:

Public and private sector partners from across Canada will work together on research and innovation to further recovery and upgrading oil sands technology, develop cleaner coal technology, reduce greenhouse gas emissions, manage water resources, improve conventional oil and gas recovery and explore alternative and renewable energy sources.

In proposing this strategy, AERI has recognized that substantial new investments in research and technology will be required to achieve the vision and implement the energy research strategy.

The strategy, if achieved, will make huge contributions to the Canadian economy, with beneficial social and environmental impacts over the next 20 or more years. The challenge is to convert this strategy into action and to harness the innovative power of Canadian engineers and scientists to generate the new technologies needed to achieve the objectives. For this reason, the initial focus has been to get the right players involved in initiating integrated "innovation programs" that solve priority problems or capitalize on significant opportunities.

Converting the Strategy into Goals

There is an old expression that if you don't know where you're going, any road will take you there. The first step after articulating the overarching strategy is to clearly define measurable goals, without which the strategy is just that: a strategy with no meat on the bones.

A process of intensive discussions among energy stakeholders, including both energy providers and energy users, has led to a set of six goals for the year 2020. These represent the bookends for Canada's energy challenge, the vision via a strategy statement and the goals that the country has determined to achieve. These goals span the entire energy system in Alberta, as it exists now and as it can become in the future.

The Canadian Energy Innovation Strategy → Six Economic, Environmental and Social Goals for the year 2020

But there are other important pieces of the puzzle that are needed to take this from a wish list to an achievable mission – a commitment to find the people, build the infrastructure, and put in place the funding to make it happen. In addition, it is critical to ensure that the right policies are in place to facilitate investment in new technology by industry. These are the Enablers. This then provides the full dimensions of the Canadian energy challenge, as shown in Table 23.1.

TABLE 23.1
Canada's Energy Evaluation Matrix™

Innovation Strategy	Enablers (Innovation Capacity)	Economic, Environmental and Social Goals related to:
Link public and private sector partners from across Canada to work together on research to further oil sands technology, develop cleaner coal technology, reduce greenhouse gas emissions, manage water resources, improve conventional oil and gas recovery and explore alternative energy sources.	Energy Innovation Network	Bitumen Upgrading • Energy Efficiency • Diversified Products • Environment
	Policy and Business Drivers • R&D Incentives • R&D Investments • Capital Investment • Regulatory Protocols • Climate Change and Water Management • Industrial Infrastructure	Clean Carbon/Coal • Coal • Biomass
		Carbon Dioxide Management • CO_2 Environment • CO_2 Use and Disposal
		Hydrocarbon Recovery • Conventional Oil • Natural Gas • Heavy Oil & Bitumen • Environment
	Innovation Framework • People • Infrastructure • Global Intelligence • Communications • Technology Management	Alternative and Renewable Energy • Hydrogen/Fuel Cells • Bio-energy • Other
		Water Management • Cross-cutting Initiatives • Upgrading • Recovery

Establishing the Goals and the Energy Innovation Network (EnergyINet)

AERI conducted an intensive consultative process involving key Canadian energy stakeholders to define the exact dimensions of the six economic, environmental and social goals. The process, called the Challenge Dialogue, has involved several provincial governments, the federal government, the private sector and representatives of various interest groups. Recognizing that the complex challenges facing the energy industry cannot be solved by any one organization alone, a flexible, virtual organization was conceived that would serve as a vehicle for collaboration among industry, researchers, and federal and provincial governments.

This has led to the establishment of the Energy Innovation Network (or EnergyINet) to link public and private sector partners from across Canada dedicated to ensure:

An abundant supply of environmentally responsible energy, creating economic prosperity and social well-being for Canadians.

EnergyINet builds on a tradition of successful collaborative innovation in the energy sector. Over 60% of Canada's oil production today is "technology oil," made possible by such inventions as horizontal wells and steam-assisted gravity drainage. The challenge now is to develop technology solutions for a new generation of challenges facing the industry. In many cases, the task is to take technology (such as new gasification technologies, catalysis, CO_2 capture and storage, geothermal energy), already proven technically elsewhere in the world or on a small scale, and make it commercially viable for the Canadian resource base.

Through this process, quantifiable objectives have been defined for each of the six Goals, as shown in Table 23.2.

Tracking Performance

Research organizations like to build their research programs around activities and to track performance against these activities. Some years ago, this would avoid serious trouble with the sponsors; there were many results to report at each stewardship meeting. But increasingly, research sponsors have expectations of making progress toward larger overarching goals. In the last couple of decades, many research organizations, both private and public sector, have been closed down for failure to achieve the expectations of their sponsors, as discussed in Chapter 21.

Having overarching goals, such as those defined in Table 23.2, puts emphasis on the goals, and the necessity for making progress toward those goals through a common vision, collaboration and mutual support.

With this commitment to achieve the 2020 goals, AERI has pioneered the application of a process to quantify progress on an

TABLE 23.2

Energy Innovation 2020 Goals

Program	Focus	Energy 2020 Goals
C1. Bitumen Upgrading	Upgrading Efficiency	Reduce capital costs and operating costs by 20%.
	Diversified Products	Develop innovative processes to upgrade 50% of production to higher-valued products.
	Environment	Develop innovative processes to reduce the environmental impact per unit of product for: - SOx emissions by 100% - CO_2 emissions by 50% - Waste coke and sulphur by 100% - Fresh water use by 20%
C2. Clean Carbon/Coal	Coal	Establish one or more demonstration plants to convert sub-bituminous coal into electricity, hydrogen, heat and chemicals (poly-generation) with near-zero emission of CO_2 and other pollutants of concern.
	Biomass	Establish one or more demonstration plants to convert biomass and mixtures of other low value carbon fuels into electricity, heat and other useful products with near-zero emissions and minimal environmental impact
C3. CO_2 Management	Environment	Develop technologies to reduce greenhouse gas emissions per unit of energy produced by 50%
	Use & Disposal	Develop technologies to use 67% of the captured CO_2 in value-added processes and products.
C4. Recovery	Conventional Oil	Develop technologies to increase conventional oil reserves by an additional 5 billion barrels.
	Natural Gas	Develop technologies to increase Alberta's natural gas reserves by an additional 25 TCF of conventional gas and 100 TCF of unconventional gas.
	Oil Sands	Develop technologies required to increase production levels to 3.0 million barrels per day of bitumen.
	Environment	Develop technologies to reduce water consumption and GHG emission by 55% per unit of production.
C5. Alternative and Renewable Energy	Hydrogen/ Fuel Cells	AERI is supporting the development of key technologies that will allow industry to produce 5% of Alberta's energy demand from hydrogen and fuel cells technologies.
	Bio-energy	AERI is supporting the development of key technologies that will allow industry to produce 5% of Alberta's energy demand from bio-energy sources.
	Others	AERI is supporting the development of key technologies that will allow industry to produce 10% of Alberta's energy demand from geothermal, solar, wind and small hydro energy sources.
C6. Water Management	Cross-cutting Initiatives	Novel technologies have been developed that will contribute to the target of 50% reduction in fresh water usage by the energy industry.
	Upgrading	Key technologies have been developed that will allow industry to reduce fresh water consumption by 20% per unit of product.
	Recovery	Key technologies have been developed that will allow industry to reduce fresh water consumption by 55% per unit of production.

annual basis, which will involve the active engagement of all of the EnergyINet participants.

The Metrics for Tracking Performance

Building on ProGrid® methodology[iii], AERI has established metrics for the cells in the Evaluation matrix shown in Table 23.1. This involves establishing Language Ladders that track performance from the current position to the 2020 targets, as illustrated in Table 23.3.

TABLE 23.3
Language Ladder™ for Long Range Energy Goals

A	The Current situation as of 2003
B	Key Enablers are in place and progress has been made toward the 2012 Goals
C	The 2012 Goals are met
D	The 2020 Goals are met

The Language Ladder shown in Table 23.3 is generic. Thirty-two specific Language Ladder statements have been developed to provide the full metrics needed to track progress toward the ultimate 2020 Goals. Examples are given in Table 23.4 for one cell in the Evaluation Matrix.

TABLE 23.4
Example of Language Ladder

Energy Innovation Strategy	
A	Alberta's energy innovation strategy is not well accepted and programs are fragmented and not well coordinated.
B	Alberta's energy innovation strategy is accepted but adequate funding has not been committed; some programs are contributing to the Alberta plan for economic development and climate change, but gaps exist and the programs are not well integrated.
C	Alberta's energy innovation strategy is well accepted and adequate funding has been committed; there is a research and technology portfolio that contributes effectively to the Alberta plan on economic development and climate change...
D	... AND the portfolio is being undertaken collaboratively by industry, government and leading R&D organizations. Funding is supplied by industry and the Alberta and Federal Governments.

The cells in the Evaluation matrix in Table 23.1 are at two levels, with the main headings defined as Level One and the "bullets" in eight of the cells defined as Level Two. In ProGrid methodology, the Level Two metrics, derived from the Level Two Language Ladders, are rolled up to Level One, which provides an internal validation of the evaluation results.

The Positioning Grid

Progress toward the 2020 Goals can be measured and plotted on the grid shown in Figure 23.1, which uses as axes the headings in Column 2 and Column 3 of the Evaluation Matrix in Table 23.1.

FIGURE 23.1
Positioning Grid

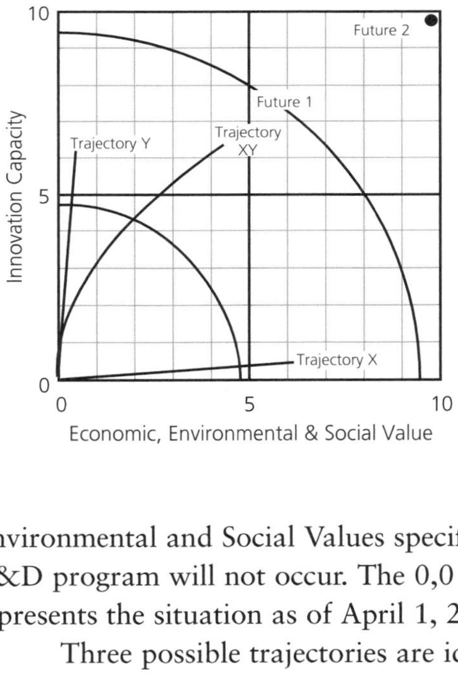

Figure 23.1 illustrates possible trajectories for the building of Innovative Capacities and the resulting Economic, Environmental and Social Values. The underlying premise is that there is a direct relationship between the two axes; without new Innovative Capacities, the Economic, Environmental and Social Values specified as the targets for the R&D program will not occur. The 0,0 position on this grid represents the situation as of April 1, 2003.

Three possible trajectories are identified.

Trajectory X describes the situation where the desired Economic, Environmental and Social Values are achieved without any increase in Innovation Capacities. If this were to occur, it would mean that the basic premise of the relationship described in the premise is not valid, as there would be no need to build Innovation Capacity to achieve the desired Outcomes/ Values. History has shown that this is not valid.

Trajectory Y describes the situation where the desired Economic, Environmental and Social Values do not occur, even though there are substantial increases in Innovation Capacity. If this were to occur, it would also mean that the basic premise of the relationship described in the premise is not valid, as no desired Outcomes/ Values would occur no matter how much Innovation Capacity is built.

Trajectory XY describes the situation where the desired Economic, Environmental and Social Values lag the establishment of new Innovative Capacities. If this were to occur, it would validate the basic premise of the relationship described in the premise because the new Innovation Capacity would result in the desired Outcomes/ Values for Canada.

AERI is using this grid to track its progress toward the 2020 Goals. (The Future 1 and Future 2 positions are different than those shown in the corresponding grid in Chapter 22. In Figure 23.1, Future 2 is defined to be the upper right hand corner of the grid, which enables the use of the full grid for tracking purposes.)

Understanding the Details

The Positioning Grid provides the ultimate measure of success, but the devil is "always in the details." The contribution of each cell in the matrix can be assessed using the chart shown in Figure 23.2.

Progress for each cell in the Evaluation Matrix is tracked with respect to the 2012 goals and the 2020 Goals. The centre of the circle represents the situation that existed in 2003, with the two outer concentric circles representing the achievement of the 2012 and 2020 goals respectively.

Annual Operating Plans

The participants in the energy innovation program have annual operating plans that will be integrated into the above evaluation process. This is requiring a paradigm shift in the management of research programs. The activities in a research program need to be evaluated with respect to the overarching 2020

FIGURE 23.2
The Contributors to Success

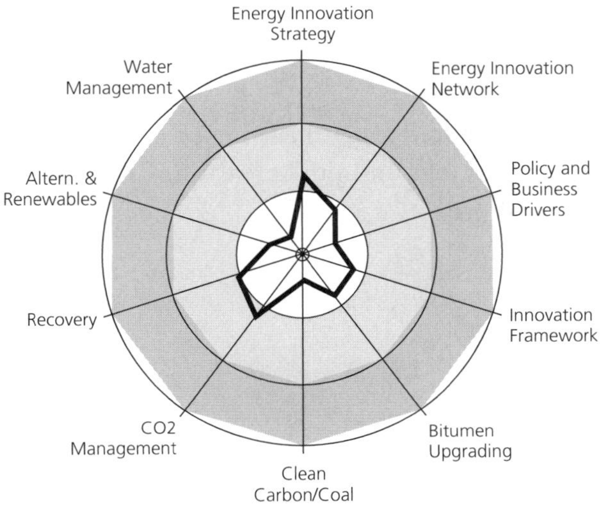

goals. For example, achievement of the bitumen-upgrading goal of a higher level of diversified products may require new catalysts or new reactor configurations. Projects designed for these purposes will be measured not by how well they achieve their internal technical goals, but how well they contribute to the 2020 goals. Projects which do not contribute to the goals may not receive support, even though they are based on sound science or engineering. On the other hand, the need for huge advances in technology will open up the pathway for highly innovative approaches that have significant risk but potentially large benefits.

Conclusions

The participants in EnergyINet have established major goals for the year 2020, which will transform the Canadian energy system, realizing major economic, environmental and social benefits if achieved. The value to Canada if these goals are met is expected to be huge. Three types of return on investment will be measured:

Financial return – Both public and private sector investors must be able to demonstrate to stakeholders that the investment has a positive economic impact

Environmental return – The protection of land, air, water and health is paramount.

Social return – In addition to enriching shareholders, the energy industry creates jobs and public wealth. Royalties and taxes support social priorities such as health and education.

[i] Oil was first produced in commercial quantities in 1858 by James Miller Williams in Lambton County, Ontario and in 1859 by Edwin L. Drake in Titusville, Pennsylvania. *Petroleum – Prehistoric to Petrochemicals,* G.A. Purdy, The Copp Clark Publishing Company, 1957

[ii] *Energy Development and Future Outlook,* Presentation to the Canadian Standing Senate Committee on Energy, the Environment and Natural Resources, Eddy Isaacs, M.P. Du Plessis, March 7, 2005

[iii] *Evaluating Intellectual Capital* – Parts I, II, III, IV, January, February, March, April, 2001, Canadian Chemical News

24 Picking up After Enron

Rob McLean – Co-President Benchmark-Action Inc.
Ron McCullough – Co-President Benchmark-Action Inc.

Getting the Rules Straight

Well-posted speed limits are essential on high-speed highways. They are designed, based on experience and the nature of the highway, to limit the potential for catastrophic crashes and subsequent risk to life and property. They are enforced to make sure not only that violators are "caught" but also to make sure that everyone knows they are enforced and that there is a risk of "being caught."

Speed limits and other traffic regulations do not, however, make good drivers or work to continuously improve the general standard of driving excellence. They are designed to limit the downside. A poor or negligent or purposely reckless driver can cause an accident at any speed; the consequences, supposedly, are simply less if the overall standard speed is lower.

In the late 1990s, some aspects of how corporations around the world were being managed were not unlike driving powerful cars on the "autobahn" with few posted limits and thus few enforceable consequences. As the complexities of corporate structures and activities grew, the old, well-established "rules" (based largely on GAAP – Generally Accepted Accounting Principles) became less able to deal with the ability of persons or groups within corporations to bend them to what they thought might be best. In some cases, this bending of the rules was well intentioned; in some cases not. Some cases had the intent of protecting or enhancing shareholder's value in the corporation; some were focused solely on the individual. Some resulted from incompetence, some from failure of process, and some from criminal intent.

The results are well publicized–Enron, WorldCom, Adelphia, Hollinger, Nortel, etc. These and others resulted in a global focus on "Failures in Governance," particularly in the light that these failures have cost investors many billions of dollars. Over and above the monetary losses has been a loss in confidence of investors in capital markets in general.

As a consequence, governments and regulators introduced both legislation and regulations to define a new set of "speed limits" and penalties for breaking these. Many of these are quite naturally designed to protect against the negative experiences of the past. They are not designed to improve standards of governance in whole, but rather to limit instances of bad governance. Significant debate goes on about whether or not some of the new regulations to limit "bad practices" are antithetical to "best practices." As an example, one initiative is to have all of the members of a board of directors as independent directors to prevent the possibility of insider dealings. This could mean that a board has no members who really know the business; such knowledge has been shown in the past to be one essential element in corporations that generate high returns for the shareholders.

Best Practice vs Staying Out of Jail

The vast majority of those involved in running companies do in fact make an honest effort to do their "best" for their stakeholders. In corporate governance there are three main groups of individuals involved: Management, Directors, and External Professionals (Auditors, Legal Counsel, etc.). Significant failures in governance have been attributed to each of these groups in various combinations, and in some cases, such as Enron, with disastrous consequences. Some of the issues were attributed to failures in due process, some to rules or regulations waiting to be bent or broken, and some to malfeasance. All occurred within a set of processes and relationships that were already complex, time-consuming and demanding on both the organizations and the individuals.

Along came the new "speed limits" with an initial focus on governance processes and financial reporting.The United States

Congress passed the Sarbanes-Oxley Act. The Canadian Securities Administrators adopted Multilateral Instrument 52-110. Stock exchanges such as the TSX, NYSE and NASDAQ revised their rules and manuals. The limits defined new regulations and obligations for companies, the individuals within them and the professional organizations supporting them. Penalties were potentially severe and implementation was to be almost immediate. The new environment was so demanding and complex that in the area of audit and reporting it was generally acknowledged that there were not nearly enough audit professionals in all of North America to do the work required to be compliant. In fact, significant numbers of corporations were given permission to delay their initial filings for just this reason.

The overriding question was:
"What do we/I have to do right now to be compliant (ie: stay out of jail)?"

But behind this was the equally important question:
"What can we/I do better to maximize value for our stakeholders?"

Pressure to answer the first question right makes focus on the second very difficult. There were, however, both organizations and individuals who were looking beyond the impact of new speed limits and were focused on improving the standards of overall driving.

Setting New Standards

The Canadian Institute of Chartered Accountants is the organization which provides accreditation for accounting professionals across Canada. It determines and publishes practice standards and manuals. It is a world leader in creating new tools and "best practice" guides to continually advance the standards of practice for not only its members but also for the clients they serve.

One such publication is *"Integrity in the Spotlight, Opportunities for Audit Committees"* (thousands of copies have been sold around the world with a second edition to be published in 2005). Written for CICA by J. Goodfellow, Vice Chair, Deloitte & Touche, and M. Sabia, both leading Audit Committee authorities, *Integrity* discussed best practices for Audit Committees well in advance of the new regulations. Reviewed in light of the practices that led to prominent audit and governance failures and the new regulations that arose, it was obvious that *Integrity* had compiled a framework of practices, which could give guidance to immediately help audit committees meet the new requirements. It was also obvious, however, that the framework within *Integrity* could help audit committees continually improve their practices in order to provide greater value to their stakeholders while at the same time improving the processes, efficiency and effectiveness of both committees and their members. A number of organizations had begun to apply *Integrity* in part or in whole based on the efforts of individuals who had read and espoused its principles.

The subject matter, however, was complex and changing rapidly. Those involved in audit committees were under intense and increasing pressures on their time and their ability to absorb new standards. Those few who were able to think beyond the pressures of just meeting new filing requirements (i.e.: obeying the new speed limits) were left alone in the open when asking:

"I wonder how others are approaching continual improvements in audit committee practices and effectiveness? How can we all become better drivers?"

Making It All Work

The authors of *Integrity* had pondered how to make an "electronic" version available. The stumbling block was how to make the knowledge with *Integrity* into easily used tools as opposed to simply publishing the book itself on the Internet.

Rob McLean, President of Matrixlinks International, a CA and former partner in Ernst & Young, worked for a number of years with the CICA in creating new frameworks and standards that push the boundaries of accounting practice and methodologies. McLean has also worked with ProGrid Values and Ron McCullough in creating innovative processes and structures in multiple disciplines. In particular, they were in the process of completing a new framework and internet-enable tool to assess and benchmark global best practices in the management of intellectual property.

McLean led a series of conversations that resulted in the CICA undertaking to provide a new service based on *Integrity*. The concept for the service was based on three key factors:

- The leading edge conceptual framework in *Integrity*
- The ability of the ProGrid methodology to organize the concepts into quantifiable measures that could be compiled and compared
- The ability of a Matrixlinks web-enabled database to provide instantaneous global access to the framework and to compile and deliver comparative data and processed information to users.

These three were combined and resulted in the *Audit Committee Performance Support System (ACPSS)* introduced by the CICA in January 2005. ACPSS uses a platform developed by ProGrid and Matrixlinks and marketed as the "BenchMark-Action" technology.

ACPSS and How It Delivers Value for Its Users

ACPSS has two primary functions:

- Assessment – the ability to have the user complete an assessment of their Audit Committee against the reference framework based on *Integrity*
  – *"How do I stack up against the standards and regulations?"*
- Benchmarking – the ability to compare an assessment to a comprehensive database of other companies
  – *"How do I compare to my competition?"*

Built into ACPSS are multiple types and levels of functionality that let the users take a major leap up from a set of information that simply tells them where they are. ACPSS, like other comprehensive ProGrid-based systems, assists the user in determining what the future should look like and what they need to do to achieve their desired future. In addition, it also provides tools that help the user manage a complex set of requirements and actions. The hierarchy of Figure 24.1 shows how these four elements integrate into a Performance Support System.

FIGURE 24.1
Performance Support System

Professional Support Infrastructure	• Linkages with professional organizations • Implementation support for corporate professionals and service providers • Marketing support for service providers	
Performance Support System	• Linked with "state-of-the-art" content • Dynamic benchmarking • Supports integration into management process	
Online Platform	MatrixLinks	• Content-independent • Taxonomy-based • Object-oriented • Structured but flexible
Methodology	ProGrid VENTURES INC.	• Language Ladders™ • Multiple time periods • Visualization • Linkage to action

The requirements facing audit committees are complex and dynamic. ACPSS is uniquely able to deal with both. The framework developed from Integrity has 114 different assessment criteria that are grouped into 27 cells in the matrix shown in Table 24.1.

Each cell represents a grouping of criteria around a subject that clearly resonates with an audit committee. Thus, an audit committee or any of its members can assess what they are doing regarding "Performance Reporting," one of the hot performance indicators of today. Similarly, the criteria can be grouped at higher levels to meet special needs.

The regulations for audit committees require that they formulate, publish and follow a Charter – a document that states exactly what the audit committee will be responsible for each year. ACPSS contains the keys to match the Charter requirements for any of the North American listing jurisdictions to the responses for any user and prepare a special report which indicates how well they meet

TABLE 24.1
Audit Committee Assessment Matrix

Reporting and Disclosure Oversight	Annual financial statements	Accounting policies	Interim financial/ continuous disclosure	Performance reporting
External Audit Oversight	External auditor appointment and qualifications	Annual audit oversight and fees	External auditor communications and relationship management	Internal audit
Risk Management and Control Oversight	Financial risk	Business risk	Internal controls	
Other oversight Responsibilities	Compliance	Ethics	Finance	
People	Independence	Qualifications and composition	Other people factors	
Information and Processes	Planning	Information needs	Audit committee meetings	Use of IT enabled tools and support
Managing Relationships	Board relationships	Management relationships		
Accountability Reporting and Evaluation	Reporting to the Board and shareholders	Minutes	Evaluation	
Outcomes	Audit, reporting and other outcomes			

the requirements as shown in Figure 24.2. The grey areas indicate where improvements are needed to meet expectations.

The system allows the user to "drill down" in specific areas where Charter requirements are not met and produces suggestions for the actions needed to do so. ACPSS presents a tool that lets the audit committee allocate time for all the Charter requirements over their schedule of meetings – and which then allows them to record their

FIGURE 24.2
Meeting Requirements

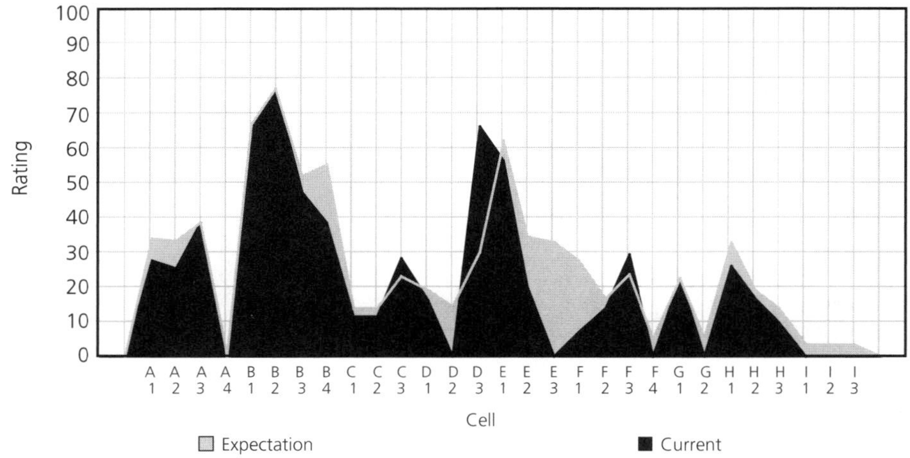

"closure" thus providing a trail that validates the activities of the committee in fulfilling its charter.

ACPSS can select and group the data in a number of relevant categories and produce instantaneous customized reports.

As each user completes an assessment they are asked to provide not only a response for where they are today, but also for where they would like to be at the end of the current reporting period and also one year after the current period.

The metrics for the assessment is based on Language Ladders defined for each of the 114 criteria in the assessment process. These Language Ladders embody the best practices from Integrity and, where appropriate, regulatory requirements. An example is shown in Table 24.2.

As a first step in being able to gain consensus and set a goal for the future, ACPSS takes the inputs from many different members or staff for a given committee and produces reports that highlight the areas of consensus and where consensus is yet to be reached.

A report is generated based on the consensus that shows what has to change in one and two years to reach the future goals. A profile of the changes required is shown in Figure 24.3.

TABLE 24.2
Language Ladder™ for Review of Accounting Policies

Accounting Policies	
A	The Audit Committee does not review and discuss the company's accounting policies and their relationship to GAAP as part of its review of the annual financial statements.
B	The Audit Committee reviews the accounting policy note to ensure completeness and acceptability with GAAP as part of the approval of the financial statements.
C	The Audit Committee discusses with management and the external auditor the acceptability, degree of aggressiveness/conservatism and quality of underlying accounting policies.
D	The Audit Committee carries out discussions with management and the external auditor to ensure that the underlying accounting policies, disclosures, and key estimates and judgements are considered to be the most appropriate in the circumstances (within the range of acceptable options and alternatives).

If, as often happens, the totality of change is seen as being too much of a task, the system is available to quickly update the goals and produce a new, realistic set of goals. ACPSS then generates action statements that indicate exactly what must be done to reach the goal–and provides tools to plan and track accomplishment of the goals.

Features such as the above, illustrative of a very comprehensive system, help an audit committee to not only "keep within the speed limits" but also help them to become "better drivers."

FIGURE 24.3
Example of Change Profile

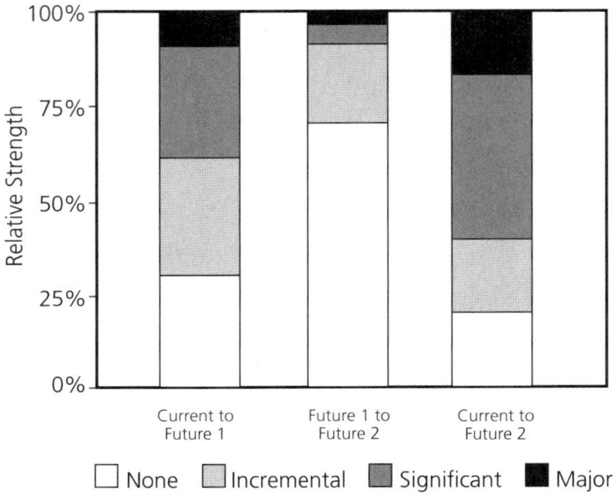

But They're Always Changing the Speed Limits

Regulators and legislators in areas such as Audit now realize that the standards and regulations must be "living documents" that evolve to meet the needs of the times. On-line systems such as ACPSS provide a dynamic response to changes in requirements. The system will be updated continuously to reflect new standards or requirements allowing users to get the latest information. Moreover, their own data stored in the system will now be updated and compared to today's requirements regardless of when they entered their assessments.

Similarly, as other users enter assessments, the data available for comparative benchmarking will grow continuously. Signing in will allow any user to see the latest comparisons at a glance.

Finally, audit committee requirements as embodied in ACPSS are but one element of a complex and evolving framework of standards, requirements and best practices being generally grouped as "Effective Governance." The platform and methodologies used for ACPSS are already being applied to other such topics. The goal: better drivers, of any type of vehicle, in any weather, on any road and at any type of day.

25 Evaluating Company Performance

Ron McCullough – Co-President, Benchmark-Action Inc.
John Kramers – ProGrid Ventures Inc.
Clem Bowman – Clement W. Bowman Consulting Inc.

Corporate Alignment

There is sometimes a long and tenuous path between the shareholders of a company, its board of directors, and various corporate and line business units. The latter may have distinctive qualities of their own and be geographically dispersed. At what stage does the transmission of visions, missions, strategies, objectives and tactics becomes so distorted that they cease to have any useful meaning? Is it feasible to measure the degree of alignment of the company's business plan as you move across and down organizational units?

The degree of corporate alignment can be evaluated using the concept of cascading matrices as illustrated in Figure 25.1. The view as seen by the board of directors (called Level Zero) can be assessed using an Evaluation Matrix of nine cells. Each cell represents a key component of the company's operations and can in turn be expanded into another Evaluation Matrix with more detailed information. The example in Figure 25.1 illustrates a specific ProGrid tool designed for this purpose with a total of 60 Level One cells.

These "Level One" views of the organization can be aggregated to provide a new Level Zero perspective, but this time representing a view of the organization as seen at the "factory floor." The two views may be highly aligned which would be the case for high-performing organizations. It is also plausible that there may be good alignment in most cells but one or two may be seriously misaligned, which would require corrective action.

Drilling deeper into the organization can be accomplished by continuing the cascade of matrices by expanding Each Level One cell into a Level Two matrix.

It is unlikely that it would be feasible or useful to drill down uniformly into all company operational areas. Nevertheless, it is certainly possible to drill down as deeply as needed to uncover hidden parts of the organization that previously have escaped the surveillance of upper management!

Company Overview at Level Zero

The first step is to set up the nine Level Zero matrices as an Evaluation Matrix™ as shown in Table 25.1, with the two overarching objectives of Organizational Excellence and Business Performance. Organizational Excellence represents the "inputs" that the company provides (Vision/Mission, Governance and Intellectual Capital) in order to capture the desired Business Performance (achieved through Products entering the Market in spite of Competition). Having the right Enablers (Human Resources, the Plan and effective Production Practices) ensures success.

A set of Language Ladders for each cell in the Level Zero matrix will provide the metrics for the evaluation, as illustrated in Table 25.2 for the Governance cell. Note that the concept of governance goes well beyond meeting regulatory requirements, which seems to be the focus of much of the current emphasis on the responsibilities of boards of directors.

A Board of Directors can undertake an evaluation of the performance of the organization with respect to Governance using this Language Ladder. A similar process for the other eight cells in the Level Zero Evaluation Matrix produces an overall performance rating, as seen at Level Zero.

TABLE 25.1

Level Zero Company Evaluation Matrix

Organizational Excellence	Enablers	Business Performance
Vision/Mission	Human Resources	The Products
Governance	The Business Plan	The Markets
Intellectual Capital	Production Practices	The Competition

Level One Divisional Evaluation Matrices

Vision/Mission		
A1	B1	C1
A2		C2

Human Resources		
A1	B1	C1
A2	B2	C2
	B3	

The Products		
A1	B1	C1
A2	B2	C2
A3		

Governance		
A1	B1	C1
A2	B2	C2
A3	B3	C3

The Business Plan		
A1	B1	C1
A2	B2	C2
A3		

The Markets		
A1	B1	C1
A2	B2	C2

Intellectual Capital		
A1	B1	C1
A2	B2	C2
A3		C3

Production Practices		
A1	B1	C1
A2	B2	C2

The Competition		
A1	B1	C1
A2		C2

TABLE 25.2

Language Ladder™ for Governance

Governance:	
A	The organization meets the governance requirements established by all relative regulatory bodies...
B	and senior management has established appropriate systems to govern the on-going affairs of the organization with effective succession plans for key positions...
C	and the Board of Directors takes an active role in overseeing the operations of the organization including evaluating the performance of senior management ...
D	and the Board of Directors and senior management have processes in place to identify and address internal and external issues that represent future threats and opportunities.

Drilling Down to Level One

Let's take the Governance cell in Table 25.1 and drill down into Level One, using the Evaluation Matrix shown in Table 25.3.

TABLE 25.3
Level One Governance Evaluation Matrix

Commitment to Governance	The Connectors	The External Impact
Board of Directors	Organizational Structure	Industry Relations
Shareholders	Audit and Evaluations	Public Relations
Senior Management	Succession	The Environment

A set of Language Ladders for each cell in this matrix will provide the metrics for the evaluation, as illustrated in Table 25.4 for the Board of Directors cell.

TABLE 25.4
Language Ladder for Board of Directors

Board of Directors:	
A	The Board has not had any active role in the direction of the organization and/or is dominated by Members of Management.
B	The members of the Board of Directors are well known in their fields of experience and have been able to provide guidance at legislatively required meetings of the Board.
C	The organization has an effective Board of Directors with a good balance of internal and external representation. Members of the Board actively participate in the affairs of the organization through frequent Board and Committee meetings …
D	AND the external members of the Board are major participants in reviewing and approving the vision and mission.

The Board of Directors can assess their performance using this Language Ladder. The board and/or other corporate groups can similarly assess the company's performance with respect to the other eight cells in the Level One Governance Evaluation Matrix. These nine ratings provide a Level One rating for Governance that can be compared to the rating for the Governance cell at Level Zero.

The other cells in Table 25.1 can be drilled down in a similar manner to obtain a full set of Level One performance ratings. These nine ratings can be aggregated to compare against the original Level Zero rating.

Drilling Down to Level Two

Suppose the Board of Directors wishes to drill down further to examine its performance over a broader range of indicators, using the Level Two Evaluation Matrix shown in Table 25.5.

TABLE 25.5
Evaluation Matrix for the Board of Directors

Attributes	Roles/Processes	Impact
Experience	Strategy and Policy	Internal Impact
Knowledge	Planning	External Impact
Independence	Performance	Strategic Impact
Commitment	Staff Relations	Leadership

A set of Language Ladders for each cell in this matrix would provide the metrics for the evaluation, as illustrated in Table 25.6 for the Independence cell.

TABLE 25.6
Language Ladder for Independence of the Board of Directors

Independence of the Board of Directors:	
A	There are some external members on the Board of Directors but members of management hold the key executive positions on the Board and its sub-committees.
B	External Board Members are in the majority and serve as Chairperson for some Board Subcommittees. The Audit and Nominating Committee members are a combination of internal and external Directors.
C	External Board Members are in the majority and fill most key executive Board roles including the Chairperson for most Board Subcommittees. The posts of Chair of the Board and CEO are separately held. The Audit and Nominating Committee members are all external Directors.
D	External Board Members are in the clear majority and fill all key executive Board roles including the Chairperson for each Board Subcommittee. The posts of Chair of the Board and CEO are separately held. The Audit and Nominating Committee members are all external Directors.

The Board of Directors can assess its level of performance with respect to the Independence cell and also with respect to the other 11 cells in Figure 22.5 to provide an overall measure of board performance. It may be that the Independence attribute may not be of critical importance to a company at an early stage of development. The Commitment cell might represent a more important characteristic. These types of considerations can be taken into account in interpreting the results, or if desired in the metrics themselves.

The performance level of the Board of Directors obtained from all the cells in Table 25.5 can be compared with the performance of the Board of Directors cell in Table 25.3 (Level One- Governance). Inconsistencies can be identified and corrective action taken.

A Summary of the Assessments by the Board

If the above course were followed, the Board of Directors would be involved at three levels:

- Level Zero – Undertaking an overall assessment of the company according to the criteria in Table 25.1, and specifically for Governance using the Language Ladder in Table 25.2.
- Level One – Undertaking the role of the board of directors in Governance using the Language Ladder in Table 25.4.
- Level Two – Undertaking an assessment of the level of Independence of the Board of Directors using the Language Ladder in Table 25.6.

Rules of Aggregation

Using the concept of cascading matrices, a comparison can be made of the degree of alignment at various levels in an organization. Each Evaluation Matrix will have a set of Language Ladders that will provide a rating for that cell. Each time an evaluation is carried out based on that matrix, an R-value can be determined as described in Chapter 1.

There are two steps to aggregating from one level to the next higher level as illustrated in Figure 25.1.

Step 1 – The R-value for a lower level matrix can be compared to the rating of the corresponding cell in the next higher-level matrix.

Step 2 – The R-values from the underlying matrices can be aggregated to produce a performance rating for the higher-level matrix. This R-value can be compared to the original evaluation rating for the upper level matrix.

FIGURE 25.1
Aggregation Logic for Cascading Matrices

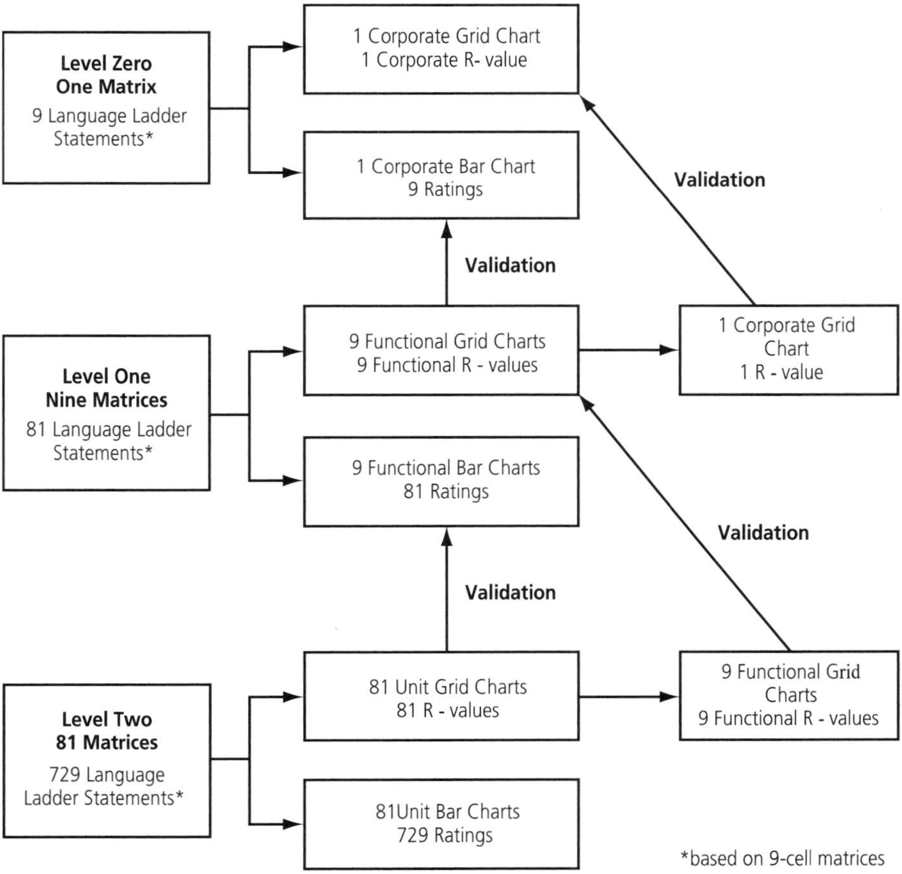

Example of Use

FIGURE 25.2
Organization Grid as seen by Board of Directors

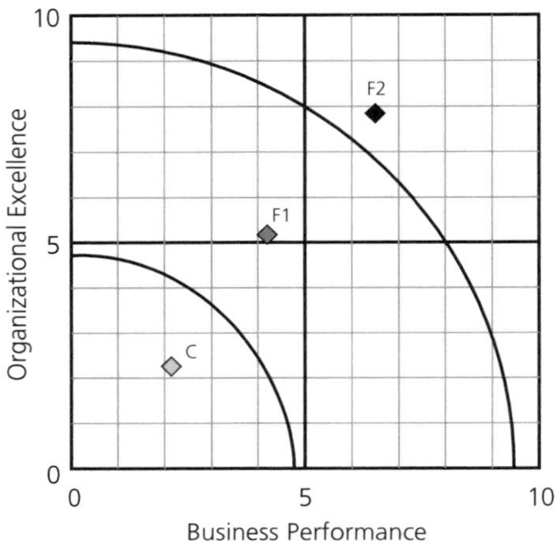

FIGURE 25.3
Organization Grid as seen by Line Management

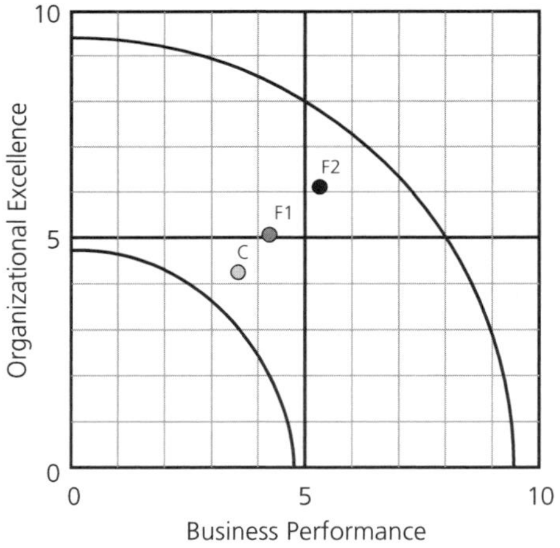

An organization as seen by the board of directors is shown in Figure 25.2 and as seen by Line Management in Figure 25.3, with the results of their Level 1 evaluation aggregated to Level Zero. Note that the spread between the current state and the two future states as seen by Line Management is much smaller than the view of the Board of Directors. Although the near future position (F1) is the same as seen by Line Management and the board, the work needed to achieve this goal is considerably different. This issue needs to be reconciled.

The Board has a more aggressive long-term objective as reflected by the position of F2.

This may not be a problem if it means that Line Management is focused on immediate tasks, and if these tasks are not inconsistent with the long-term aspirations of the organization.

The Evaluation Matrix in Table 25.5 identifies the criteria that a Board of Directors would use for evaluating their performance at Level Two. A Board could evaluate their current position and their

FIGURE 25.4
Current Board Performance

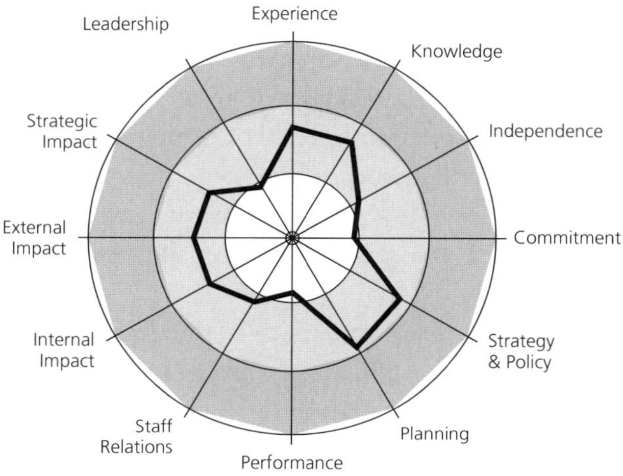

FIGURE 25.5
Desired Board Performance in Three Years

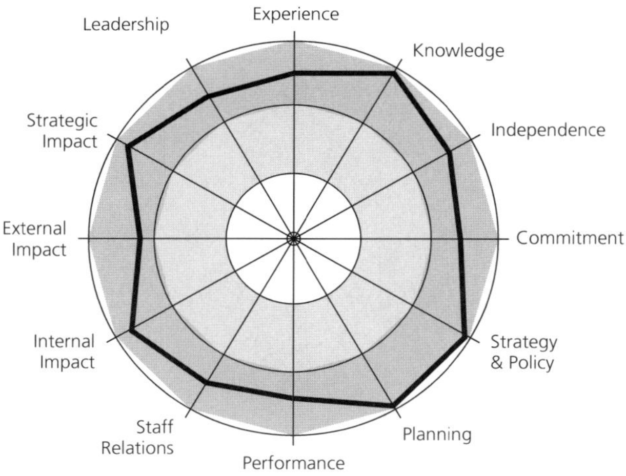

mid-term target in three years. An example of an assessment is shown in Figures 25.4 and 25.5. The second circle from the centre indicates expectations are met (C ratings) and the zone between that circle and the outer circle indicates expectations are exceeded.

In Pursuit of the Desired Future State

In Chapter 24, we described how the issue of governance in the corporate world has resulted in an array of new regulatory requirements. These represent the reaction of governments to solving blatant acts of malfeasance and fraud. In this Chapter 25, we have laid out a methodology in which corporations can attain high levels of performance that meet the fiduciary requirements expected by regulatory authorities and at the same time, meet the expectations of shareholders.

The methodology is more complex than the decision-making tools that were outlined elsewhere in this book. But the information that is needed is no different than what is required for the effective management of any organization. Once the overarching objectives established by the Executive and approved by Shareholders are established, the means to achieve these objectives requires that all parts of the organization are in alignment and that performance is measured and reported in a full and comprehensive manner. The actions required to move from the current to desired future states should be known and understood by all stakeholders.

26 A Time-Tested Tool Box

John Kramers – ProGrid Ventures Inc.

The Practitioners

In this book, a large number of practical applications of the ProGrid® methodology have been presented by organizations faced with a major decision, issue or re-engineering task. Each organization started from a similar point, with values, priorities and expectations that had to be met. In some cases, these were prescribed in legislation. In other cases, they were internally derived benchmarks that were driven from cost and or competitive pressures. Each organization formulated Evaluation Matrices to match the challenges that they faced, and then constructed Language Ladders to provide the metrics to make decisions and guide future action. However, from this point on, the pathways were unique and specific to the task at hand. The original developers of the methodology were astonished at the variety of approaches that users developed and the versatility of tools that were employed. For several years, User Group meetings were held to compare ideas and approaches. These meetings have now been superseded by an informal network of information exchange between users.

The Software

Early practitioners of ProGrid used a combination of commercially-available spreadsheets for each application or opportunity. These were linked to another spreadsheet to provide a "sort table" where all applications were ranked according to how well they met the objectives. For the first competition of Materials Manufacturing Ontario (see Chapter 10) 225 spreadsheets were generated (one for each application) and linked to the master "Sort" spreadsheet. In 1998, ProGrid software was modified and an MS Access database with Visual Basic code served as the process controller. Application data stored in the MS Access database was transferred to a calculation module (MS Excel spreadsheet) and the results transferred to a master report module (also a MS Excel spreadsheet) that was then saved as the report for each application. A high degree of customization was required to set up the software to meet the needs of specific users.

With experience, it became apparent that many of the software requirements were similar for all users. Software programs were developed that were independent of the commercially available programs, using Visual Basic. In April 2002 ProGrid-Decision Manager Professional was introduced, a fully independent software package that included database, calculations, viewing of results in real time and a report-generating capability in one package. As data are entered (manually or electronically imported), calculations are carried out in real time with the results seen instantly. This is especially useful for meetings where the committee wishes to see what happens if they provide a "committee," "final review" or "consensus" rating for each criterion. Some committee members may be reviewers and, after seeing new information provided by other committee members, may want to change their ratings. These changes can be entered and the revised ratings are immediately available. The software offering has been expanded to include two "entry level" products (Advisor and Advisor SE) and two "full featured" products (Decision Manager Premium and Performance Manager).

Entry-level products are designed for the personal or organizational user when there is not a large number of applications to evaluate and when the evaluation process does not include more than six evaluators. The "full-featured" products are designed for a larger volume of applications/opportunities and more complex evaluation processes, which may include a "final review" by a management committee or a Board. In the summer of 2005 the "full featured" products were re-branded as *Global*Evaluator and *Performance*Evaluator to more fully reflect the nature of the ProGrid methodology – to evaluate opportunities that lead to an action. The tool kit's offering in the evaluation spectrum is shown in Figure 26.1.

FIGURE 26.1
ProGrid Tools coverage of the Evaluation Spectrum

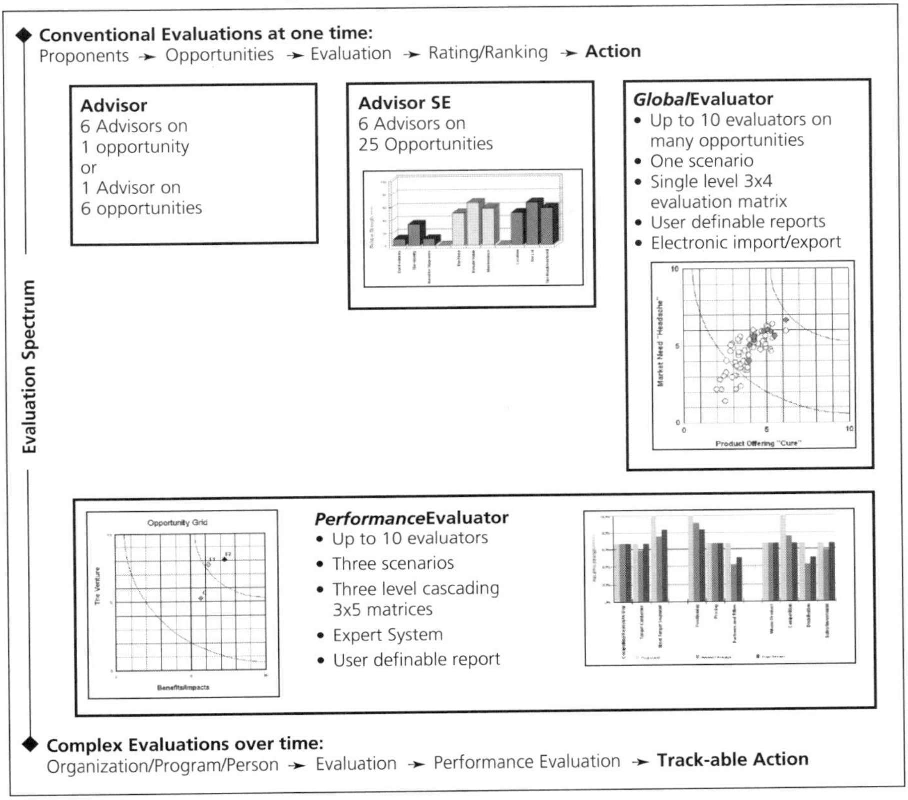

Products in the tool kit are differentiated whether their main purpose is for *"Conventional Evaluations"* of one or many opportunities at one time (e.g. evaluating R&D grant applications); or for *"Complex Evaluations"* over time (e.g. organizational, technology or personnel performance evaluations) from the top to the bottom of the chart (the evaluation spectrum) and the number of evaluations from left to right. The products do not have content. The user provides the content with assistance from a ProGrid practitioner. Content packages that represent a "solution" to a "problem" faced by the user have been developed and are explained later in this chapter. This content includes overarching objectives, an Evaluation Matrix and Language Ladders.

To illustrate the capabilities of the ProGrid tool kit, typical applications are shown below.

*Global*Evaluator and its predecessors have been used to evaluate such areas as:

- selecting among competing projects or alternative courses of action, when resources are limited
- selecting technology commercialization partners
- screening requests for support by venture capital organizations
- selecting applicants for positions in an organization and for promotions and performance appraisals integrated into effective human resource management
- awarding scholarships for students and faculty members
- allocating "bonuses" to participating partners
- purchasing equipment or consulting services

*Performance*Evaluator can be used in a "performance evaluation" or "benchmarking" mode to:

- evaluate organizational excellence and business performance of an organization
- measure performance of a Board of Directors or its individual members
- benchmark performance of research organizations
- develop and evaluate progress of operating plans
- facilitate strategic planning
- measure effectiveness of philanthropic organizations

These are examples of the applications by various ProGrid users, but there is essentially no limit to the range of applications. The easily-understood graphical results can be communicated to management and to all stakeholders involved. The ProGrid products are fully independent Windows-based programs. The reports and charts that are generated contain the information and graphics illustrated in the next section.

The Charts

The graphical output that is generated by *Global*Evaluator and *Performance*Evaluator is illustrated in Figures 26.2 through 26.6. *Global*Evaluator generated Figures 26.2 and 26.3. *Performance*Evaluator generated Figure 26.4, 26.5 and 26.6.

FIGURE 26.2
Individual Assessor Ratings

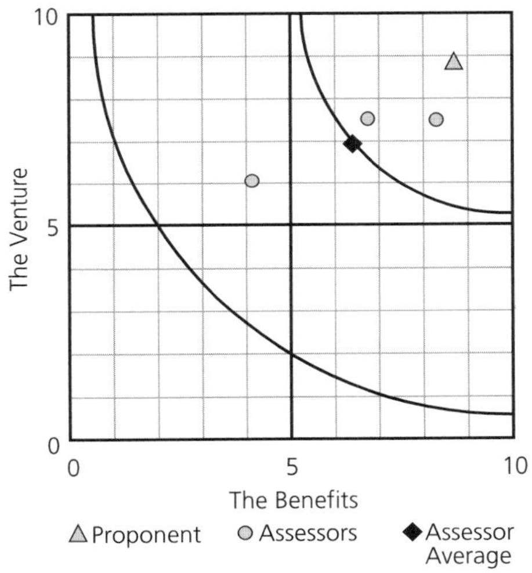

Individual Ratings

The ratings of three evaluators (circles), the average rating (diamond), and the rating of the Applicant (Triangle) are shown in Figure 26.2.

FIGURE 26.3
Comparison of Opportunities

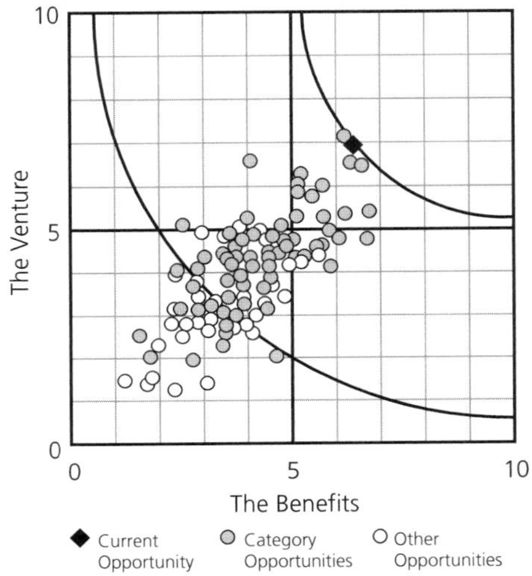

Database Comparison

The rating for the current opportunity is compared against the other opportunities in the database, which can be divided into different categories, in Figure 26.3

FIGURE 26.4
Comparison of Three Scenarios

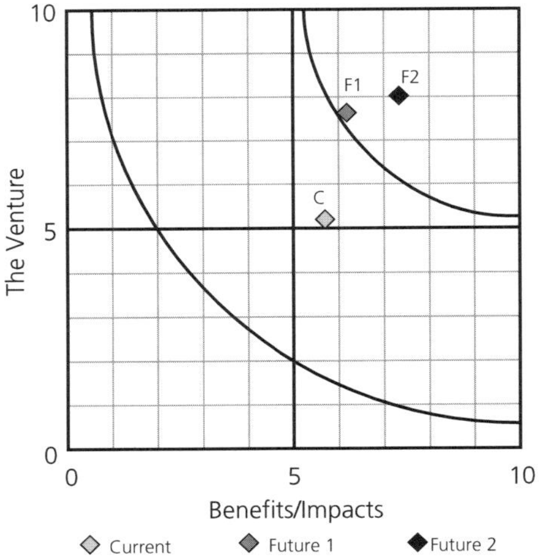

Scenario Comparison

Three scenarios, such as: the current state (C) and two desired future states (F1 and F2), one of which could be a short- term future and the second a strategic long-term future, are compared in Figure 26.4. A series of action statements are also generated that indicate what events must take place to move to the higher scenarios.

The Profile Chart

The strengths and weaknesses of the opportunity in the assessed criteria, for the selected scenarios, are shown in Figure 26.5.

FIGURE 26.5
Profile of Strengths and Weaknesses

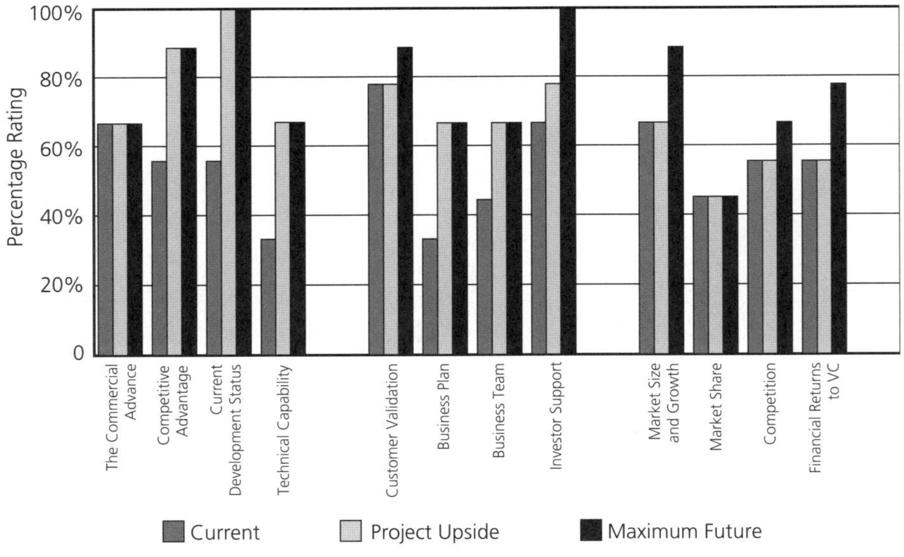

Complying with Expectations/Regulations

How the opportunity compares (for each evaluation criterion) with all the other opportunities in the database and how close each criterion comes to meeting or exceeding expectations, is shown in Figure 26.6.

FIGURE 26.6
Compliance Chart

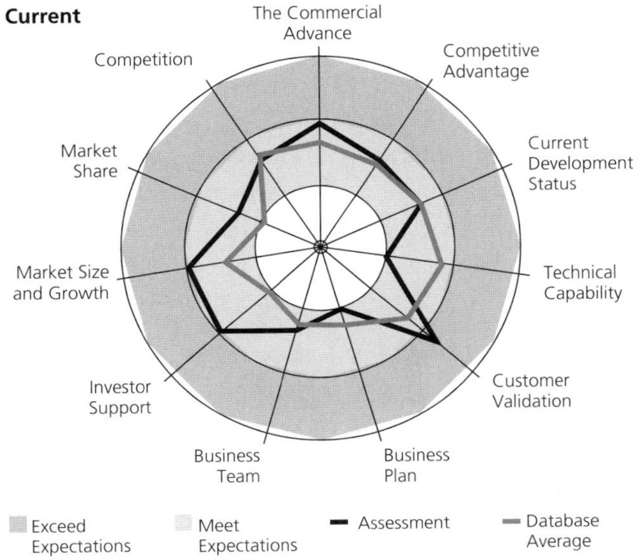

In addition to the above charts, the software generates other specialized charts and tables including a series of reports with comments that each evaluator has provided for each criterion and a summary comment. The final ranking sorted by the overall score for the opportunity, the ranking for the "inputs" or the "outputs", or by any of the individual criteria is also provided. The program generates electronic opportunity and evaluation forms and will automatically import this data into the database, thus eliminating the time and errors of manual data entry.

Action Statements – Creating desired future states is a key step in strategy development, but raises the question of how to get to these new states. The ProGrid methodology provides a powerful tool for this task, called Action Statements. Referring back to the illustrative Language Ladder™ in Chapter 1, the spaces between the steps in the ladder are as important as the steps themselves. The actions needed to move from one step to another are embedded in these spaces. For example, suppose an organization is at level A in the Language Ladder shown in Table 26.1, and believes it can get to level C in three years.

The Action Statement that would be generated by the software would therefore be:

"Building on the commercialization strategy, develop a comprehensive business plan that identifies necessary resources, contains clear goals and milestones and is accepted by all key stakeholders."

The software would generate a number of action statements equal to the number of factors in the Evaluation Matrix for each of the desired future states. This list can be prioritized and embedded in the organization's operating plan.

TABLE 26.1
The Business Plan Language Ladder

	A Business Plan should identify the markets you intend to enter and how and where you have or intend to obtain all necessary resources to bring the products / processes / services to market. Schedules and milestones should be presented for all key activities accompanied by the actions needed to reach the milestones. Please select which of the following statements best describes your business plan.
A	A commercialization strategy has been developed and documented.
B	A preliminary business plan has been developed. It identifies the key factors to be addressed in commercializing the concept.
C	A comprehensive business plan has been developed and accepted by all key stakeholders. It identifies all necessary resources and contains clear goals and milestones.
D	A comprehensive business plan has been developed and pursued successfully for at least two years. All critical goals and milestones have been achieved or exceeded.

*Performance*Evaluator provides a graphic that indicates the level of change required to go from scenario 1 (Current) to scenario 2 (Future 1) and then scenario 3, as shown in Figure 26.7. By re-evaluating the organization at specified future times, movement on the chart, or lack thereof, would become clearly visible, with no place to run, no place to hide!

FIGURE 26.7
Change Profile

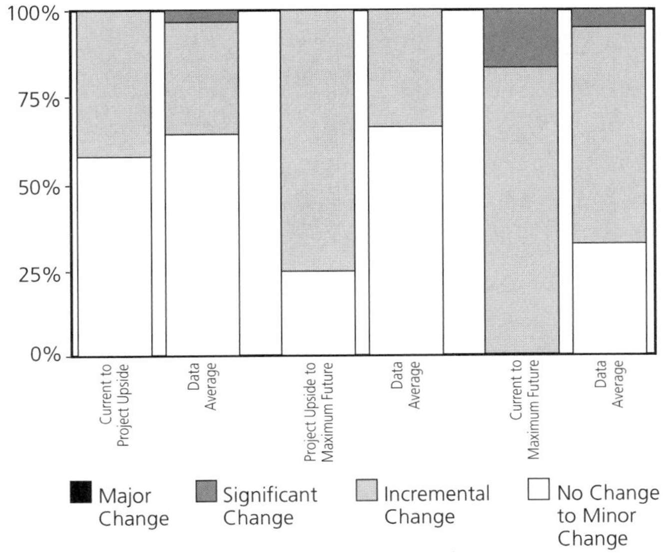

Evaluation Charts – Having several charts in view at one time has proven to be a useful feature for committees that meet to review applications/opportunities. Four key charts are shown in one display in Figure 26.8.

This display shows the Grid plot (with the proponent position and the evaluator positions as well as the evaluator's average), the Profile chart identifying the strengths and weaknesses, the database plot that shows how the current application ranks versus the other applications under consideration and the Evaluations Table that shows each evaluator's ratings and the variability of these ratings.

From this multiple chart view, the user can drill down into more detail for each of the charts by clicking on the magnifying glass button. If this is done for the lower right corner Evaluations Table, ratings can be modified and saved, and criteria and overall comments can be accessed. In other words, from this one chart all the evaluation information needed to take an action is available.

FIGURE 26.8
Evaluation Charts View from *Global*Evaluator

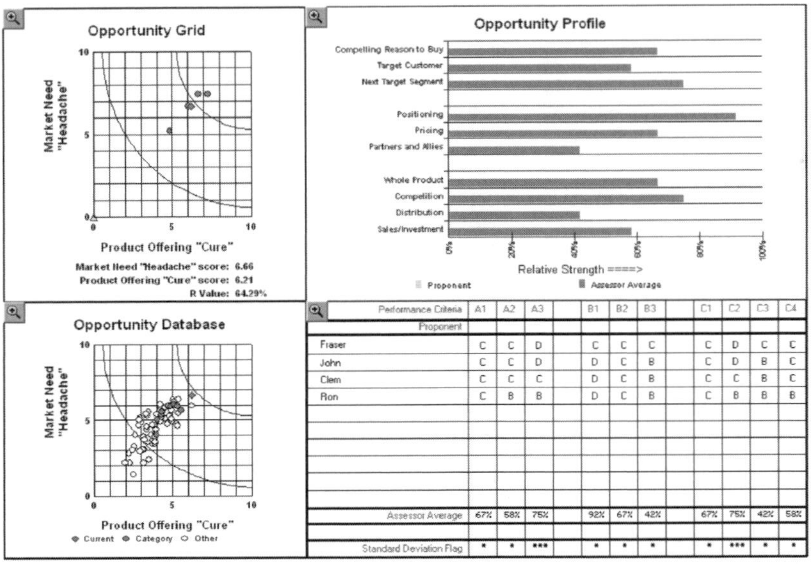

The Content

In the previous section, examples of the software are provided with illustrative content. It is the content that provides meaning to the software. Over time, some standard content packages have been developed, called Library Packages. These packages contain a series of tested library products that contain the Evaluation Matrices, Language Ladder Statements and Action Statements in a database that forms part of the *Global*Evaluator and *Performance*Evaluator software products.

Examples of these Library packages are:

R&D Projects was developed to evaluate proposals submitted for funding to research granting agencies, or for a corporation to evaluate projects submitted to management for funding. This package has the Evaluation Matrix shown in Table 26.2.

TABLE 26.2
The "R&D Projects" Evaluation Matrix

Quality of the Project	Enabling Factors	Benefits/ Impacts
Technical Advance	Project Plan	Technology Transfer
The Researchers	Capacity	Direct Benefits
Validation	Collaboration	Indirect Benefits

In this example critical aspects of a research project (*Technical Advance, The Researchers* who will carry out the research project, and *Validation* of the research direction) are evaluated along with the Enabling Factors (*Project Plan, Capacity* to do the research, and *Collaboration* with other experts or researchers) to have the desired outcomes (*Transfer* of the research results to others along with the *Direct and Indirect Benefits*) to the goals and objectives of the granting organization).

TA Basic evaluates a new or emerging technology with respect to two overarching objectives: Technical Assessment and Commercial Readiness, and uses the Evaluation Matrix shown in Table 26.3.

TABLE 26.3
The "TA-Basic" Evaluation Matrix™

Technical Strength	Enablers	Commercial Strength
Technical Framework	Commercial Readiness	Market Characteristics
Level of Verification	Proprietary Strength	Margin and Profit Potential
Excellence of the Project Time	Technological Durability	Commercialization Channels

The methodology evaluates the maturity of the technology and identifies the current state and potential future states, and an accompanying set of actions. It can be undertaken by a panel of stakeholders, augmented by at least one non-stakeholder, who collectively have a sound knowledge of relevant scientific, technical, and market issues and a good understanding of existing and potential competitive offerings. TA Basic represents Level Zero for the detailed technology analysis (ProGrid-TA) described in Chapter 20.

Venture evaluates a technology-based venture with respect to two overarching objectives: Venture Attributes and Commercial Value, and uses the Evaluation Matrix shown in Table 26.4.

TABLE 26.4
The "Venture" Evaluation Matrix

The Venture	The Connectors	Commercial Value
The Commercial Advance	Customer Validation	Market Size and Growth
Competitive Advantage	Business Plan	Market Share
Current Development Status	Business Team	Competition
Technical Capability	Investor Support	Financial Returns to the VC

The methodology is used to screen investment opportunities as the initial evaluation step prior to proceeding to more detailed due diligence. The tool evaluates the maturity of a technology and identifies the current state and potential future states, and an accompanying set of actions. It can be undertaken by a panel composed of the proponent, prospective investors and experts who have a sound knowledge of relevant scientific, technical, and market issues and a good understanding of existing and potential competitive offerings.

Research Organization evaluates a research organization with respect to two overarching objectives: R&D Management, and Benefits/Impacts, and uses the Evaluation Matrix shown in Table 26.5.

TABLE 26.5
The "Research Organization" Evaluation Matrix

R&D Management	Connectors	Benefits/Impacts
Mission/Vision	Alignment to the Business	Corporate Impact
Portfolio Development	Technology Acquisition/Application	Industry/Public Impact
Program Management	Performance Management	
Human Resources		

The methodology emphasizes both the tangible and intangible factors that determine the difference between maintaining the status quo and achieving pacesetter performance. A powerful feature of the methodology is the identification of both the current state and potential future states, and an accompanying set of actions. The tool is applicable to both public and private sector research organizations and can be undertaken by an organization's Board of Directors (or an equivalent body representing the "owners"), and/or senior management.

Philanthropic measures the effectiveness of philanthropic foundations with respect to two overarching objectives: Governance, and Impact, and uses the Evaluation Matrix shown in Table 26.6.

TABLE 26.6
The "Philanthropic" Evaluation Matrix

Governance	Operations	Impact
Accountability	Alignment with Objectives	Strengthening Grantees
Financial Stewardship	Grantee Selection Process	Funding Influence & Leverage
Engagement	Grantee Interactions	Effect on Field
Endowment Performance	Staff Interactions	Program Impact

The methodology emphasizes both the tangible and intangible factors that determine the difference between pacesetter performance and ineffective stewardship. A powerful feature of the methodology is the identification of the current state and potential future states, and an accompanying set of actions. In a 1999 Colorado Trust report, it was noted: "Foundations most often direct their evaluations at the activities of their grantees, only rarely subjective themselves to the same level of scrutiny, accountability and discomfort [i]." Governments are expecting Foundations to achieve high levels of accountability consistent with the tax benefits they receive. The criteria in this program for measuring the effectiveness of Foundations use many of the concepts and indicators recommended by the Center for Effective Philanthropy[ii].

The next three library products: Corporate; Governance and Board of Directors, involve drilling down to evaluate performance of an organization from Level 0 (Corporate – the 40,000 foot strategic view), to Level 1 (Governance – criterion A2 in Corporate), to Level 2

(Board of Directors – criterion A1 in Governance that explores how well a Board of Director performs). Each of these Library products can also be used by itself to do a specific evaluation for a defined purpose, as discussed in Chapter 25.

Corporate evaluates a company with respect to two overarching objectives: Organizational Excellence and Business Performance, and uses the Evaluation Matrix shown in Table 26.7.

TABLE 26.7
The "Corporate" Evaluation Matrix

Organizational Excellence	Enablers	Business Performance
Vision/Mission	Human Resources	The Products
Governance	The Business Plan	The Markets
Intellectual Capital	Production Practices	The Competition

The methodology emphasizes both the tangible and intangible factors that determine the difference between commercial success and failure. A powerful feature of the methodology is the identification of both the current state and potential future states, and an accompanying set of actions. This tool is applicable to publicly traded corporations and can be undertaken by a company's Board of Directors and/or Senior Management.

Governance evaluates the governance of an organization with respect to two overarching objectives: Commitment to Governance and the External Impact, and uses the Evaluation Matrix shown in Table 26.8

TABLE 26.8
The "Governance" Evaluation Matrix

Commitment to Governance	The Connectors	The External Impact
Board of Directors	Organizational Structure	Industry Relations
Shareholders	Audit and Evaluations	Public Relations
Senior Management	Succession	The Environment

The methodology emphasizes both the tangible and intangible factors that determine the difference between pacesetter governance and ineffective stewardship. A powerful feature of the methodology is the identification of both the current state and potential future states, and an accompanying set of actions. This tool is applicable to both private and public organizations and can be undertaken by all those involved in governance, shareholders, Board of Directors, and senior management.

Board of Directors evaluates the performance of a Board of Directors with respect to two overarching objectives: Composition and Impact. Board of Directors is available in two versions:

1. to evaluate the overall performance of a Board of Directors,
2. to evaluate the performance of individual Directors.

The Evaluation Matrix shown in Table 26.9 is used for this version.

TABLE 26.9
The "Board of Directors" Evaluation Matrix

Attributes	Roles/Processes	Impact
Experience	Strategy and Policy	Internal Impact
Knowledge	Planning	External Impact
Independence	Performance	Strategic Impact
Commitment	Staff Relations	Leadership

The Library packages described above provide a starting point in developing a customized "solution" to an evaluation challenge. It is the power behind the ProGrid methodology that allows an organization to build an Evaluation Matrix with Criteria and Language Ladders that are based on their own priorities, values and expectations.

[i] *Using Evaluation to Improve Grantmaking: What's Good for the Goose is Good for the Grantor,* Colorado Trust, Denver, Colorado, March 1999

[ii] *Indicators of Effectiveness – Understanding and Improving Foundation Performance*, Center for Effective Philanthropy, Inc., Boston, MA, 2002.